"Carole Dean's book *The Art of Film Funding: Alternative Financing Concepts* is a 'must have' tool for every independent filmmaker today. Now in its second edition, it has even more indispensable information to take you through every step on the way to financing your film. She covers all the bases, with experts in every field like crowdfunding, grant writing, trailer creation, legal concepts, and distribution paradigms. Carole provides much needed encouragement for the daunting task of getting your film produced by giving you all the essential tools on every page of the book. Buy it if you really want to get your next film made!"

— Maureen Ryan, professor, Columbia University, author of *Producer to Producer: A Step-by-Step Guide to Low-Budget Independent Film Producing*

"*The Art of Film Funding* should be considered the new filmmaking bible. Carole's book goes far beyond film funding to the very foundations of successful filmmaking. She couples her intimate understanding of the mechanics and logistics of getting a film made with the more ethereal, yet equally important aspects of the filmmaker's mindset and motivations. This book provides a blueprint for making films that matter, that are successful, and that create immense value in the world."

— Jilann Spitzmiller, Philomath Films & DocuMentors (*www.documentaryhowto.com*)

"In her updated edition, Dean blends the experience of grassroots filmmakers with the savvy of experts. Dean transcends the how-to approach by instilling in the reader a feeling of empowerment that grows page after page and leaves you with this valuable short end: believe in yourself."

— Chelo Alvarez-Stehle, documentary filmmaker

"Carole, you've done it again. You've shared your own knowhow and gotten some amazing filmmakers to add theirs, too. You picked my heroes, the people I read and follow every day. And I'm overwhelmed to be included in that group. This is the book I needed when I first started making films; I'm glad it's finally out there."

— Norman C. Berns, producer/director/consultant (*http://reelgrok.com*)

"*The Art of Film Funding* provides readers with proven strategies, valuable insights, and an in-depth understanding of the art, science, and business of funding films."

— David Vasile, president, Dazzle Entertainment

"*The Art of Film Funding* gives you the tools you need to make your dream a reality. Carole refers to it as an art for good reason. It's all subjective, there are many different forms, but in the end, you're putting together your own personal masterpiece. This book will help you achieve that!"

— Bobby Mardis, producer

"If I had a book like this twenty-five years ago, I'd be writing screenplays and getting them produced. In *The Art of Film Funding*, Carole Dean has laid out, in simple, entertaining, and informative terms, how to overcome the hardest roadblock in the creative process — how to raise money to get what you've created on the page, on the screen!"

— ... Digital Sales Director,

"*The Art of Film Funding* is the bible of the film industry — if you have a project and you want money, this is the definitive work on the subject of developing, planning, crafting, communicating, securing, and funding your dream."

> — Lori Pye, PhD, director, The Institute for Cultural Change

"It's a jungle out there, with so many great projects amidst the tightening of funding sources, and this book will help ease the squeeze."

> — Arthur Dong, Deep Focus Productions

"Carole Dean has established herself as one of today's most passionate voices on behalf of independent filmmakers. This book continues her tradition of expert practical advice that guides you step by step through various realistic strategies to finance your film. Yes, there is a winning state of mind, and this book reveals how to achieve and maintain it."

> — Rodney Vance, director, Film and Television, Pacific Union College

"Carole Dean has years of experience both as a producer and a funder and her new second edition is full of nuts-and-bolts information from both sides of the fence, told in a conversational and heart-felt manner. Of special interest to filmmakers will be the in-depth interviews with experts in the field, and an extensive appendix chock full of references. A great new addition to the filmmaker's lexicon."

> — Morrie Warshawski, consultant and author of *Shaking the Money Tree*

"*The Art of Film Funding* gives you the tools you need to make your dream a reality. Carole refers to it as an art for good reason. It's all subjective, there are many different forms, but in the end, you're putting together your own personal masterpiece. This book will help you achieve that!"

> — Tom Malloy, actor/producer, author of *Bankroll, 2nd Edition*

"I tell all my students that the real path to success in film is to take the reins yourself and just do it. Of course, the first step is the script, but after that, I recommend that all my students read *The Art of Film Funding*. Carole Lee Dean's book is a compendium of information that would take years of struggle in the business to learn. It gives you the tools you need to get the funding on your own to make your first (and future) film. Read this book! Make your film!"

> — Paul Chitlik, clinical assistant professor, Loyola Marymount University School of Film and Television, screenwriter for *The Twilight Zone* and *Alien Abduction*, WGA Award Nominee, GLAAD Award Nominee, Genesis Award Winner

"Although I am still in the process of reading and making notes from this book, I have learned that preproduction funding takes as much artistic skill as directing and editing, and that this is the most critical stage of the film. Thank you for this, and for all I continue to learn from this great resource!"

> — Helen Hall, producer, Zero Point Productions

"A quantum leap above and beyond the first edition of this instant must-have classic. All the direction a filmmaker needs to secure funding. Plus, this edition contains a treasure trove of information about the filmmaking process itself."

> — Don Schwartz, *CineSource* Magazine

"The beauty of this book is that it's not just theory; there are interviews with people who've actually done it and who have been involved with the filmmaking process. This book takes a realistic look at what it takes to get your film funded."

— Nathyn Masters, owner, Timecode Mechanics

"I have gained amazing insight and benefited beyond my expectations from reading *The Art of Film Funding* by Carole Lee Dean. This book is an essential and powerful guide for independent filmmakers. It is easy to read and contains numerous golden nuggets in every chapter. I appreciate this book because Carole provides invaluable tools and exercises."

— Alicia Brauns, independent filmmaker

"Hurray for Carole Dean! At last a comprehensive approach to film funding. Her book is the Bible for securing financing for films."

— Joe Tornatore, producer/director

"Whether you work in film, TV, or new media, Dean's book is a terrific guide not only to funding your project, but to thinking about your work in a way that's often difficult for artists and creators: as a product that must be sold and made. Sure, artistic freedom and vision are important, but if you want to succeed in this industry, you must have a grasp of its creative and business sides. This book is a wonderful, easy-to-read start to doing that."

— Chad Gervich, writer/producer (*After Lately*, *Wipeout*, *Cupcake Wars*), author (*Small Screen, Big Picture: A Writer's Guide to the TV Business*)

"Carole Lee Dean answers the question — the most pressing question — filmmakers have: Where am I going to get money to make my movie? Writers who prefer life inside their own heads suddenly have to become sales people, who actually initiate interaction with individuals and organizations with deep pockets. Dean takes the screenwriter from script to pitch to trailer, offering insights from filmmakers who've grabbed those golden purse strings."

— Mary J. Schirmer, screenwriter/producer/instructor (*www.screenplayers.net*)

"Carole Lee Dean does everything from the heart. With her second edition of *Film Funding*, she does it again: expanding documentary funding strategies to include features and converging technologies with state-of-the-art crowdfunding strategies and Transmedia approaches."

— Heather Hale, writer/director/producer (*Snitch*)

"I run a website for emerging documentary filmmakers and I most definitely recommend this book. For most filmmakers, the whole process of fundraising is a great big mystery. As filmmakers, we want to make films, not ask people for money! Those two things really take two very different personality and skill sets."

— Faith Fuller, president, Desktop Documentaries

THE ART OF
FILM FUNDING
ALTERNATIVE FINANCING CONCEPTS

2ND EDITION

CAROLE LEE DEAN

Published by Michael Wiese Productions
12400 Ventura Blvd. # 1111
Studio City, CA 91604
tel. 818.379.8799
fax 818.986.3408
mw@mwp.com
www.mwp.com

Cover design: Johnny Ink *www.johnnyink.com*
Book interior design: Gina Mansfield Design
Editor: Paul Norlen

Printed by McNaughton & Gunn, Inc., Saline, Michigan
Manufactured in the United States of America

Library of Congress Cataloging-in-Publication Data

Dean, Carole Lee.
 The art of film funding : alternative financing concepts / Carole Lee Dean. --
2nd ed.
     p. cm.
 Includes bibliographical references.
 ISBN 978-1-61593-091-3
1. Motion picture industry--United States--Finance. I. Title.
PN1993.5.U6D35 2012
384'.830973--dc23

                         2012003411

This book is dedicated to my family:
Carole Joyce, Eliza Lauren Dean, Cinda Jackson, Susan Bradley & Beth Bolding

TABLE OF CONTENTS

FOREWORD

Feature documentaries are an integral part of the ongoing independent film revolution, continuing to keep pace with their fictional peers not only at the North American box office, but in other revenue windows as well. Moviegoers eager to see intellectually stimulating, well-crafted fare continue to go to the theater to see documentaries, resulting in attendance figures that have increased the value of these films in ancillary and foreign markets, and to equity investors. With their growing potential to bring back profits to private investors, feature documentaries have reached another plateau. There is now enough data to create business plans for them that mirror the forecasting structure of plans for fictional films.

The film audience has a wide taste in theatrical documentary subjects. From 2009 to 2011, successful nonfiction features varied from *Waiting for Superman* to *Exit Through the Gift Shop, Babies, Inside Job, Cool Hair,* and *Catfish.* Another indication of the nonfiction film's ability to perform financially was the apparent distributor rush to pick up documentaries before the 2011 Sundance Film Festival began. While in previous years, five to six films usually were acquired from the day that Sundance films were announced until the start of the festival, in 2011 distributors picked up twenty during that same time period. Nine of those films were documentaries. Before 2000, there weren't enough theatrical docs that had earned significant revenues to make the discussion interesting enough to write a business plan that would tempt investors. Michael Moore's 1989 documentary *Roger and Me* began the emergence of the nonfiction film as a credible theatrical release. Then, in 1994, *Hoop Dreams* was a major success. Similarly successful, but very different in tone were *Crumb* (1995) and *Buena Vista Social Club* (1999). However, there still weren't enough theatrical docs to make a reasonable projection.

Michael Moore made a major financial statement in 2002, when *Bowling for Columbine* earned $21.2 million at the North America box office alone. With investors and organizations being more willing to fund documentaries, a treasure trove unspooled on the theatrical screen in 2004, causing critics to anoint it "the year of the documentary." In addition to the extraordinarily successful *Fahrenheit 9/11* and *Super Size Me*, some of the other documentaries released that year were *Control Room*, *The Corporation*, *Riding Giants*, *Metallica*, and *Touching the Void*. These were followed over the next four years by a slew of successful documentaries with even more widely varied subjects, including *Mad Hot Ballroom*, *An Inconvenient Truth*, *Man on Wire*, *Religulous*, *March of the Penguins*, and *Shine a Light*.

In putting together a business plan for a theatrical documentary film, there are two slight differences from the traditional plan. First, the target markets have the same genres plus an additional group that can be discussed — the documentary audience itself. Nielsen Media Research estimated that 85% of U.S. television households watch documentaries. This audience apparently was unwilling to wait six to twelve months for a film to get from the multiplex to their home. In addition, the growth of reality television also helped documentary films build their growing theatrical audience. Since every documentary has a clear subject, be it political, economic, musical, sports-themed, and so on, the corresponding market segments can be quantified.

A second difference in creating a business plan for a documentary is that the spread of years for comparative films needs to be longer. Enough fictional features are released each year to have enough data within a five-year time span, which is as far back as one should go due to changes in audience numbers, inflation, and other economic conditions. As documentaries are more sporadic in their subject matter and timing, I often use seven to eight years of data in order to have enough films to create a statistically significant forecast.

Emerging technology has been a major boon to the performance of all films in both marketing and sales. Films can be downloaded to cell phones, iPods and iPads. In addition, with more than one billion people worldwide on the Internet and the explosion of social media, self-marketing of films has become an important method for filmmakers to interest the public in their work. Without incurring additional costs, it is possible to supplement a distributor's strategy by spreading word-of-mouth "virally" to interest groups, all of whom have email lists and their own websites. This creates the potential for exponential growth in exposure and influence. With their large communities, finding "friends" on Facebook (currently 600 million unique users) or other sites in a social network is fairly easy. In addition, Twitter (currently 150 million unique users) has become a force in the success of many films. Fans blog reviews on their own web pages or even make a video recording of their reactions and post these to YouTube, their own sites or a social networking page, thus informing friends and web surfers about a film and influencing their opinions.

The establishment of a website for a movie by the filmmaker, as well as the availability of the websites belonging to special interest groups, allows the sale of films directly to individuals around the world and provides forums for alternative voices to be heard.

Although there is not enough data to project the number of sales from these sites, the revenue return from these ventures is expected to grow in the next five to ten years. One thing I do know — whatever outlets become financially viable, the funders will be there with you to reap the rewards.

Louise Levison
Author, *Filmmakers and Financing: Business Plans for Independents*

ACKNOWLEDGMENTS

JanEva Hornbaker McKeel did a marvelous job editing the book. She is a talented writer and filmmaker with extraordinary skills in research and a great sense of humor.

Special thanks to Carole Joyce, Richard Kaufman, Brianna Medley, Pilar Walsh, Peter Hungett, Jim Hague, and Will De Los Santos for their support and information.

It's my grant sponsors that deserve the most credit. From 1992 when I started the Roy W. Dean film grants I have been graciously supported by the top people in our industry. One woman who was a finalist for the grant said it for me: "I want to win for the contacts. The donors to the grant are the top people in the film industry!" If you are ready to shoot your film, please know that these names are the people in the industry who sincerely care for and nurture their clients. These companies donate to my grants because they want to give back to filmmakers. They are listed in the back under the Production List.

PREFACE

Thank you for all of your suggestions from my first edition. I've incorporated them in this second edition in which the concept is raising money and *saving money for features and documentaries.*

You asked for information on distribution. Included is an interview with David Vasile of Dazzle Entertainment as he outlines his criteria for accepting features or docs. The creator of the Hybrid Distribution, Peter Broderick, focuses his chapter on maximizing the Internet for sales and distribution.

Tom Malloy, actor, producer and author of *Bankroll*, outlines funding concepts that brought him millions for his last three features and documentary. Entertainment law specialists Mark Litwak and Corky Kessler share important legal and paperwork issues to save you time and money.

Maureen Ryan, Academy Award–winning producer for *Man on Wire*, let me print a chapter from her brilliant book, *Producer to Producer*. It explains music rights, what the "Most Favored Nation" payment process is and how it can skyrocket your music costs. Too many people under-budget music and this information is most important for your budget.

I often hear filmmakers say, "I am shooting next week and hope to get what I need for my trailer." Bill Woolery (trailer editor of *E.T.* and *The Usual Suspects*) tells you how to be sure you get what you need for your trailer.

Kent Hamilton, V.P. of Truman Van Dyke, helped us with the insurance chapter so you know what is mandatory and what's optional. Paige Gold, lawyer for artists, has great advice on how to read and understand contracts. Michael C. Donaldson writes an entertaining piece on fair use that fully outlines how you can save money and avoid pitfalls; Rosemary Rotondi explains how beneficial a researcher can be for archival footage.

From the Heart is now a fiscal sponsor/partner with IndieGoGo. Danea Ringlemann, co-founder of IndieGoGo, contributes a chapter on understanding the crowdfunding concept. This is a wonderful way to raise money and create your audience, and I have included an outline for a successful crowdfunding campaign.

Britt Penrod, V.P. at Raleigh Studios, and Maia Kaufman from AbelCine Tech give us insights on creating relationships and saving money on stage and equipment rentals.

No book would be complete if we didn't touch on the concept that you are in charge of the money, it's *your* film, and when creating the budget you can decide how to shoot the film based on the funds you think you can raise. Norman Berns, producer of *Kundun, The Writing Code*, explains this in detail in his Budgeting chapter.

Sara Marmoorie and Jesse Deeter, *Who Killed the Electric Car*, let us have a copy of their brilliant Transmedia proposal. This may be a first look for many filmmakers to know how to make their film an Internet work of art. It is the way of the future. This outline is for a documentary, but the same concept can be used for features. It's a new day and anything is possible with the Internet.

The back of the book has a comprehensive list of grantors and a production list of top people in our industry that sincerely care about filmmakers, no matter what your budget.

Everything in the book is written to empower you to fund your film.

INTRODUCTION

You are a filmmaker because you are an artist and a visionary. Where else are you going to find a job that encourages you to create something based on your ideas and thoughts, then get to see it all dance across a twenty-five-foot screen? What other career gives you the opportunity to design something that has the potential to inspire so many people? Filmmaking is a passion that infuses every fiber of your being. It challenges you to reach your potential, and allows you to observe the world from a unique perspective.

Film production is also one of the most demanding careers you could choose. During the course of your career you will be required to make an endless number of artistic decisions that will ultimately affect the final outcome of your film. Each stage of production is paved with potential pitfalls. If you mess something up in production, you'll pay dearly for it in post. Of course the upside to the frenetic pace of your chosen career is that you will never be bored. Filmmakers seem to thrive on all the twists and turns that come with the job, and they love to talk about their latest war stories.

Just grab a double cappuccino and a table at Starbucks over on Hollywood Boulevard and you will hear it all, from passionate debates over the best camera and the latest editing equipment, to a broad range of esoteric criticism on some rogue director's bizarre shooting style. What you probably won't hear is the excited banter of filmmakers discussing the latest in funding.

There is more to filmmaking than stepping behind a camera. A film's life does not begin with production and end with postproduction. There is another stage that is equally important. I'll give you a few hints: Decisions made during this stage will determine the very essence of your film, including where it will go, who will see it, what it will say, and whether or not it will survive. It is a stage that occurs long before you dust off your camera, and it requires just as much artistic skill as directing and editing.

You were probably going to take a wild stab based on the title of this book and guess preproduction funding, only the part about it requiring as much artistic skill as directing and editing threw you, right?

Preproduction funding is the most critical stage of your film's life. If you don't learn the latest funding techniques and marketing trends, you will not survive in this industry. Your future career as a filmmaker and the integrity of your film are both on the line. Do you still want to set this book down and get right to the art of directing?

If you do, you're not unlike the majority of those filmmakers over at Starbucks. By the way, have you ever wondered why there are so many filmmakers sitting around drinking coffee in the middle of the day when they could be out there making movies? Maybe it's because they don't happen to have a couple hundred thousand dollars lying around to support their film habit.

If you don't have funding you don't have a film. You might be able to pull off a small project with the help of your little plastic buddies, Visa and MasterCard (along with whatever you can manage to squeeze out of good old mom and dad), but if you do not learn the art of funding, your film career is going to be very short.

Believe me: I know what I'm talking about. I've watched too many talented filmmakers pack up their cars and leave town because they were hocked up to their eyeballs. It's not easy to produce a film when you're working all day at Kinko's and tending bar on the weekends so you can pay off the debt from your last project.

There is another reason why the funding stage is so critical. The very heart of your film begins with the funding process. The tasks you complete during the funding stage will take you deeper into your project than ever before. Your project will start to come together and will take on a whole new perspective as you explore and write about the background of your story, the style and structure you will use to tell the story, and all the other elements that go into your proposal. Creating your budget — as daunting as that seems — will take you into the heart of the film and open your eyes to changes you may want to make in your script to save you tens of thousands and still tell the same story. Once you start with your business plan and find what you need to give to get the money, then you are really starting to create your film. It's all creative, especially the money side. Dov S-S Simens of HollywoodU.com thinks funding is such an important part of the filmmaking process that he gave it its own special category, which he calls the "pre-preproduction" stage.

Too many filmmakers think the process of funding their films is going to be a long uphill battle that will suck the creative juices right out of their veins. Maybe this is because they can hear the dull echo of doors slamming before they even get started. Once you start to entertain ideas like this, you are doomed! Your belief system is the most powerful asset you have in financing your film. Trust me.

The money is out there. You just have to know how to find it. No, I haven't been living in a cave. I know times are tough. I have heard the grim economic forecasts. I have sat through meetings where board members drone on and on about how the economy has dramatically affected funding for the arts. However, the Internet has given us so many wonderful ways to raise money. You can reach tens of thousands with your film. It's learning a new skill, raising money with the new social media. All of this is to your benefit, and it's all outlined for you to use your creative juices to plan your film's financing.

According to the Foundation Center:
1. Overall, foundation giving reached an estimated $42.9 billion in 2009.

2. The Foundation Center estimates that foundation assets rebounded slightly in 2009 — rising 3.3% to $583.4 billion and that giving will remain flat in 2010. As the economic recovery falters, the outlook beyond 2010 remains unclear, but there continues to be potential for modest positive growth in 2011 foundation giving.

Now, how much did you say it was going to take to get your film made and distributed? We are talking billions of dollars here! Individuals and corporations are giving away billions of dollars to support the arts.

Several articles on the net say that Wall Street and other major investors are considering movies as a good investment.

The amount you need to make your film represents a tiny drop in the bucket, so what's stopping you from going out there and getting your piece of the "funding pie"?

If you believe your film is worth the effort and the money that it is going to take to produce it, and if you believe that you have what it takes to become a great filmmaker, then you owe it to yourself to take the journey toward discovering the art of funding your films. Along the way I will introduce you to ideas and concepts that I have picked up after more than thirty years in the film industry.

Throughout this book you will also hear from successful industry professionals who share insights and strategies that will help you make your filmmaking dreams a reality.

Just one more thing before we take off. I travel light. There's no room for negativity on this train, so you are going to have to leave your excess baggage at the station!

Note: We cannot guarantee the legitimacy of the claims made by any of the entities listed in this book and strongly advise that you obtain legal counsel before you discuss any specific agreements regarding your project with any online or off-line entity.

CHAPTER 1

COMMIT OR BE COMMITTED

The guideposts or books will only tell you the road
or the direction for the destination.
You must make the journey and experience the
joy and the victory.

— Sai Baba

You've got an idea for a film. Great! So does my neighbor's daughter, the man who sold me this crummy computer, and the pizza delivery boy. My plumber pitched a film that will gross ten times more than *E. T.* while he unclogged my sink!

So what sets your idea apart from the rest of the naked city's untold stories? What makes your story so special that investors and grantors are going to want to hand you their hard-earned money and let you take it to Tinseltown to produce a film?

I've read grant applications that start off, "I am thinking of making a film about the secret lives of moths. What do you think?" Even if the concept was crackerjack, the filmmaker's lack of confidence and commitment to the project makes me (along with every funder I know) nervous enough to pass.

With that in mind, I have devised a list of questions that every potential filmmaker should answer before committing to a project. This is not one of those *Cosmo* quizzes where you add up all the "A's" and "B's" and subtract all the "C's" to get some arbitrary score. If you answer each question honestly your answers will reveal your level of commitment to the film.

List three compelling reasons why this film should be made.

Describe your connection to the story and explain why you are the one who should make this film.

Who will benefit from this film? If your primary purpose in making the film is to prove that you can do it, or to make money, then that's what you should put down. Just be honest.

Are you willing to quit your job for the next three years and accept the financial consequences that will accompany this decision?

If not, can you produce the film in your spare time?

How many hours a week can you put into this film?

How long can you drive your car? Will it last the next three years with minor repairs?

Describe your audience by markets including niche and sub-niche.

How will you find your audience? On the Internet? Tell me in detail.

Are you prepared to market the film and distribute it yourself if necessary?

Are you willing to work for three years on this film without getting paid?

Explain why this film is important to you.

You should now have a healthy concept of the reality of filmmaking. If your answers tell you that this is not the film you are willing to make these sacrifices for, then don't do it. If, however, your answers reflect that you are willing to make the sacrifices necessary to make this film, that you are fully committed to your project and nothing can stop you, then read on. This book was written just for you.

Of course that doesn't mean this is going to be a cakewalk. Producing an independent film is a lot like draining an alligator pit. Most of the time you are so busy fighting off alligators that it's easy to forget why you went in there in the first place! That's why you're going to carry the answer to the last question with you wherever you go. When things get hairy, take it out and read it again. Remember where you are coming from and focus on that energy.

SECRETS TO SUCCESS

The Soul never thinks without a mental picture.

— Aristotle

Two equally talented filmmakers set off to make their fortunes. One ends up securing a three-picture deal at Miramax while the other ends up parking cars in West Covina. What is the key ingredient that separates these two filmmakers? Is it film school? I doubt it, since the majority of successful filmmakers out there did not graduate from film school. Is it wealth? Hardly.

Try creativity and vision.

"Cool, Carole! I've got creativity! I've got vision!"

I'm sure you do, grasshopper, but stay with me. Successful filmmakers know how to apply their creativity to the entire project, from the first spark of an idea, all the way through preproduction, production, distribution, and screening. Successful filmmakers understand that funding their project is as much an art as producing it.

My good friend Lynn Preston, who lives outside Sai Baba's compound in Puttaparthi, India, told me a beautiful story about the power of visualization. One afternoon while Sai Baba and several men were engaged in a planning meeting, Sai Baba pointed to a site on the map and announced that they would build a hospital with a new school and a new housing complex close by. When one of the men interrupted Sai Baba and asked him where the money would come from, Sai Baba looked at the man and simply said, "From wherever it is now."

That is such a simple way to manifest. Sai Baba did build the hospital, the school, and the housing complex. He brought the money from wherever it was at that time into his coffers and created his dreams. This is a key element to manifesting money. Don't worry about where the money for your film will come from; just know that it will come to you from some bank, from some corporation, or "from wherever it is now." Once you make the decision that your film must be made and that you are the right person to make it, see and feel that money in your bank account and continue to focus on the finished film.

THE JOURNEY

It is our duty as men and women to proceed as though the limits of our abilities do not exist.

— Pierre Teilhard de Chardin

The journey starts upstairs in your head. You must be ready to throw away any preconceived ideas about the funding process. The economic forecasters were right. Times have changed — there is more money than ever! You just have to learn to go outside the box and look for it. That is what this book is about. It is about adopting new ways of thinking when it comes to funding your film. It is about recreating some of the old methods and accepting new ones.

Dr. Dave Smiley hired me to mentor him in my Angle program. He was living in Florida, recently divorced, retired as a prison physiologist, and according to him, was living in an apartment with so many boxes he had a small path to follow in and out of the place. He had been listening to the CD from *The Secret* and had become a believer in the art of attraction. He wanted to make a film on weight loss because that was a subject he was familiar with and knew he could help people.

Dr. Smiley always said, "I don't know where the money is coming from, I just know that it is coming." In two years from the first contact he had moved to California, raised just under a million dollars and completed his film, *The Inner Weigh*. He was marketing the DVD and setting up affiliate programs. That's what you can do with your mind! Two years from prison physiologist to Hollywood producer. I can't take any credit. Dr. Smiley did it all with his total faith in himself and his film.

When I was a kid I listened to a radio program called *Let's Pretend*. Every Saturday morning I would tune in my radio and take off on a wonderful exotic trip. I never left my home but you could never tell me that. As far as I was concerned I was right there alongside Miss Nila Mack and her cast of Pretenders on every one of their magical voyages.

I'm sure you have similar memories of playing make-believe. Remember how real it all seemed? To help fund your film, you want to recapture that child-like faith that will enable you to see, hear, and feel your goals.

When I want something I put it in writing first. This helps me clarify what it is I really want. Begin by writing down your goals. Describe exactly what you want to do and what the outcome will be. Draw pictures if you like, just include as much detail as you possibly can. You want to be able to see the money and feel the confidence that it brings to you knowing that others fully support you in the filmmaking process.

Once you have outlined your filming goals, get a mental picture of how you will fund it. Picture your bank account with a large balance and see the date. I once wanted a certain amount in my account by November and while I didn't get it that year, I had it the next year! This taught me that exact dates with years are very important.

See a check with a large amount of money and see yourself depositing it in your account. Visualize your dream by believing that the money is here and do not be locked into any one grant or donation or investment from a specific person. Just know it is yours and it will come from — wherever it is now. Believing will open your mind and allow you to continue without being blocked by fear.

Next, verbalize your dream. Discuss it at the beach or on a long walk with yourself. That's right, how does it feel when you verbalize your dream? Do you get a queasy stomach? If so, your body doesn't agree with your mind. You may be asking too much too fast. Keep talking until your body and mind are both able to accept your verbal description of your dream and especially with the dates when you intend to manifest them.

The more detail you use the better, because detail helps you visualize exactly what you want. Be sure to put a lot of passion in your visualization; passion manifests.

This is how you empower your dreams.

Start with an idea.

Write it down.

Visualize.

Emotionalize.

Keep it to yourself and don't share your goals.

There are books that will help you with this part of your journey. My second book, *The Art of Manifesting: Creating Your Future* will help you master the art of clearly defining your goals and explain how to manifest using new concepts from quantum physics. Also on *www.fromtheheartproductions.com* are several videos on creating your future. They are free, and have ideas to fund your film. Also, Wayne Dyer's book, *Change Your Thoughts — Change Your Life* is beneficial. Throughout my career in the industry I have witnessed the success of some very strange films while excellent projects fell by the wayside. This led me to the realization that there was a missing ingredient in filmmaking that was not spoken of in industry circles. I first believed the missing ingredient was passion; however, I looked deeper and saw that many filmmakers who found themselves blocked halfway through production had plenty of passion. Some were so dedicated they were working sixty hours a week so they could scrape together the funds to complete their film, but it still wasn't happening for them. No, passion is an important ingredient, but it is not the secret ingredient.

It soon became apparent that the missing ingredient is faith. You must have faith in yourself and faith in your film. The funding starts in your mind, you are the creator. We attract what we think. So, the very things we feel we can attract, like fear of failure, insecurity, loss, self-doubt — you know, those issues that are usually foremost in a filmmaker's mind. "Did I choose the right format?" "Should I have gone with the more experienced editor?" "Am I going to be able to pull off the pitch of a lifetime when I walk through that door?" Your own self-confidence is the first thing you need to shore up.

These books and audios will help you understand why many of your dreams have not materialized and they will give you the tools to change your life. They will help you be aware of the power of your mind and prepare you for *The Art of Film Funding.*

THE POWER OF SOUND AND WORDS

The thought that comes from your mind should be pure;
the words you utter should be true and sweet
and the work you do should be sacred.

— Sai Baba

It was a perfect day in the Bahamas. The air was clear and the 80-degree water below offered amazing visibility. As I dove off the platform of Martin Woolen's grand yacht, *The Mustard Seed,* I was greeted by a kaleidoscope of comical fish along with an amazing assortment of exotic creatures, all coexisting amid a spectacular coral garden. It was a sight that soothed the soul.

I was joyfully exploring this underwater wonderland when another guest from the yacht swam toward me, pointed out a giant lobster, then without warning, aimed his spear gun and sent his spear into the tail of the brightly colored creature. The lobster emitted an ear-piercing scream as it writhed about. I will never forget that sound; it taught me the awesome power of sound to convey emotions.

Many creatures emit sounds or change colors to express themselves. The octopus is one of the greatest underwater communicators. When they are hungry they change colors to disguise themselves from unsuspecting prey, when they feel sexy they change colors to attract a mate, and when threatened they change colors to confuse their enemy. It seems for the octopus every single thought is on display in living color! The octopus is so talented that he can even emit a cloud of black ink that resembles his own shape, a phenomenon called pseudomorph, meaning false body.

We also become what we believe. You are a very unique being. Look at the talents you possess and cherish yourself. Never ever put yourself down. My father, Roy W. Dean, used to say, "If you can't say something nice about a person, don't say anything at all." This proverb also applies to what you say about yourself. You have been chosen to impart art, beauty, and knowledge to the rest of us. Everything you do is a reflection of you. If you put yourself down you also put down your film and reduce your image to your crew, so hold yourself in the highest esteem.

The words we use to describe our dreams and our aspirations hold an immense power to create and manifest. Think about the words you use to create things in your life. How many times have you made plans for the future and verbalized your plans? Once spoken, your plans are like a fait accompli. What you have said comes true even if you are not aware that you verbalized this plan in the past. Be responsible and choose your words carefully when verbalizing your hopes and dreams. Above all, be kind to yourself.

As an artist you also have a profound responsibility to choose the best sounds and words to project your message. Your audience will walk away from your film with images embedded in their senses. Once you show something as fact, many people will store this information forever and it will become part of their belief system.

Alison Landsberg coined the phrase "prosthetic memory" to describe a phenomenon that occurs when memories that are not organically based, are nonetheless experienced with one's own body through various cultural technologies, such as film and television. According to Landsberg the experience of film "might actually install in individuals 'symptoms' through which they didn't actually live, but to which they subsequently have a kind of experiential relationship."

Landsberg's studies have shown that prosthetic memories derived from watching films can actually "become part of one's personal archive of experience."

If you move to the concept that you are shaping minds and assigning emotions and beliefs with every picture, every word, and every sound, you will realize how important your words, sounds, and pictures are to humanity. This is especially true when pictures are enhanced with words, sounds, and music. You must be in control of your script and take great care during the edit if your audience is going to receive the message you want them to receive.

You should always be asking, "Do these words convey the message I want to impart to the world? Do the sounds convey the meaning and emotions I want my audience to remember?"

Sound is one of the most powerful tools you will use in your film. Sound can create and sound can destroy. It can shatter glass, and can even produce subtle patterns in sand. Sound can lower or increase blood pressure. When martial arts experts shout "KI-AI!" during impact, they are using sound to focus all of their internal energy. Kiai, also known as the spirit yell, literally means to concentrate one's life force or energy.

There is a scene in *Bobby Deerfield* when the film's terminally ill heroine waits for a noisy train before she releases the most unforgettable scream. The entire theatre can feel this woman's anger, grief, despair, and help-lessness. I was so impressed that I went home and tried to do the same thing. I put on a CD, cranked it up full-blast, and I let it rip. It was very disappointing. All I could manage to come up with was a squeaky, stifled little shriek. I immediately went to work on improving my scream and can now go up against some of the best screamers out there. Sound strange? Try it! I find it amazingly therapeutic and frequently will use it to release all sorts of pent-up emotions. Of course this therapy should be used with caution as it can elicit some strange looks, not to mention a police officer or two at your front door!

Sound conveys energy and meaning to your audience. It is up to you to make sure it conveys the meaning you want to project.

Tips on Production with Xackery Irving

Jack London once said, "You can't wait for inspiration. You have to go after it with a club."

That is exactly how Xackery Irving made *American Chain Gang*, a documentary that explores the controversial revival of prison chain gangs in the South. Xackery is a hunter. He is always moving; always observing. He stalks the human condition with a camera and takes deliberate dead aim on his subjects to produce documentaries that make a difference.

In an interview I chatted with Xackery about how he captured the idea for *American Chain Gang*, how he raised the funds, and how he managed to stay focused while surrounded by such a hostile environment.

Xackery, I heard that after *American Chain Gang* was released, the practice of using chain gangs was actually outlawed in Alabama, so you now have an important historical document. I would like to know where you got the idea for this film.

What initially sparked my interest in the subject was a magazine photo essay depicting the resurgence of the chain gang labor program in Alabama.

The striking black-and-white images of the officers and inmates in these prison fields inspired me to make a film about this experience. I couldn't get the subject matter out of my head. I thought, "This would translate into a compelling documentary."

I began the process of researching the history of chain gangs in the U.S.

Though, as a responsible documentarian, I didn't want to go into the research with a strong preconceived notion driving me, I did find some accounts of horrible brutality and neglect that chain gang inmates had been subjected to for more than a century. Leasing prisoners to coal mines and factories where they were forced to work without pay and under harsh conditions — no heat, chained to bare metal beds, and no medical attention whatsoever. The idea confounded me that a practice with this legacy could be brought back to our society.

I felt it was a very powerful subject. I took a trip to Alabama and received permission to spend time at the Limestone Correctional Facility and meet people who would later be in the film. I was completely hooked.

I knew there were good stories here. I saw white supremacist inmates chained to and working with their African American prison mates. I saw the resentment and hatred among the inmates that were chained together. I saw the resentment inmates had for their officers. I listened to the officers share their perspectives on overseeing men who were deemed by society as "too dangerous to be free." This was clearly an emotionally charged environment. I felt drawn to the challenge of telling this story with the clarity and complexity that it deserved.

It's an amazing process to watch the story unfold, isn't it?

When I was in Alabama shooting, we spoke on the phone a few times and I remembered your advice. You said, "You must remember that a film is a living thing. It takes on a life of its own." I think the idea was, that as a filmmaker, your responsibility is to foster the growth of this "living thing" and follow it as it takes its own path. You explained that I could contribute my own vision as I pursue the story, but I had to let go and focus on catching on film the reality of the story and subject I was portraying. You instilled in me that it can be refreshing that you don't have control of how the story and production unfolds. That lesson stayed with me.

During production, I did heed your advice and dedicated my focus to catching these moments as they happened.

How do you see the process of filmmaking?

Some people say filmmaking is like architecture. Your blueprint is your script, or outline, you have a crew and a cast to procure and assemble the materials. Everything is constructed in postproduction. Narrative filmmaking produces a structure based on your initial script.

Documentary filmmaking, in this architectural analogy, is more like log cabin building, I think. In production, you are gathering the timber, the raw material of your story. When you go to the edit suite, that's where you really make the film. These raw materials now exist and you can't redesign or retrofit them to match what you had written in your treatment. You have to put them together pretty much as they exist. You may have a detailed plan when you start, but once you get into the edit room your story is really what you have in your footage.

How did you make your vision of the film into a reality?

I think the most important thing one needs to do during this planning stage is to become very organized. You need to have a good treatment, a solid pitch, and a clear presentation of what it is that you want to achieve in the film. I found that having a well-written proposal is as important as any aspect of production or postproduction. Become an expert about the subject matter you want to follow. Research. Get to know the people you will be following, so that you can bring the story alive when you describe the film you want to make. Do all this, and have a clear, itemized budget so that you can describe how funding will be used to produce your story. Being prepared to answer questions about the film in a clear and definitive way will show potential investors and collaborators that you are focused, organized, and prepared to start the journey.

So the search for funding begins.

I applied for the Roy W. Dean grant in New York because I knew that if we got the grant, we could get started on principal photography right away. I was chosen as one of the five finalists, and the next step was to pitch the film in front of a judging committee and an audience. The opportunity to create a verbal pitch at the National Arts Club challenged me and, ultimately, forced me to sharpen my focus of subject matter of the film.

(The night Xackery pitched his film at the National Arts Club, he and Ann Stern were neck and neck for first place. The judges were going back and forth, agonizing over the decision before finally awarding the grant to Stern.)

(Xackery did not walk away with first place that night, but it was far from over for this tenacious filmmaker. His passion and dedication to his project really came through in his pitch, which is why I decided then and there to find a way to help him realize his dream. I dug some ASA 50 & ASA 400 16mm stock out of the vault and donated it to him so he could start shooting.)

It really does start with the concept and the pitch, doesn't it? What advice can you give filmmakers about pitching their projects?

I think it is always good to practice your pitch. You will need to inspire a lot of people to help make your film a reality. I learned to constantly practice pitching. Even when someone has passed, they have given you an opportunity to practice. Ask for feedback and use it to make your pitch better.

The other good thing about pitching people is that it forces you to be very articulate about the vision and direction you want to take with your film. It becomes a good process to listen to ideas from others and go over logistical scenarios. This prepares you mentally by stimulating creative new approaches for how and what to shoot.

What is the most difficult challenge when approaching potential donors?

It is important to be very clear about conceptual and practical details of the project you are asking them to support. If one is asking for someone's time, money and energy, it helps if you can present a clear, concise snapshot of what steps you need to complete your vision of the film.

When you communicate this with enthusiasm, it can be contagious. You want to ignite that spark in the potential donor.

Documentaries are special in this way as they are usually centered on a social issue or a particular subject. You are selling a film about something that you have to examine and explore. You want to help change the world's perception through this exploration. This can be very powerful. Find the people who share this goal and you'll be more likely go get funding.

So there you were with your vision and some donated raw stock. How did you keep the momentum moving forward?

I think once I started shooting, everything else sort of came together. I gathered the resources needed and kept the crew size and budget small.

Once we finished production, I put together a five-minute teaser reel to present to distributors. This helped communicate what our film was about and gave a sense of the editorial style of the finished film. I met with HBO and others. The reel got the interest of a foreign sales agent who carried the film when we completed post.

We needed that five-minute piece to get the film sold. It was much more effective to have this to make a sale, than to just have a treatment or business plan. I think it is easier to sell your project if you have film or video to present.

I learned this from George Stoney while I was at NYU. He is a pioneer documentary filmmaker. His other legacy has been to advise many fledgling filmmakers how to develop their craft. He read the treatment for

American Chain Gang and he was the first one who impressed upon me the difficulty of raising money with a "paper" version of your film alone. You have to shoot something, he said, to show them your vision.

When you were filming *American Chain Gang*, you were one-on-one with some pretty tough characters. What advice can you offer other documentary filmmakers on how to approach the interview?

Your subjects are the ones who tell the story of your film. So, it's a partnership. And it can often be an uneasy one. This is part of the journey you described during our phone conversation when I started. You have to be up for the challenge of following a story even when it follows a path that defies your expectations. Some of the inmates we followed had made some personal decisions that were heart-breaking. You have to follow the story wherever it leads you.

How do you win your subjects' trust, especially inside a prison?

I think to develop this partnership, get them used to the camera. They are in a very vulnerable position, putting themselves in your hands. Let them look through the viewfinder and roll some film or tape (or digital media) on them. This will allow your subjects to empower themselves to tell their story with you. If you impose your sense of storytelling "authority" on them too much it could hinder a powerful connection. If they feel and know they have the ability to express themselves in their own words then you have opened the treasure chest of great character moments. This happened with a couple of the inmates when we let them roll the camera on the crew. We sat with one inmate a few afternoons without shooting. When he was ready, we began following him. He gave us some pretty candid interviews as a result.

What important lessons have you learned about the art of the interview?

Albert Maysles was at the National Arts Club the night of the Film Grant presentation. I believe he was one of your judges. Afterwards, he talked to me about the project and offered some advice. He said that it is more effective with two people talking on screen and sharing an idea rather than just one person talking to camera. It seems like an obvious thing, but it works so well. Instead of getting an idea just in an on-camera interview, he said, try interjecting the idea when your character is speaking to another subject. If this idea is discussed between two people, or even argued over, it can be a much more dimensional way of exploring that idea.

It allows the audience to see the information unfold between two people so it seems more organic and real.

That being said, there are times when a straight-to-camera interview is the best way, and sometimes the only way, to get an idea across in your film. Build on the trust you build with your subjects to get an honest and strong interview.

If you had the opportunity to go back and do this film over again, what would you do differently?

I would have focused on fewer subjects and stuck to them like glue. I would have covered even more interactions between the main characters and the people in their lives. I think the most compelling thing to see in a film is people in conflict overcoming obstacles to get what they want. I would have covered even more scenes that demonstrated the conflict and struggles they were enduring. I think that's something to strive for in my next documentary.

As a documentary filmmaker you are constantly shooting life as it unfolds. What tips can you offer new filmmakers?

I like to shoot my own films. Operating camera can keep your crew size sometimes to just one person. If you are not comfortable with shooting, then hire good people you can trust. And be present but unobtrusive. I think the more time you spend with your subject, the easier it is to get the great scene.

It is like hunting; you get the shot or you don't. The wonderful thing about it is, the more you shoot and are in this environment you begin to anticipate how the action will come across and you can get into position and get the material.

What have you done since the completion of *American Chain Gang*?

I have been producing, shooting and directing nonfiction television programs. Making my own film prepared me for this career.

As well, I have just completed production on my first narrative feature, entitled *Nothing Without You*. Though it is a tightly scripted psychological thriller, I used a lot of the lessons learned while making *American Chain Gang*. I kept the budget modest by operating camera myself and using a small, locally hired crew in a small city. I shot the film in a vérité style. My shot list was made, sometimes, after blocking was completed, which gave the sense that we were "catching moments" of the story.

The film was self-financed. We didn't wait for big investors; we just started shooting when we were ready and worked within a tight budget to make the film. Like *American Chain Gang*, I learned to go after the project with care, focus, and a little relentlessness.

CHAPTER 2

THE PERFECT PITCH

I don't know how the word pitch first became synonymous with the art of describing a film, but it seems appropriate. The film pitch is like the baseball pitch in that it is critical to the outcome of the game. Pitching is a team effort. While it is the pitcher's job to get the ball over the plate, it is actually the catcher's job to tell the pitcher what kind of ball to throw.

The catcher (potential investor) sends signals to the pitcher (you) if you are looking for them. Is the person you want to pitch a conservative? If so, then you want to pitch tax deductions, state incentives, write offs, etc. They are interested in return on investment or tax deductions. They want to handle money in a way that benefits them. If the person you want to pitch is what I call a "high flyer," someone who looks for potential from investments but will take chances, then you want to pitch the sizzle. It's being an executive producer, seeing his name in the film credits, being on the set, cast parties, and the thrill of opening night!

Because your catcher is your investor or funder, if you pay attention to your catcher you will have a better chance of winning the game. You know that you might have to adjust the speed and the trajectory a little here and a little there, depending upon to whom you're pitching, but the goal will remain the same: you've got to connect the ball with the glove. To do this you will need to create a pitch that will sell, and you need to work on it until it is perfect. This is one of the most important steps in the *Art of Film Funding*.

In the Appendix you will find a list of funders. Don't even think about getting up there on the mound and going after these funders until you have perfected your pitch.

Go back to the questions in Chapter One that every potential filmmaker should answer and expound upon your answers.

1. List three compelling reasons why this film should be made.

2. Describe your connection to the story and explain why you are the only one who should make this film.

3. Who will benefit from this film?

Plus, tell me what the urgency is: *why make this film now?*

Write the story of your film. Keep writing until you run out of steam, then walk away and let it sit for at least two days.

Sometimes when you start writing you open a floodgate of creativity. Keep a little notebook in your pocket during the day and on your nightstand when you go to bed so you can jot down ideas as they come. Remember, an unwritten idea is an unfinished idea.

Now go back to your notes and edit everything down to two paragraphs or less. This becomes the first part of your proposal and the beginning of your pitch. The pitch must convey the meaning of your film while capturing all the passion, intrigue, drama, or humor of your story. It must move the audience and leave them wanting more. That's why they fund you; they want to see the film finished.

Writing a pitch is like writing poetry or the lyrics to a song. Use words that give the utmost compression, force, and economy. As you work on your pitch, read it out loud. How does it sound? Does it roll off your tongue or does it sound clumsy? Rewrite it, read it out loud, then rewrite it again. Keep working on it until the words have just the right rhythm and pace.

VISUALLY DESCRIBE YOUR FILM

A pitch must visually describe your film. This is the first mistake most people make. They leave out adjectives. When you tell me that your hero is tall, dark and handsome, I have a visual. Add creative or nerdy and I have an even better visual, plus I have some "feeling" for him. The words you choose are paramount to creating the image for your potential funder. Your words must conjure up a vision of your film so as you speak them, your catcher can imagine your completed film. Visually describing your film is the most important part of the pitch.

We don't talk the way we write. I learned that from the first production I made. I wrote a script about my unique process of evaluating used tape. My company bought "1" and Betacam tape from TV stations here and abroad. Then we processed it on evaluating machines, repackaged it, and sold it to other TV stations! We had lots of fun doing this and we made a very nice profit. So when my friend, IATSE Director of Photography Geno Talvin, promised to shoot this "little video" for me as a gift, I sat down and wrote a script that was the same as the copy I wrote to sell my evaluated tape. He looked at it and said, "This won't work." Just as simple as that he summed up my two weeks of writing. He knew from shooting thousands of pages of dialogue that my script was the written word and not the spoken word. Well, I was adamant that it was perfect and I stood my ground. Geno, the D.P., just smiled that knowing smile and said, "We'll use a lot of your short ends on this production!" And right he was: after seventeen rewrites we finally had a decent script.

Please don't make the mistake I made. Write your pitch, then speak it and rewrite it until it sounds natural. Actually if you can catch yourself on tape talking about your film, that is the best way to create your pitch. Use words that you normally use in conversation and you will see the difference between the written and spoken word.

A STICKY STORY PITCH

What do you think is the most important element of your pitch? After listening to thousands I think it is a *"sticky story,"* not just a story, but one I can easily remember. When you pitch someone it's an opportunity to spread the word about your film to all their friends, right? Yes, but only if they can remember it. *Made to Stick* by Chip and Dan Heath says that "too often you are cursed with too much knowledge." Bringing that wealth of info into a simple sticky story is the key to the perfect pitch. I highly recommend this book.

A "sticky story" is one where you take all the knowledge you have on your film and transform it into a *simple story*, one that is easy to remember. The first rule is to keep it simple, find the core of the idea. You may have paragraphs of info; keep taking things away until you can't take anything else out or you lose the essence.

Step one, find the core. Think of journalists who create lead copy for articles and you get the story in a few words. They prioritize. So can you. This simple story needs something *unexpected*; this is to be sure you get their attention. You might ask a question that the film needs to answer. It can be a surprise like a shocking fact or a point of interest they will remember or a massive change in direction for the film.

You need something *concrete*, like specific people doing specific things. Or give them some facts. Concrete ideas are easy for people to remember and they create a foundation.

Credible information makes people believe your story. This can be a place for truthful core details, and please make them as vivid as possible. We need to see your film from the pitch.

Emotion is next. I say, "Touch my heart and I reach for my pocket book." We communicate through the heart chakra, so touch me with your story.

You can do this through one of your characters, let me feel them. When you pitch me your "sticky story," I want to walk away with your film in my mind forever. Then I can tell my friends that I invested/donated to your film and brag about it. They can then tell their friends about this wonderful film and on and on it goes. This is what you want.

Remember, you have carried this film for several years and your audience is just hearing about it. That's why brevity and a sticky story are needed to transmit your knowledge to someone who knows nothing about it. This is an excellent way to create your pitch.

Find these elements of a sticky story: unexpected, concrete, credible and with emotion from the long draft you made. They are there, just put them into this format and begin to pitch yourself, then family, then friends. Soon no one is safe!

THE WINNING PITCH BY JOHN MCKEEL

Just the thought of standing in front of an audience scared Jim. He wasn't alone. A recent survey showed more people are afraid of public speaking than dying, so Jim worked very hard to memorize what he thought was a great speech. He wrote and re-wrote it until every word was perfect. Unfortunately, when it came time to deliver his talk, Jim was so nervous he forgot what he was going to say. He stumbled over his words. Jim stopped frequently and his eyes naturally rolled to the top of his head as he tried to remember those perfect phrases he had so meticulously constructed. He lost contact with his audience and the speech was a total bomb.

You've written a great proposal, but now you have to pitch it. Never confuse the written word with the spoken word. They are two completely different forms of communication. Beautiful writing can sound stilted and pretentious when read aloud. Great literature doesn't guarantee great performance, so prepare an oral presentation orally. This is so important I'm going to repeat it. Prepare an oral presentation orally.

How is that possible? You know your material. You've lived and breathed your project for a long time. You've talked about it with friends, family and probably perfect strangers, so your first exercise in the preparation of a great oral pitch is to sit down in a room by yourself and just start talking. Let the words come as you describe your passion. As you talk about it, certain sentences will stand out. Quickly jot them down and then keep talking. Again, remember this is an oral presentation, not a written proposal. Don't write down any more words than it will take to remind you of the thought. The key is to get back to talking as soon as possible. It's an oral presentation, so we are preparing orally for it.

If you are having trouble getting started with your talk, answer these questions out loud. Imagine that I am right there with you. Now let's talk:

1. Your film is a jewel with many facets. Can you describe some of these facets and some of the other themes I will see in your final project?

2. Now, if you had to choose only one theme, what is the most important facet? Why?

3. Who are you making this film for?

4. You seem very passionate about your project. Why?

5. Tell me about some of the characters I will meet in your film.

6. What do you hope people will take away from watching your documentary?

7. The three most important topics to address in your pitch are:

   ❧ What is this film about?
   ❧ Why make it now?
   ❧ You have to convince us our money won't be wasted. Tell us why you will see this film through to completion.

After an hour you should have pages of great sentences that will trigger great thoughts. Now it's time to find your theme.

Look over those pages of sentences you just wrote down. Do you see any themes? It's time to take out more paper and write a different theme on the top of each page. Now copy all of the sentences that relate to that theme onto that page.

Take a break. Have a cup of coffee. Play with the kids and then come back to your notebook. Look through all the pages. One will stand out. You've done it! That's your theme for this pitch, but how will you organize those random sentences into an organized pitch?

Try giving a three-minute talk from just the notes on that particular page. A couple of things will happen. First, a natural rhythm will develop. You'll discover you need to say this before that. A rough outline will develop. You will also find that some of the sentences aren't as powerful as the others. Discard them and you will be left with pure gold.

(John McKeel wrote this for my monthly newsletter to filmmakers. If you want to be on the mailing list for information like this, please sign up on the first page under newsletter at *www.fromtheheartproductions.com*.)

KNOW WHO'S WHO

At a seminar one of my students asked me how I pitched my Roy Dean Film Grants to get my donations. I was stunned. It took me a minute to realize and explain to him that I was the grant. It was part of me and my pitch changed with each potential funder. First I analyze their needs. Usually this may be a matter of minutes; since I know the benefits of the grant, I only need to assess their needs.

But I do not always close someone at the first meeting. Why? Because if they don't know me or know the incredible films we have supported with the grant, then I would waste a potential funder by pitching too hard too soon. In an instance like this, at the first meeting, you need to make a good impression. Please, don't over pitch. Remember, funders don't fund films, they fund you. Make an excellent impression; find a way to get their card by saying you may want to ask them for advice in the future.

Before I approach someone to donate to the Roy Dean Film Grants that we give yearly at From the Heart, they need to know who I am. I explain that I have been giving grants since 1992 for films that are unique and make a contribution to society. We have helped produce over thirty-five films. So my passion comes out when I talk about our success stories. I tell them that I believe we are creating filmmakers as well as films.

Your potential donors need to see and feel your passion for your film and you need to know who they are. You first meeting will always be to make an excellent impression and to learn all you can about them. Who are they? What do they do? What is their passion?

During this "interview" you can access a lot of information. People like to talk about their companies, their potential future, and where the company will be in five years. In America many people are their business; when they talk about their business, you get to know who they are. This is important. You must know their needs before you can get a donation or a discount or advice.

Usually when I first meet someone whose company could become a donor to my grant, I take mental notes to outline who they are but I do not pitch them. Not yet. When asked what I do, I tell them about my grant for filmmakers and keep the conversation focused on them. If you have found someone with tons of money then you want to know all about that person before you make an "ask." We will cover this more in "Perfecting Your Pitch."

BECOME THE FILM

Your pitch may be the only chance you get to tell someone about your film. You may find yourself standing next to the head of Sundance acquisitions at a crowded cocktail party, or you may find out that the grumpy little old lady sitting next to you on the plane is a wealthy entrepreneur who got bumped to coach. You may be up against some heavy hitters, so make sure you are always ready with your perfect pitch.

I know a documentary filmmaker who raised $5,000 while standing in line at the grocery store. How? Because she created a short pitch under two minutes that truly engaged people and she learned how to take advantage of situations. When someone asks you what you do, you must respond that you are a filmmaker.

Forget that you are a computer guru in your day job; if you really want to make that film, then let everyone know you are a filmmaker. That's what she did. While waiting in line, the man ahead of her began to chat and when he asked what she did, she immediately responded that she was a filmmaker and pitched him. Her film was about Greece and he said, "I'm Greek and my family came from Greece." She took his card and followed up with a phone call to discuss her film and his benefits by donating to the film; she got a check for $5,000.

The biggest mistake filmmakers make with their pitch is not focusing on the story. They often give you the history, why it needs to be made or, heaven forbid, the technical information. They will even tell you how they are shooting on the latest XYZ tape-less camera. This can be distracting. You want them to listen to your story.

Most funders don't know anything about cameras and they don't really care what type of editing system you have, so stay away from technical information in the pitch. Only mention it if someone asks you.

Please don't say you are making a film because you need to get a message to people. As Mr. Warner said, "If you want to send a message, go to Western Union. If you want to make a film, tell me a story."

What is paramount to financing is people fund stories.

Morrie Warshawski came to L.A. and taught a seminar with me. One of the most profound things he said was, "I can tell in thirty seconds if your film will be funded." Can you imagine? Morrie is right: You have thirty seconds to grab your potential funder or investor, and you can only do that with a brilliant, engaging story, passionately told.

I believe you must become the story. Remember the film *Fahrenheit 451*? This film is set in a future society where books are not allowed. It's a time when people must live only by the controlled information on their television sets, which is a horrid thought, right?

The hero of this film is actually a fireman who is in charge of burning books and he becomes curious and decides he must understand what is so evil that he has to burn books, so he steals one to read. Naturally he becomes an avid reader and soon realizes the importance of preserving books as works of art. Eventually he is forced to flee the city and live in the woods with people who become their books. The only way this band of book lovers can legally live in this society and not own books is to memorize them, every word, every comma, and every paragraph.

That's what you need to do. You must become the film. When you can see the film, when you know every scene, when you know every point you want to make in your story and when you and your film are inseparable, then your pitch moves from your head to your heart. Now you are communicating with people because we communicate through our heart chakra. You need to touch people's hearts to reach them, especially when you want to be funded.

Originally they said that the heart pumped blood to the body. Now the scientists say, "Whoops, we made a mistake. The heart would have to be the size of a Mack truck to do that, it pumps blood to the lungs and other systems take over for the rest of the body." I believe some day they will say that our creativity lives in the heart. Think of what you do when you are touched; your hand immediately goes to your heart. Don't tell me that great works of art did not originate from the heart, not when you can see the Pietà and gasp at its beauty. Clint Eastwood won an Academy Award with *Million Dollar Baby* because he touched our hearts with the love the three main characters had for each other.

We communicate to each other through heartfelt feelings. If you want to make a point in your film or connect with your audience, then use words that touch people's hearts. This is what people want to hear, heartfelt stories. That's what they want to fund. You don't have to use the word love. It's all about nurturing, caring and supporting each other.

THE WIND-UP AND DELIVERY

You need to have the same level of confidence when you pitch to Sheila Nevins at HBO that you have when you pitch to your best friend. This confidence will come with practice and from knowing with complete certainty that you are presenting a great story that people will be interested in.

You and your pitch need to become inseparable. Write it down and carry it with you. Stick it in your purse or backpack. Sew a special little pocket for it in your swimsuit; just don't leave home without it. I want you to whip it out wherever you are and practice. Practice it on the bus driver. Practice it on your doctor's receptionist. Practice it on your imaginary friend while you are stuck in traffic.

When you go to Starbucks and they say, "How are you today?" I want you to pitch them your film. Pitch your film to the checker at your local grocery store, your cleaners, your pizza shop, and your mailman. Let everyone in your life know you are making a film. It's another way for you to practice your pitch, and they will be so impressed to know you are a filmmaker. To them you are in a glamorous business. These people will be the first ones you invite to your funding parties and they will be a good support group for you. Get their emails and ask for support with your IndieGoGo.com crowdfunder.

PERFECTING YOUR PITCH

- Give individual one-on-one pitch sessions to everyone in your family and be sure to write down their comments and questions. As you pitch your story, pay close attention to how they respond and listen to what they say.
- Are they excited about the story?
- Do they act like they want to know more?

- ❖ Does your pitch stir up interest and stimulate questions?
- ❖ Remember, potential donors are likely to ask some of the same questions that your family and friends ask. Don't forget to research and follow up on all of their questions so you can be ready with good answers. If a question is asked repeatedly, consider addressing the issue in your pitch.

No matter how hard you prepare you will come up against some questions that you don't have the answer for. Just be honest. Explain that you are still in preproduction and that you have not worked out all the details yet. Try to anticipate challenging questions and don't be afraid to memorize your answers.

Your project is still in its infancy. This is the critical stage when everything will start to jell, so pay attention. Sometimes pitching your project will bring you some great ideas. That's what Xackery Irving discovered when he pitched his idea for *American Chain Gang*. The more he pitched, the more feedback he got. He listened and ended up using several ideas that evolved out of discussions from his pitch that improved the film and saved him money.

Practice your pitch and practice your answers until your delivery is smooth and convincing. Become one with your pitch. Memorize it until it is part of your DNA. This is the beginning of funding your film.

It is important to create several pitches. First is the elevator pitch. You want to literally be able to tell someone the outline of your story from the first to the eighth floor and be able to hand them your card and leave them wanting more.

The second pitch is under two minutes. This is the visual description of your film passionately delivered. You may have to disappear and jump up and down several times to rev yourself up, but the passion you have for your film can be contagious and it must be part of the pitch.

Once you finish, say nothing... absolutely nothing. That's paramount to the funding process. Give them some time to process what you have just said. Remember, you have been carrying this film for years and this is the first time they have heard about it.

Don't continue on because they must have time to gather their thoughts. Wait for them to say something. Usually they will ask you a question about the film. Wonderful, this is what you want, you have engaged them. They are interested. Now what do you say? Well, if it is a good question to answer, answer it and let them have time to respond.

If it is not a good question to answer, then beg the issue just like the politicians do. Answer the question with a follow-up to your pitch. This follow-up has more details on the story and may even include why you are making the film and why you are the only one to make it.

I have so many wonderful filmmakers who call me to pitch their films. Usually during the first two minutes I have questions for them and I wait until they finish to ask my question. If they understand how much we can handle at one time, they will stop talking, those who don't keep going for five to sometimes fifteen minutes. By the time they are finished I have forgotten whatever it was I wanted to ask and definitely forgotten any comments I wanted to make.

I have a beautiful garden of flowers all growing in the sand at my beach house in Oxnard Shores because of these long pitches. I just go outside and work on my garden knowing nothing will stop them until they run out of steam or pause for another espresso. Please don't do this. Realize that your job is to engage people with your pitch, not overwhelm them.

After several weeks of pitching your project to friends, patient family members, and complete strangers, your pitch should feel as comfortable as your favorite pair of blue jeans. Your pitch will be on a much higher level and will contain the elements that will capture the interest of anyone you speak to.

Remember, it is a good pitch if: It tells an engaging/sticky story, it communicates how your film will make a difference, it creates a sense of urgency, it works, and you get funded!

CHAPTER 3

THE PROPOSAL

*Your vision will become clear only when you can
look into your own heart...
Who looks outside, dreams; who looks inside, awakes.*
— Carl Jung

Reading proposals is a passion of mine, which is a good thing, since I read over five hundred proposals and view over a thousand DVDs a year for my Roy W. Dean film grants. Filmmakers frequently ask me how they can improve their applications.

First, remember that grantors or investors are usually under a deadline to read and make a decision on something that should never be judged: your art. Your potential funder is probably reviewing hundreds of proposals, one right after the other, so find a way to make your proposal unique.

I consider the introduction or synopsis to be the most critical element in the proposal. It is the first thing I read when I pick up a new film proposal because it tells me how compelling the project is and reveals how passionate the filmmaker is. It should tell me a visual story of the film. Sponsors use the synopsis during the selection process as a way of categorizing and separating one type of film from another. If your synopsis is dynamic and is strategically placed on your application, it will remain active in the sponsor's mind.

This is where your sticky story works for you. It's important to have a concise overview of the film that gives us that visual description and tells a story with emotion, surprise, concrete information, credibility, etc. I can pitch you films that entered my grants over ten years ago because I can remember their sticky story.

MORE INFORMATION TO INCLUDE

Mention any creative fundraising ideas you are using in your application. For example, filmmakers often barter with other filmmakers to get their projects completed. Donors like to see filmmakers who use creative funding techniques.

If you are making a documentary on food, do you offer to cook a healthy meal for a $500 donation? Tell us your creative ideas for funding.

Tell us what you may be offering for large donations.

Are you planning a crowdfunding campaign? If so, what are you doing before the launch to ensure success? Outline it for us. (See Chapter 10, "The Roar of Crowdfunding.")

I usually call my finalists and discuss their film application. When possible I give them guidance and suggestions on how they can improve their proposal. The most important thing I tell them is to submit again next year! Cathryne Czubek, the producer for the wonderful film, *A Girl & A Gun*, applied three times before she won.

Something wonderful happens when you win one grant; most people win another or get some important recognition. It's in the consciousness now, and you are moving with the universal speed to finish your film. You are in the "field of infinite possibilities," as Dr. Chopra says.

Winning one grant leads to success with future grants, so mention prior grants that you have won in your cover letter and any awards anyone on the crew won.

Use a PR person to promote your accomplishments and you can easily pave the way for even more funding and distribution.

Avoid using technical jargon in your application unless your proposal is to a grantor who has specifically asked for technical information. The people reading it will not know what a 20 to 1 zoom is nor will they recognize the latest digital camera you want to use. This can be confusing and divert them from the real issue of your film.

A funder who was speaking at a conference I attended told the audience about an applicant who entered her grant competition seven times! Each time the filmmaker asked the funder how he could improve his application and he incorporated their ideas in his proposal when he applied the next year. The filmmaker finally won on his seventh try. Many times the information given to filmmakers by grantors can improve the film, so entering ITVS, for example, can benefit you with advice. I give a personal consultation to everyone who enters my grant competition. Of course you enter to win, but if you don't, you want to know why! That's very important. Take everyone up on the consultation and take good notes, it will benefit you for the next grant.

Once you start on your journey you are committed. Never give up. You may have to apply several times, but don't despair. I tell filmmakers to stand by the suffragettes' motto, "Never Give Up!"

If you have made mistakes there is always another chance for you...
you may have a fresh start any moment you choose,
for this thing we call "failure" is not the falling down,
but the staying down.
— Mary Pickford

UNDERSTANDING PROPOSAL WRITING

A Conversation with Writer/Filmmaker JanEva Hornbaker McKeel

When I came across JanEva's proposal during our Roy W. Dean Media Grant competition, I was struck by how well she managed to capture the heart of her story. I found her proposal to be exemplary and asked her if she would share her secrets for dynamic proposal writing.

Eva, what is the number one rule of proposal writing?

The number one rule of writing anything is to understand who your readers are and what you are trying to accomplish. This sounds like two rules but actually they are very integrated.

The film proposal is a tool designed to sell two things: your idea for a film, and your ability as a filmmaker to successfully produce, market, and distribute your film. You need to know everything you can about the organization you are applying to, and more specifically, the person who is going to read your proposal. If you are going to convince them to invest in you, this is what it boils down to.

The funder's deadline is three weeks away. What are the first steps toward creating a perfect proposal?

The first step is to make sure your project fits the sponsor's funding guidelines. Once you have determined this you need to dig in and start researching the organization and the people behind the organization.

Read their mission statement and jot down key words and phrases used to describe the goals and objectives of the organization, then go to your proposal and use these same key words to describe your project. It's absolutely essential that you make a connection between the funder's goals and the goals of your project. This shouldn't be a stretch if your project is a good match with the funder.

Funders support interests that are closely tied to the source of their funds, so find out who is funding your funder. You can get this information right off their website or from their tax return.

How did you organize your proposal?

My education background is in library science and information technology, so I studied grant writing in college. However, when I went to write my first film proposal I found very little information that was geared specifically toward putting together an effective film proposal. I read everything I could find and researched a lot of different funders on the Internet and made a list of what each of these funders wanted, then I made my outline based on this list.

Did you find a lot of variation in what funders wanted?

Oh, yes. Some organizations only want a one-page synopsis while others want something that resembles a doctoral dissertation. I put together a general outline based on my research. That way I had all the information in one computer file. You are going to need all of this stuff anyway for distribution and marketing so my advice is get it together early on and customize it to each funder.

Customizing it is the key, isn't it?

Definitely. It's essential that you follow each funder's guidelines to the letter. If the funder doesn't ask to see a budget, don't include it. If they want a two-page synopsis, make sure you only send two pages. And make sure you address each individual funder's goals and objectives.

Funders want to be able to scan a proposal and immediately come away with information — what the film is about, the filmmaker's approach, style, goals, and objectives. They can do this if the proposal is organized into clearly defined headings.

You did not sacrifice style. Your proposal was not a dry, analytical treatment. What can you share on how to achieve style in the proposal?

You have to give your reader all the information they need to make an informed decision, but how you say it is as important as what you say.

You are describing your ideas for a motion picture so it is essential that you show your reader instead of tell your reader what you intend to do. Ezra Pound said, "The image is more than an idea. It is a vortex or cluster of fused ideas and is endowed with energy." If you are going to energize a reader with your ideas then you have to do more than just describe your project; you need to actually transport your reader into your film.

Your opening paragraph does just that. Can you take us through the process of how you wrote this?

Sometimes when you're writing about something that you're passionate about it just flows, but this can be dangerous. It's critical not to miss any key ideas, so I start by writing down exactly what it is that I need to communicate. Then I rewrite it adding descriptive words.

Could you take your opening paragraph here and break down the process?

Sure. I write the information I need to convey, which is: World War II ended over five decades ago, yet thousands of Americans are still missing.

As you can see, this sentence provides information, but it does nothing to help the readers conjure up a visual picture. Like most filmmakers I think in pictures, so I go back and rewrite the scene as I see it. One of my favorite writing teachers used to say, "Walk your reader through the corridors and hallways of your story." I think the best way to do this is to remove yourself from your story and approach it completely fresh, as though you've never been there.

You're so familiar with your story it's easy to forget that the scenes are only in your head. You can't just say, "This story is about explorers who look for lost Americans," and expect your reader to see that fantastic scene that is in your head.

Close your eyes and picture the scene, then put it down on paper. Sometimes it helps to take the concept you want to describe and reduce it to one scene, then work from there. You have to add physical detail, because physical detail is going to pull your reader into the story.

So using this opening paragraph as an example, I worked in some descriptive words and ended up with: The battlefields of World War II fell silent over five decades ago, yet more than 78,000 young Americans still lie in shallow makeshift graves, rusting wrecks, and abandoned battlefields thousands of miles from home.

Shallow makeshift graves and rusting wrecks give the reader some very vivid pictures. Young Americans — who could read that and not be moved? You have to describe your locations, describe your subject, and describe your subject's actions so the reader is transported into the scene. What if I write: This film will be shot in Europe and Asia as we follow searchers on different expeditions to find missing Americans.

Again, I've given the reader the information, but that's not my only objective here. I want to show the reader. So I add description to give it energy: We will follow unique explorers across dramatic backdrops of Europe and into the deepest jungles of Asia as they search for the scattered bones and the rusted dog tags of young soldiers.

The trick to effective writing is to layer descriptive language with specific language so you don't end up with something that is too vague. You want to create mood but you don't want to overdo it.

How do you know when it's too much?

When you sacrifice clarity for style you've gone too far. Funders don't want to read through tons of adjectives to get to the point. Make sure your proposal clearly demonstrates what your film is about and what you are trying to do. Save descriptive words to illustrate your subject, your location, if you have a dramatic location, your subject's motivation. Good writers control their style to match their purpose.

What is your biggest proposal writing challenge?

Usually if I'm writing my own proposal the biggest challenge is to know when to stop. When you're writing passionately about your subject it's tempting to keep going. Pretty soon you end up with something that resembles the Los Angeles phonebook.

Once you've mastered the art of creating these wonderful paragraphs that draw the reader into the story, your next step is to chop it down to the minimum pages allowed. It's the hardest thing but it's a necessary part of the writing process. You just have to do this, knowing that your best work is going to be what is left after you have eliminated all of the fluff and repetition.

William Strunk was really big on omitting needless words. He said, "Vigorous writing is concise," and he said that "a sentence should contain no unnecessary words, a paragraph no unnecessary sentences." I think a lot of people think that omitting needless words means they need to cut down their sentences and paragraphs to the point where they sacrifice style, but this is not what he meant.

Strunk went on to explain that you do not include unnecessary words and sentences, "for the same reason that a drawing should have no unnecessary lines and a machine no unnecessary parts." You're not going to leave out an integral part of a drawing to make the drawing smaller. You're not going to leave off an essential bolt to make the machine lighter. Strunk said, "Make every word tell." That's a very powerful statement. I think most filmmakers can relate to this because this is the essence of good filmmaking. Make every scene count.

Eva, how do you stay on track?

The best way to stay on track is to work from a design. That way you're not going to veer off in a direction and write about things that are not essential. Know exactly what you are trying to accomplish, then develop an outline so you achieve all of your points.

PROPOSAL OUTLINE

Now that you're inspired, let's put these suggestions to work. The following outline works well for funders. Use this guide as your standard outline and add additional elements according to each sponsor's specific requirements.

Log Line and Title (from Carole's point of view as a grantor)
The log line is a one-sentence description of your film. I know you are saying, "But this film is too complicated!" You might as well make it a challenge to yourself because everyone has to do it. Finding the story points and creating your one liner will stand you in good stead when you write your script. It's the full story in a nutshell. When you think, "Should I follow the main character's wife?" read the log line. It's there to keep you on track; it's the backbone of your film.

Richard Kaufman tells the story of the a writer who handed in an envelope with "Romeo & Juliet on crack" sprawled across it. That sold his script. The film was *Panic in Needle Park*.

It's a process. Write what you think are the elements of the film. The "who," the person the film is about, the "what" that happens to him and the "how" it's solved. This is way too much information but it can be a start. Then find the core of the film, keep removing words until you get down to one good sentence. This is the best tool you have for marketing your film, it's your elevator pitch, it's pure gold and totally worth the effort.

Blake Snyder, author of *Save the Cat!*, says that irony is the key element in your pitch. When you read Netflix's outline on films you will agree that irony is the main ingredient. We love irony. So find that irony in your film and use it for your log line. Blake also says that on Saturday night when your friends are deciding on a film and you choose "Gunfighter" your friends will say, "What is it?" and if you can't give them a good logline they will normally say, "What else is showing?" This film just lost four customers because that log line wasn't clever, ironic and engaging.

That's how important this one-sentence log line is. So please, write it first and stay with it.

Once you have a paragraph or even a few lines, you are moving in the right direction. Keep working to reduce what you have and make it shorter, smarter and ironic. You may wake up in the middle of the night with a great one liner, keep a pen and paper close to the bed, I do, and I get the best ideas in the middle of the night. Wayne Dwyer says that 3 a.m. is the magic time and he gets up and uses that time to connect with the universe and write.

Log Line Examples
A top student becomes the school slut to boost her popularity. (*Easy A*)

A career bank robber hits a roadblock when he kidnaps the bank manager and falls in love. (*The Town*)

A backwoods Tennessee loaner plans his funeral while alive so he can attend! (*Get Low*)

You need to see the movie in your mind or part of it from the log line, that's really what drives people to the movies and DVD rentals. This works when you are pitching studios, grantors and investors. They can usually tell who the audience is from a good log line and that's the most important element to them. Just make sure the log line says what the movie is and we get a visual of the film with an ironic twist.

Next is a title that will stick. Usually great titles are one word, some two words. Make it easy to remember. Word of mouth is your best marketing tool. When Jane tells Dick to see a newly released comedy called *Remember Me*, he has to remember it! Make brevity a key for your title.

Log Line Construction

by Rodney Vance, Director of Film & Television Program at Pacific Union College, a member of the Writers Guild & Academy of Television Arts and Science, and President of Singular Entertainment

Whether you use it in a pitch meeting or as a way to focus your story, a great log line takes you a long way toward selling your screenplay.

So what's a log line? And how on earth did it get that name?

A log line is a one-sentence summary of the story in your script. Major film studios such as Warner Bros., Universal Studios, and Disney used to have script vaults in which they stored screenplays. Script readers "logged" scripts into the vault along with a "log line" that was placed on the cover or on the spine of the script. This made it possible for studio executives to quickly scan the scripts in the library and select those that matched the type of story they wanted to film.

Since a log line is so short, a lot of information has to be communicated in just a few words. Who is the story about? What happens? Who benefits? These three questions are answered in the subject, verb, and direct object positions in a sentence.

Let's look at some examples.
- A wealthy businessman falls in love with a hooker he hired for the weekend. (*Pretty Woman*)
- A handicapped mercenary soldier inhabits an alien body to learn their culture and abandons his human body to save the aliens from his fellow mercenaries. (*Avatar*)
- Three hung-over bachelors sift through the wreckage of a Las Vegas bachelor party for clues to where they misplaced the groom. (*Hangover*)

The most important thing we need to know "who" the story is about and what their primary role is in the story. The most important thing to know about the "who" in *Pretty Woman* is that he is a wealthy businessman. That's far more important than his name, how old he is, what kind of business he does, how many ex-wives he has, etc.

The most important thing to know about the "who" in *Avatar* is that he's a disabled mercenary soldier, a man of action who no longer has full use of his body. This all-important characteristic sets up his actions for the rest of the story.

The most important thing we need to know about the "who" in *Hangover* is that they are hung-over bachelors. The entire story rides on this central characteristic. What led to the hangover? What happened during the hangover? How does it turn out? The answers to those questions form the story: beginning, middle, and end.

Next you want to know "what happens." A good way to know you have a major problem in your story is to be unable to answer this question in a few words. Any story that requires a description of many scenes and events to answer this question is a story that isn't focused on what Aristotle so long ago called a "unity of action." In *Pretty Woman* our wealthy businessman falls in love. In *Avatar* our disabled mercenary inhabits an alien body and uses it to save his "new" people from human invaders. In *Hangover* our hung-over bachelors sift evidence for clues.

Notice that all of these verbs are active and visual. In a movie, the story can only be told through what can be seen and heard. We don't hear the character's thoughts, or smell what they smell, or touch what they touch. We can only see what they see and hear what they hear. Falling in love can be seen. So can inhabiting an alien body, saving friends, and sifting evidence. Avoid variations on the verb "to be" here (is, was, will be, etc.) because they communicate little or no information.

Our log line has now told us "who" the story is about and "what happens." Now we learn "who benefits." In *Pretty Woman* the beneficiary is the hooker the wealthy businessman falls in love with. In *Avatar* it's the alien race. In *Hangover* it's the groom. With these three elements in your log line, any reader can have a pretty good idea of the gist of your story. You can pitch your movie at a cocktail party or in an elevator without boring your listeners. Professionals can decide immediately whether or not they want to read your script.

Here are a couple of other things to note about your log line.

1. A good log line reveals the genre of your script. It's easy to see from the examples above that *Pretty Woman* is a romantic comedy, *Avatar* is science fiction, and *Hangover* is a comedy.

2. In a good plot, the "who," the "what happens," and the "who benefits" connect, often in an ironic way. It's ironic that a wealthy businessman, a highly desirable bachelor, falls in love with a hooker. It's ironic that a soldier saves an alien population from his fellow soldiers. And it's ironic that bachelors at a bachelor party lose the groom, the man who represents the purpose of the party. That kind of irony gives a "twist" to the story.

3. A log line is not a tag line. The tag line is the line put on the poster of the movie to get an audience to buy a ticket. The log line is the one-sentence summary of your story designed to sell your script.

In summary, a log line summarizes your story in one sentence that reveals who the story is about, what happens, who benefits from the action, the genre, and the story's twist.

Introduction/Synopsis (from Carole's point of view as a grantor)
Your introduction is the most important part of the film proposal (after your log line). Potential funders want to see two or three dynamite paragraphs that visually describe the film you want to make. If your project is a documentary, chances are you don't know what the final product is until you've finished your final edit. That's okay; just tell the story. People fund engaging stories. Don't let them get lost in paragraph after paragraph about the history. Tell the story of the film you intend to make from your research.

Creating this visual description of the film is an excellent exercise to help you, as the filmmaker, visualize what your story really is about and how you plan to tell the story. It is an exercise that will take your film to a new dimension. Focus on these three paragraphs because they are what make funders stop, sit up straight, and visualize the film with you. Once you've got our attention, we will read every single word. Follow Eva's outline below. If your film is engaging, and you've put it into a concise outline, you will go to the top of the pile.

Background and Need

Acquaint the reader with essential information about the background of your story and your main characters. Don't bombard the reader with information. Give them just enough detail to capture their attention and motivate them to keep reading.

Next, explain why you want to do this film and why it will be of interest to others. What specific concerns will be addressed and why? Who will benefit and how? What will your film accomplish? And, most importantly, who is the market for this film? Tell me that you know your audience. You have met them on Facebook and connected to them or they are now sponsors of your film. Never say "Everyone will love this film." That seldom happens. Find your core audiences. Niche marketing, as Marc Rosenbush teaches, is the key to successful film marketing.

Now you will insert the hook! You have already determined that your film fits the sponsor's guidelines for funding. Now carefully study the sponsor's mission statement and use it to create an original statement that demonstrates how your film relates to the sponsor's specific goals and priorities. This is a critical part of your proposal, and it is something that most of your competitors will overlook. I always know when you have read the guidelines for my grant because most filmmakers say, "My film is unique and makes a contribution to society because…." These are my criteria and filmmakers use that to explain how their film fits our requirements.

Approach, Structure, and Style

This is where you will describe how to approach your story as a film-maker. Structure is the framework that holds up each element of your story. Describe how your story will unfold and how the subjects will move through each of these elements from beginning to end. Is your story an intimate personal journey or an exposé? Are you going to use narration? Is there a connective thread that will tie all of the elements of the story together? Sponsors want strong stories that have strong characters. How will your subjects relate to each other and how will they impact the story? Will your subjects experience personal growth? Will they help others grow? How will they carry the story forward through the conflict, the climax, and the final outcome? How will your audience react to the dramatic tension and what will they learn by the end of the story? Describe how your film will stir viewers to action and inspire them to make a difference.

Documentaries can be character driven or concept driven. In America we love films that are character driven, whereas Europeans like concept-driven films more than we do. If your film is concept driven, I suggest that you take some of the characters and wrap your proposal around them for the American audiences.

We want to know who these people are. Are they parents, religious, hard-working, caring, giving people? Tell us the essence of the person and give us some visual description. If you can't put a picture in the proposal, let us see and feel your characters through your words.

If you are shooting life as it unfolds, you may not know the final outcome. Explain this, then describe several possible outcomes and explain how you will approach each of these scenarios. Remember, a story does not have to have a clear-cut solution to have resolution. An open-ended film that leaves unresolved issues can be even more compelling than a story that reveals how the lives of the characters or events turn out. Style includes all of the techniques that will give your film its own unique quality or tone. This might include camera work, lighting techniques, cinema vérité or your interview style. Include everything that will project your personal imprint onto the story. Avoid getting lost in a lot of technical detail. Instead, explain (show) how a certain technique or style will be used to carry the story forward or illuminate a specific character.

Avoid describing one specific approach unless you have completed all of your research and are convinced there is only one way you can tell the story. Research can reveal twists and turns that can dramatically alter your approach, and changing approaches once a sponsor has already funded you can be sticky. If you are not sure which way you will approach your story, describe several approaches that you are exploring and explain how your subjects might respond to each of these approaches.

Coming up with an idea for a film is easy; nailing down the best approach is the hard part. If you have not decided on an approach, exploring and writing about different methods and ideas will draw you closer to your project.

Theme
The theme is what your story is about. If it is difficult to pinpoint an exact theme then your story is probably underdeveloped. Don't worry, dig deeper and do more research. Your theme will emerge as you continue to research and write.

When I first started researching the idea for *Searcher for Souls* I concentrated on how the ongoing consequence of war affects a family for generations. It was an important theme but I knew something was missing. It was only after I went to Europe and spent two months researching my subject that another theme began to unfold.

Philippe Castellano is a French explorer who has spent over twenty years searching for lost American flyers who fell from the sky during World War II. As I followed and observed my subject I began to notice remarkable similarities between Philippe and the young American flyers he was looking for.

As you research your story, don't forget to stand back and observe. Look for hidden themes that connect the elements of your story.

Share your information online with your Facebook friends and see what gets the most attention. You have such a great opportunity to find which elements of your story are most interesting to your online audience. Use your online portals to help you with the theme.

Audience, Marketing, and Distribution
Your sponsors and people from your website, Facebook and Twitter contacts will want to know about your intended audience. Is your film about a subject that has worldwide appeal? Do you plan to target a specific

community? Is it educational or commercial? How will the market support your audience and how do you intend to distribute your film to this audience? Give statistics that support the size of your audience and explain how your film will appeal to these audiences. Never say "everyone" will love this film. You need to know the new demographics, as Peter Broderick outlines in his chapter.

How have you approached distribution? Are you pursuing a specific network or cable television market? Does your film have a rental market? Will it be featured in public libraries, museums, or university collections? Will you enter your film in festivals? Sponsors want to see that you have a distribution plan and that you are exploring several options. Provide copies of letters of support from key individuals, networks, and anyone that can help support the fact that your film will be seen.

Will you have a digital download? What other portals do you have connected? In today's world it is best to plan on self-distribution and be prepared to show the world who and where your market is from the people you have connected to your film on your social networks and website. This gives you much more power with distributors. You can show them demographics and numbers. There is more for you to do than to say I will take it to this and that film festival. We want to know you have identified your audience and can successfully market your film online.

Budget

Your budget must be a reasonable projection of how much it will cost to produce, distribute, and market your film. Make sure your budget is consistent with the production ideas you have described. Explain where you plan to come up with the rest of the funds to meet your budget. This is also where you will describe how you will use the award if you should win.

For a budget template, see Norman Bern's chapter on Budgeting and his website *www.reelgrok.com*.

Remember, each budget is different, based on your needs and your industry contacts. You should get each number so that you know what the kitchen sink budget (which has everything you want in it) and the bare bones, I-can-do-it-for-this-amount budget. I can't tell you which one to submit, you need to decide. I will say that I saw a brilliant filmmaker lose a grant because she under-budgeted her post. My judges are filmmakers so you can't fool them, they know everything!

Make sure you include a brief statement acknowledging the goals and objectives of the foundation and make it clear that you will use the award accordingly. Let the sponsor know how much you need this grant and that it will be used to create a film that will help advance their cause.

A film budget can have many hidden elements that can come back to bite you. If your budget is too big you might scare off a potential sponsor. On the other hand, if your budget is not in line with your production ideas, a potential sponsor may feel you are too inexperienced or unrealistic. There are budget templates and budget software programs out there to help you create a budget.

Entertainment Partners is a donor to the Roy W. Dean grants and we highly recommend them. They have excellent budget programs. Check them out at *www.entertainmentpartners.com*.

FILMMAKER'S STATEMENT AND BIOGRAPHY

Include a short biographical sketch of each of the principal filmmakers, with pictures if allowed. Describe any film grants that you have won and sponsors that you have secured. Be sure you attach the appropriate documents in an appendix. Include past awards and notable achievements as well. Attach letters of recommendation from industry professionals, letters from key officials supporting your project, and letters of support from industry mentors and advisors. Tell us the organizations you belong to, and if you donate your time, explain where and why. If you won any awards from college on, include them. This is the time to promote yourself.

If you need to brush up on your writing skills, Eva suggests William Strunk's *The Elements of Style*, now available online at *http://www.bartleby.com*, and Purdue University's online writing lab located at *http://owl.english.purdue.edu*.

Both of these resources feature search engines that allow you to easily find answers to your writing and grammar questions. Just remember, if you hire a professional writer to help you with your proposal you need to make sure your passion is projected in the final proposal. Too often other people don't have your commitment and it can show in the proposal. So rewrite it if necessary.

The most important thing is never give up! Keep applying for those grants and keep your project in front of potential funders. For a list of experienced grant writers, see *www.fromtheheartproductions.com*.

TIPS FROM A GRANTOR

This is a visual industry, yet only 10% of the applications I receive include pictures, which always amazes me. Since the person reading your proposal is probably very visual, consider dropping a few pictures or graphics into your proposal.

How about submitting a picture of yourself with your application? Include a photograph taken during your last film shoot — something that shows you in action, behind the camera giving direction. Even if it's just your student ID, put that shining smile on the page and let us see who you are! Passion, perseverance, and personalization are what you need to win grants, so don't be afraid to put your heart on your sleeve to win that grant!

How many grants have you entered? Tell us about them so we can see how determined you are to make this film. Do you really want this grant? Are you willing to dedicate the next three years of your life to produce this film? Find a way to communicate your dedication in your proposal. Include a personal film statement. Tell us what is driving you to make this specific film. That tells us you are in for the long haul. No matter if things get tough, this film is so important that you will not give up. I must feel that in your words.

Grantors want compelling films.

The first two paragraphs must be dynamite, knock me off my seat!

Be impeccable with the truth.

Do not commit to things you cannot do. Sponsors can tell when you are overstating.

The people reading your budget know if it is unreasonable.

A guaranteed audience, such as a commitment from a cable station, puts you on top. Or over three thousand fans on Facebook who like your film is also very good.

Having a dozen Strategic Alliances with your niche audiences is important to us.

Do you have a fiscal sponsor? Tell us their name or that you are looking for one.

Demonstrate solid marketing and distribution plans, and explain your outreach distribution.

List names of your partners or sponsors for the film. We want to see a nice long list.

Have you secured a distributor? Go into detail about anyone you contacted or any advice you have from consultations on marketing.

Explain who your market is and how you are reaching them.

Can you market this film yourself? If so how will you do that?

Bringing a scholar or expert on board as a mentor will shift the scales to your advantage. (Be sure to read Peter Broderick's chapter on distribution.)

Explain how your film relates to the goals of your grantor.

Is your project one of a kind? If so, explain and include support information.

If there are projects in the marketplace with a similar message or subject matter to yours, make sure you demonstrate how yours is unique. Give specific information about your audience and include the full demographics. Tell us all the social media outlets you are using to create your following for the film.

We want to know you have identified your audience and know they are following the film.

Attach letters from major donors to your application as a form of support. Music and picture rights must go in the budget; they are expensive and donors look for this.

Put your name and the name of your film on submitted DVDs. When donors are reviewing scores of tapes, they often get interrupted and it's easy to confuse DVDs.

Please don't use insulated bags that are lined; plastic boxes and bubble wrap are a better choice.

CHAPTER 4

THE PLAN:
FROM AN IDEA TO A TRAILER

We are all in this boat alone together!
— Lilly Tomlin

There are so many things to do when you start making a film that it is imperative to have a good plan. You know you must have a fantastic trailer to raise money. So how much is that going to cost you? Probably about $10,000 for a documentary and for a feature about $20,000. Creating your trailer is an important goal. Once you have created your pitch (see Chapter 2) and your proposal (Chapter 3), you are ready to follow these guidelines to get your film company set up and complete your trailer.

1.   Find **a fiscal sponsor** for your film. A fiscal sponsor is a nonprofit company. All donations are paid to them and they disburse funds to you, thus making the money given by your donors tax-deductible. People like to write checks to a nonprofit company and they like knowing that someone is monitoring the film. Women Make Movies (*www.wmm.com*) and From the Heart (*www.fromtheheartproductions.com*) are fiscal sponsors. At FTH we are constantly uploading information on film financing for you. We are partners with IndieGoGo and can help you raise money online as your fiscal sponsor. We also review your proposal and trailer and give you advice on financing your film. When looking for a fiscal sponsor, ask, "What's in it for me?" Make sure you feel you are getting something for your 5 to 8% fee.

2.   When people approach From the Heart to be their fiscal sponsor, I immediately tell them that if their checks are to be paid to them personally, or to a DBA, we must issue a 1099 at the end of the year for miscellaneous income. We suggest they form an **LLC**. There are lots of places online, such as www.ehow.com where you can set one up for around three hundred dollars. This may take six weeks to complete.

3.   Open a **bank account** in the name of your LLC. Where's the money to open the account? Try your mother or grandmother and tell them you need this to become an entrepreneur. Believe me, someone in your family will be glad to donate to this worthy cause.

4.   Now that you can receive donations as tax deductions you are all set to start your **Internet work**. Facebook is a must to fund your film. Use their newest landing page to advertise your film. Lots of wonderful new things emerge daily, so stay current and use Facebook to start a dialogue with your potential audience. You need to find your audience online. Use Google and search for organizations and forums on your subject matter. Post on these forums and send people to your Facebook page and website. Get as many people to "like" your film on your Facebook page as possible. You are now building your audience and these are potential donors. You might even try an online ad and ask a question pertaining to your film. Example, "Do you like Shakespeare" is what Jilann asked for her *Still Dreaming* film and she received a good number of new friends.

5.   Create a **budget for the trailer**. See the chapter by Norman Berns (*www.reelrok.com*). Every budget is different. It is based on who you work with, where you get your rentals and the prices you negotiate. This is where your skills as a producer are most important. You must have a good budget; even if you are not sure of some things, include everything you believe you will need and you will have a beginning number.

6.   Set up your email names on a **mailing company** so you can stay in touch with your donors every other month, always giving them the latest and greatest news on your film. You might use *www.constantcontact.com* or *www.ratepoint.com*. Both are very helpful. Don't think it's hard to create a fantastic newsletter; you can get personal help from both companies.

7.   Decide how best to use **your time**. For docs, Morrie Warshawski draws a circle and says you usually get 50% of your money from people, so how much time do you want to put into people? If you decide to put 50%, then cut the pie in half and write people.

8.   Next, how much time do you want to spend on grants? Is your film a good fit for a lot of grants? If so, put 20% for grants. How about corporate donations? What amount of time do you want to give that? Put it on the chart. Letter writing is a brilliant way to get money. We have a sample letter for you with a card that Cid Collins Walker mailed to her potential donors and they returned the cards to FTH with their checks. Look on *www. fromtheheartproductions.com* under financing information. This can be another time-eating funding possibility. Chart it out and see what you can do with your time. For a feature you want all your money from people. You need to allocate time for creating your business plan, choosing your casting agent. Make a chart of how to spend your precious time.

9.   **What's in it for me?** The crowdfunding companies have shown us how much people want something back. So be sure to find gifts for donors that are linked to or have a relationship with your film. List these amounts and items on your website and your Facebook page. Example, a man I know is Indian and in our brainstorming session he revealed that his mother and brother are excellent cooks. So we talked about a price for him to come to your house and bring an authentic Indian dinner for six people. Use the idea of your film and create gifts around it to make people want to give you the larger donations. Think laterally.

10.   Consider using a **crowdfunding organization** like IndieGoGo. You can use it with a fiscal sponsor. From the Heart works with IGG and your donors will each have a tax deduction, plus you do not have to reach your goal to get your funds. IGG will forgo the 9% fee. Read the list of things you need to do before you go live with your campaign. (See the IndieGoGo and From the Heart websites.) Once you go live you will be very busy blogging, chatting on Facebook and sending emails to your film lists. Total dedication will enable you to reach your goal.

11.   Now you need to collect some **partners** for your film. This means you look for nonprofits that are supporting the issue of your film. Kitty

Farmer is making a film on the healthcare, or lack of, that the U.S. Government promised the Native Americans. She calls it her "circle of partners." She focused on this for several weeks. Each day she made calls and pitched her film to like-minded organizations. She found twenty organizations who want to support her film. How does this help you? Well, if each organization has five hundred members, multiply that by twenty and now you have a large database of people who care about your issue. Your job is to keep them informed with your *www.ratepoint.com* or *www.constantcontact.com* newsletter. These are people you don't know but who will donate to help you reach your goal through crowdfunding.

12.   Finding partners is first. You start with some of these nonprofit websites like *www.guidestar.org*, *www.councilofnonprofits.org* and *www.foundationcenter.org* for the subject matter of your film. Each organization has instructions on its site to help you. Then get on the phone and explain how your film will benefit their members. Find what they need and offer them something special that will excite them and let their members know about your film. Ask them to link to your organization and to post those two dynamite paragraphs explaining the overview of the film on their website. Arrange to send them your newsletter to forward to their members. You want to create a good rapport with them and find support and money from their members. Be sure to add these sponsors to your proposal and website. You will impress grantors and donors.

13.   Next you need the **money to make the trailer**. Your platform is set, you have a bank account, a pitch and a proposal, sponsors, website, Facebook page, perhaps a blog and you have people connected to you and your film. That's perfect. Review your timetable, telling you how much time you want to put into each area of fundraising. You may want to focus on the people section first. Decide if you want to call people to donate to a yard sale, create a funding party or a dinner funding party or do a letter campaign. You will find all of these in the book plus an outline of forty-three things to do for your funding party. Make plans, set dates for these events, and start your next funding adventure.

14.   You may want to listen to my free online information on **manifesting and creating your future** on the From the Heart website. It's very

important at this phase to be able to receive. You want to be sure that you are functioning at the highest level possible. Remember, there are infinite possibilities waiting for you.

15.   Before you shoot anything for your trailer, I recommend you have a consultation with a trailer editor to understand how to get what you need before you shoot. Read Bill Woolery's Chapter 6 on preparing to shoot your trailer so that when you shoot your **trailer** you will have an **outline** of what you need. Consider posting daily about creating your trailer and once it is finished put it on your site. Also consider creating a ninety-second trailer for sponsors to put on their website with a link to your site. Now you are really networking. Remember the people reading your website and blog don't know that filmmaking is 90% hard work and 10% filmmaking. So dazzle them with "Hollywood" production information so they keep coming back to your site or your Facebook page. Then tell them where you are now in the funding process and make another "ask" as you need more money.

16.   Look for **development money** from places like *www.sundance.org* or *www.cinereach.org* or *www.chickeneggpics.org*. Go to the Appendix for a list of organizations.

17.   **Apply for the Roy W. Dean grant** or any other grant and get feedback on your materials. You need to hear from people who see hundreds of films a year. Apply even if you think it's too early just to get some feedback. They won't forget you. Keep applying, that's the secret. Never give up.

18.   Through your IndieGoGo campaign, your funding parties, your garage sale, your friends and loved ones who want to see you succeed, you should now have the money for your trailer.

19.   **Celebrate**: you have just reached your first milestone.

CHAPTER 5

BUILDING THE FOUNDATION
FOR FUNDRAISING TRAILERS

A Conversation with Fernanda Rossi
The Documentary Doctor
(www.documentarydoctor.com)

Internationally renowned speaker and story consultant Fernanda Rossi has doctored over 300 films, including two Academy Award nominees (*The Garden* by Scott Hamilton Kennedy and *Recycled Life* by Leslie Iwerks), as well as hundreds of trailers, many of which received funding from ITVS, New York State Council for the Arts, and National Film Board of Canada.

Fernanda Rossi has also been invited to give presentations and seminars for major world conferences and organizations such as HotDocs, Sheffield Doc/Fest, and SilverDOCS. Her columns and articles have been published in trade publications like *The Independent* in the U.S. and *DOX* in Europe. She is the author of the book that, according to industry professionals, is the bible on demo production: *Trailer Mechanics: A Guide to Making Your Documentary Fundraising Demo.*

In your book, *Trailer Mechanics* — which, by the way, is excellent and I recommend to all my students — you state: "In order to connect with your film in a meaningful way you need to align your values to the theme of the film." Please explain why this is important.

Thank you for recommending my book, Carole. Filmmaking as a process has three components. One is the story, the other is the filmmaker and the third is the viewer. In order for the story to work, filmmakers have to know why they are making this particular story and what motivates them. Value is their strongest connection with the film.

The other two ways to connect to a film are fascination and moral obligation. The first one is when we come across something that infatuates us: an exhilarating event, or an exotic experience. Moral obligation happens when we witness an event that needs attention: saving the whales or banning child labor in Africa. These elements are very important in getting a filmmaker started, but they are not enough to get him or her through the perils of the long and sometimes exhausting filmmaking process.

The value, on the other hand, is a deep, reliable source of motivation. A value is part of our belief system; it is with us every day, all the time. Our values conform to our inner compass and deal with reality and decision making. Therefore if we find what part of our values are represented in the film and understand the film as an extension of our inner world, then our connection and commitment to it is much stronger.

The second function of value is to give coherence to the story. It's an invisible thread that brings all characters and themes together, in that case the value serves as the premise of the film. Fascination is not a very good thread for a film; it is difficult to fascinate an audience for ninety minutes. Moral obligation makes films very preachy, contrived and even propagandistic. Value is not seeking to convert but to share a point of view in a more subtle way.

To summarize, I believe that the story is not frozen alone in space; there is a filmmaker and an audience. Value is the first organizing principle to bring all these elements to work together in a cohesive manner.

You state that in production, filmmakers' abusive behavior and procrastination are often a display of their creative fears.

I see it every day!

How can we help filmmakers recognize this and get back on track?

In all professions there is a big underestimation on how our emotions play into our professional performance. Athletes are probably an exception. In sports, they appear to be very clear how mismanagement of your anxieties can affect the outcome. They train, concentrate, meditate, and visualize, they do whatever it takes to minimize interference. In the corporate world, the emphasis is not on the emotions, but at least they do address all complementary aspects of a job, from decision making to leadership.

It seems in the film business — this might be very subjective, because I'm immersed in it — everybody is eager to spend the money and time taking every workshop on shooting, editing or writing, and there is very little attention paid to management or emotional issues that diminish a good outcome.

Yes, from my thirty-three years running three corporations simultaneously, I know that when someone gets angry easily or is often rude to people, it usually means they are overwhelmed or ill.

Yes, filmmakers are part artists and part business people. There was a Harvard business book that said a filmmaking project is nothing but a temporary corporation. A film project and a regular corporation share more characteristics than we want to admit. Filmmakers should take all the same workshops that a CEO takes!

Another factor to take into account is our own endorsement of such misplaced behaviors. We equate abusive behavior with the unmistakable mark of genius. We put up with the most outrageous conduct, convincing ourselves that the pain is worth it because we are in the presence of sheer brilliance. Conversely, we downplay nice people as probably not too talented. But I'm not so sure that anybody's film is worth anybody else's suffering or mistreatment.

There is a romantic vision of the artist as a tortured, troubled person. Beethoven or van Gogh might have been difficult, but that doesn't make every moody person a Beethoven or a van Gogh. Far from that, I believe those type of artists are successful in spite of themselves or most likely they succeed thanks to the legion of tolerant and skilled people around them.

The reason artists have tantrums of various types is because they don't understand the creative process and can't manage the fears that come along with it. The creative process is very anxiety provoking. There are lots of decisions to be made and a lot of judgment to endure. It gets intensified by the financial pressures and amount of money required to make a film.

Understanding the role creative anxieties play in our performance and relationship with others is crucial for the completion and success of a project. I would dare say that fear is the shadow of value. Value is the positive force that moves the project forward and fear is the negative pull that threatens the completion of the film. You can't have one without the other, but we can all learn how to manage them to our advantage.

Very true! So how can a filmmaker understand this?

The first step is to be aware of our creative process and fears, to identify when we are reacting to the very process of creating and wrongly taking it out on our colleagues or ourselves. There are many ways to deal with all the stresses of filmmaking, but just awareness is a great start.

Among the many situations that emerge from mismanagement of fear, there is one that interests me very much because it is particular to filmmaking and collaborative arts in general. I call it "re-owning" and it stems from the fear of losing control or authorship of the film.

Filmmaking is a collaborative art; therefore there is an overlap of creative processes. A filmmaker not only has to deal with the challenges regarding the making of the film, but also must manage everybody's creative input and anxieties. And as I said before, people barely know how to manage their own creative process, let alone the process of a group of others.

"Re-owning" then happens when a director or producer mismanages the input of his or her team. Let's say somebody gets called to participate in the project. This person — whether shooter, editor or a consultant, like you or me — makes a significant creative contribution. Or maybe the director lets someone else take the lead for a while in order to take a mental if not a physical break and replenish. In an ideal scenario this situation will balance itself out, no problem. The filmmaker welcomes and acknowledges their input, thinks about it, evaluates it, and takes action without losing his or her vision and center. Unfortunately this is not the case with everybody all the time. Most likely the concurrent creative process of several people creates friction. A filmmaker might feel threatened that he or she is losing control over the project. In order to "re-own" the project, the filmmaker has to "kill" the witnesses and messengers. This killing is metaphorical, of course, but very real in terms of fights, firing or not giving due credit to those who contributed to the film. The filmmaker becomes the worst enemy of the film, trying to hold on to authorship in the most detrimental way, by alienating others.

The Academy Award winners, nominees and other very accomplished people I have had the pleasure to work with were for me great examples of how to create healthy collaborations. What I observed in them is that yes, they are dedicated and talented with good stories to tell, like many other people. But above all, they were gracious. They believed in abundance, in sharing and collaborating — as in a real exchange, not as in "you all help me and you only get a pay check, if that." They understood that a filmmaker has to first be a listener, then a doer, first a giver, then a taker and always a skilled manager of everybody's creativity. Because the team sincerely felt part of the film, they pushed the project forward creating good opportunities for the filmmaker, whether by word of mouth or just general good karma!

Yes, the crew became one unit working together with a unified vision. Actually, this united vision creates the film.

Exactly. The film is important, but the filmmaker's personality and the market circumstances are the determining factors for success.

Now, regarding the making of the trailer, how important is it to identify whether a film is topic or character driven?

Extremely important, it's the first set of questions to ask when getting ready to plan, write, shoot, or edit a trailer. It will determine the structure of the trailer and lead you to new questions.

Is this a topic-driven or a character-driven film?

If character-driven: Does this character have a goal, an obstacle or opponent? Or is this just the description of the life of the character?

If a topic-driven film: What's the main issue? Is it a conflictive issue?

What are the secondary angles of this topic?

The answers to the above questions can serve as guidelines to start the structuring of the fundraising trailer. From there the trailer can keep growing and finding its own voice.

How do you recommend someone take fifty hours of footage and create a less than ten-minute fundraising promo?

I think I will begin by saying what not to do. Part of our fears and our procrastination get us to do a lot of labor-intensive things that look like work but are not directly involved with telling the story. Sometimes those activities that are always costly and time consuming, like logging or transcribing, are necessary at some point in the film but are not indispensable to develop the trailer or story.

The other factor that reinforces the idea of doing these activities before cutting a trailer is the fact that we are still working with methods that were right twenty years ago when people shot only thirty hours of footage. For thirty hours, it made sense to log everything and transcribe everything to cut the film. Back then fundraising trailers didn't quite exist. Today the average filmmaker is shooting 120 hours. And they are going by a methodology that worked before Final Cut Pro or Avid entered the market, before there was a DVD or digital cameras. We can't use the same techniques we had for twenty hours when we have this many more hours of footage today and expect the same results.

However, sometimes filmmakers shoot just for the trailer and have less than ten hours of footage. Even then I suggest using more intuitive approaches, which are less labor-intensive and focus on story development. Approaches that make more business sense if the point is to get the fundraising trailer done efficiently so more money and support can be brought to the film.

The more I consult and witness this process, the more I realize it rarely makes sense to log everything, at least not all in one pass. It seems more efficient to build the story from memory and confirm the impact of those memories by looking at that specific material only.

Let's say we shot something a month ago and there are a few scenes that still come to mind strongly whenever we think of that time. If it made an impression on the filmmaker, it is going to make an impression on others. Therefore memory is the best selector of material. You can select ten moments you like. Then start logging just that, and apply the questions above to guide you in how to organize that material.

On the other hand, if we go and log everything, everything becomes important again, making it difficult to choose what to include in the promo. Besides, it takes a week to view fifty hours and that is if you work all day. When I used to be an editor, I did not want to be stuck with one project for a year so I was forced to develop techniques that would help me edit faster and have more fun. Even though I would have made more money doing it the long way, for my sanity, I had to come up with ways to shorten my own editing time.

List Your Top Ten Scenes

This is a brilliant idea, to list the ten things you remember the most to start the fundraising promo.

Yes, it's more organic and it serves the story better. More importantly, it's working for a lot of the filmmakers I consult with. And their editors are happier too. But I think I can already hear readers saying, "What if I miss a scene that is really important. What if I forget something?" I know of filmmakers at the premiere of their film wondering if they left something out! If a scene was that good it is very unlikely a filmmaker will forget it. If something was left out and you didn't remember it until the day of the premiere, it probably wasn't worth keeping.

That's once again a manifestation of fear that can sometimes lead to procrastination. When people are about to lock picture for trailers or rough cuts, this fear comes up and they delay locking picture for several weeks. They go back and look for something they may have forgotten. "What if" becomes their mantra. And rarely, they do come up with something, but I doubt that the one scene they found is going to make such an important difference in the outcome of the film overall. This is, of course, different from purposefully looking for scenes when the story presents holes.

Going by memory is an initial step. Eventually we have to go through other footage. But it's a way to make the process manageable so the story can emerge organically.

Do you tell people when they are shooting to make notes of their favorite scenes?

I think it is better for the shooter/filmmaker to be present, alert and sensitive to what's going on in the moment. Sometimes appearances can be deceiving, that's why when working by memory we still have to go to the footage and check. Because when you are on location the situation can be very powerful but when you see the tape later on, that something that moved you may not feel the same. Filmmakers try to convince their editors to use something by saying, "Oh, if you had been there," and that's the point, we weren't. If it doesn't come through the footage and we can't feel it, then it is not going to get a reaction from the audience.

You normally teach filmmakers to use the "Who, What, Where, and Why" in the fundraising trailer. Do you consider these part of the main story structure of the trailer?

Yes, they are an intrinsically important part of the character-driven model. For the concept-driven model I recommend figuring out the theme and assortment of related scenes that add to or contradict that central theme. A fundraising trailer is a one to twenty-minute audiovisual pitch of the film. To use more familiar wording, it is a short without an ending. People tend to think that a trailer or promo is like a music video. Nothing can be farther from the truth. Grant foundations or development departments of a network don't want to see something flashy. That only proves that you have a skilled editor. It doesn't prove that you have a story or what type of access you have to a character or that you have a distinct voice and style for this film.

The only way to prove you have a story and an engaging character or set of interviewees is by showing some scenes. In addition, we have to create a final scene that shows there is potential for the story to grow, namely a cliffhanger. It is obligatory to have this element for every trailer. A fundraising trailer or promo with a definite conclusion is doomed to fail because any grantor or broadcaster who sees a wrapped-up story can say, "Oh, thank you for sharing. Nice little story." The story is complete. We have closure. Then what's the point of telling a longer story about the same topic? But if we have a short without an ending, then we want to know more. The cliffhanger gives the promo the sense that there is something else that can be explored in the longer version of the film.

These are just the foundational elements of the structure of a trailer. It gets a bit more complicated after that. There is a way of choosing the "Who," the "What" and the "Why" to determine the main theme.

When I watch promo tapes for the grant, I like to see something engaging in the first minute. Would you agree?

The first minute is extremely important. This is where the true artistic craft comes in. The first minute generally sets the tone and style for the piece. We have to convey the "Who" and the "What" of the character or main theme if topic driven right away.

It's important not to start with a long explanatory text. For some reason people seem compelled to throw in a long statement saying, "This story started when." I call it the didactic syndrome. We all want to be understood, and sometimes make great efforts in explaining everything just in case someone doesn't quite get it. Trailer audiences are industry people. They will get it without long small typeface scrolls. This does just the opposite. It kills any expectations the viewer may have had from reading that text saying it all upfront.

The same goes for long monologues, whether these are voice-over narration or talking heads. If somebody is saying something, it better be a shocker, something really meaningful and short. I like to start a trailer with vérité footage if at all possible. Close-ups of engaging, charismatic characters are good too, if they are, once again, saying something that relates to the Who and What.

There are lots of exceptions, of course. These are just some primary guidelines. The main exception to consider is "invested audiences." If a person — individual donor, grant maker or broadcaster — is very interested in the topic or the filmmaker, then you can have the worst trailer in the world and still get funding. But for most of filmmakers this is not the case. When competing for a grant among hundreds of projects, a well-crafted trailer can make a difference.

I see lots of promo tapes where the filmmaker uses a card with words to move the film along so you have a bit of information. Do you like to see cards?

Full screen cards with text from top to bottom with black background in the middle of a trailer tend to stop the flow of the story. It's a risk, structurally speaking. I'd suggest to use text on moving images instead, i.e., vérité footage or actuality footage as they call it in the U.K.

The text should be information that helps move the story along, complementing the images that we are seeing. Text and images are two completely different formats and they have to flow together whether it's simultaneously or consecutively. Integrating them can be a challenge. The sentences have to be thought out very carefully. Each word counts, because each word can become an asset or a distraction. I favor sentences that are simple, direct, and not more than two or three lines at a time in the lower third of the screen.

Do you think independent filmmakers should create a promo and just shoot one scene?

My motto is "better something than nothing." Years ago we could get away with just a synopsis, a piece of paper, and the promise of shooting something someday. Today it is impossible to do fundraising for an audiovisual medium without, well, audiovisual material, unless you are requesting funds for production development. The technology is there, available, and that's great, but it raised the bar of demands on filmmakers. There is no excuse not to have something to show to potential funders when cameras and desktop editing software are so accessible.

If the only thing the filmmaker can present is just a scene, so be it. They can complement that with some photos and a voice-over narration. This is better than nothing.

There are cases where a trailer is not possible. Let's say the story takes place in another country and no development grants came through yet. Then the filmmaker can use visual research material to put together an audiovisual presentation.

It might not be a trailer, but perhaps a PowerPoint program that explains the project. These are extreme cases, desperate measures. For crowdfunding, I saw filmmakers shoot themselves pitching their project and that was their trailer!

A filmmaker got into the finals of our grant with a PowerPoint program and a heartfelt presentation telling us the story of the film.

Yes. Ultimately you want your project to have a chance. Sometimes you just want to put a foot in the door, creating a precedent for your project. Paper and black ink can be compelling. Some filmmakers are very good writers. If you are competing with other people who are presenting the same type of material, great. But in the "scissors, paper, stone" game of fundraising, visuals beats paper!

All this information is very important. Fernanda, how did you become interested in story structure?

I became interested in structure very early on. When I was eleven we had to write an essay on a novel we'd been reading in class. I presented a drawing showing the structure of the story and the character's arc. I couldn't name it that, but I knew it represented the spine of the novel. The teacher said, "Not sure if you are lazy or just understood it so well that you don't need words." Fortunately he was working on his Ph.D. in literature, so he said, "Your analysis of story structure is very good." Maybe thanks to that validation early on today I do what I do the way I do it. I was even more lucky then when my film degree required several courses on semiotics. My work on story structure is based not only on that thorough study of theory, but also the experience that comes from working hands on with the filmmakers.

The creative process is essential for this process and I integrate it into the consultations. The wakeup call came by the hand of a well-intentioned teacher in my degree. I had been a prolific writer as a child and in my teens. Writing was fun and liberating. I even made drawings of my short stories and performed slide shows with them. There were no rules, just the joy of telling a story.

Once in film school this screenwriting teacher would ask in the midst of us writing a script, "Now what's the conflict... what's this and what's that?"

I got a writer's block that lasted three years. I'm grateful to her because this caused me to become interested in how the creative process works. That's when I realized that story structure and creativity go hand in hand, many things interconnect. I added the creative process as another area for research and my consulting practice.

And last I got interested in business etiquette and how interpersonal relationships affect creativity and filmmaking. I get many emails from all over the world with all types of questions. And behind each question — no matter where it comes from — you can see there is a bigger question that exceeds the issues of the film. Filmmaking is just another path to whatever we are meant to do. It's not just all about getting the money for the film. It is also about growing and learning from the film you are making. To use the process of filmmaking as a mirror to see who we are and what we are contributing to society.

Yes, and to enjoy the process! Fernanda, people praise your work. Everyone I send to you is exceptionally pleased with the outcome. You must love what you do.

Thank you. Yes, I completely love what I do. It's very satisfying to me to research story structure and then have the chance to share it with other filmmakers who put that theory into action. Unfortunately story consulting, like every consulting profession, has a low entry bar. Anybody who can say something mildly articulate about a film and put up a website offering their services is in business today. Hopefully filmmakers are savvy and check the consultant's track record and confirm it with third parties. That's why I'm so grateful to you and what you do, I want to also say here, that you met me early in my consulting career and you were one of the first ones to get what I was trying to do. Since then you have been an invaluable mentor for me. I'm very grateful for that.

Thank you, Fernanda, for the inspiration you bring to us by your story structure theories and teaching.

CHAPTER 6

CREATING YOUR TRAILER

With Bill Woolery
(www.BillWoolery.com),
editor of trailers for **E.T.** *and* **The Usual Suspects**

TRICKS TO TRAILER EDITING

Bill Woolery has been a donor to the Roy Dean Media grant for many years. I have seen filmmakers win our grant with good trailers and once Bill donates his time they become incredibly compelling. The changes are astonishing. Bill can bring materials to life and have you totally engrossed in the film from the first few seconds, which is the key to a successful trailer. If you don't grab my attention as a grant funder in the first thirty seconds, you may not make it to the finals.

I asked Bill to tell me what filmmakers should know about trailers. It's most important to know what you are doing before you shoot. I hear filmmakers say I am "hoping to get enough materials for a trailer." You really need a plan before you shoot.

FUNDRAISING TRAILERS

Bill, at what point in a project's development is it time to create the fundraising trailer?

First, let me say I think the trailer is a key element — if not *the* key element — in getting your project past the planning and thinking stage and into a form that will attract attention. If you're smart you'll consider this potential right from the beginning. Even if you're just beginning to put together your website, I guarantee the site will be more effective if it includes a video. It doesn't have to be a fully constructed trailer at that point. But anyone visiting a website these days expects to "see" something.

In the initial planning stages of your project, it pays to think seriously about what your trailer will contain and what it will look like. There are several different types of trailers. Normally, the first kind you're going to be dealing with is a fundraising trailer.

This brings up **the Catch-22 problem**: funders want to see a trailer before they contribute, but you can't show them a trailer until you have the money to shoot it.

This is an obstacle almost every filmmaker making a fundraising trailer has to deal with. There are several ways to solve it, *but not having a trailer is not one of the options*. For many people, you don't have a "real" project unless they can see at least a sample of film on a screen.

So, let's say you have a small bit of seed money to get things started, but not enough to shoot any of the key interviews or location setups. Consider making a **teaser trailer** that would give the viewer a good approximation of your concept. These are also known as **sizzle reels** because their main purpose is to generate interest and buzz for your project.

These kinds of trailers often utilize video stills or video clips that you can pick off Google or YouTube. It's been my experience that material you find on the Net is usually not a problem to use — at least, for a fundraising trailer. But it's best to avoid obvious trademark brands or images of people who might take offense. The nickname for this approach is "rip-o-matic." The images are almost always interspersed with **title cards**. It's the best way to communicate your story.

A surprisingly good montage-style teaser trailer can be made with these elements. Throw in some effective music and snappy pacing, and now you've got yourself an affordable trailer to show.

Now, if your project is biographical or involves a subject that's more on the somber and poignant side, the montage idea can still work. But replace the title cards with voice over to give it a more human touch.

Let's move on to the next phase of the project. By this time, the teaser trailer has done its work and some money has been raised, perhaps enough so that the filmmaker can think about shooting. What comes next?

Well, usually the main question becomes: what to shoot first. And here the filmmaker's thoughts should turn to the creation of the fundraising trailer.

FUNDRAISING TRAILERS — THINGS TO CONSIDER

- Remember, your project is going to live or die by the quality of its fundraising trailer.
- Envision your trailer. If this is a problem for you, take time to view other trailers online — both commercial entertainment and documentary ones. For fundraising trailers you have to go to specific project websites. Watch all you can to get a feel for their structure and pacing.
- Understand that there will no doubt be multiple versions of your fundraising trailer. The first one will probably be quite short and simple. As the project expands and new material is added, it will morph into bigger and stronger versions.
- Next, mentally construct the trailer in your mind. Imagine your viewer being moved to tears or delighted or surprised by the scenes they're watching. At this point, don't be too intellectual about how to present the documentary story, just visualize what a dynamic trailer of your material would look like. Imagine yourself watching that trailer and being impressed with it.
- Through this process you will be able to discover which scenes might work best in the trailer.
- Use what money you have to shoot those scenes first.

Fundraising trailers are just one of many types of trailers. Can you describe some others?

Well, first I have to say that this involves applying specific labels to something that has an infinite number of variations.

Filmmakers often use different labels to describe the various types of trailers. We're talking about an art form here, so it doesn't fit cleanly into categories.

And there's the much-debated discussion about **how long should it be**. It's a question I'm asked many times and my standard reply is, "A trailer should end just before it gets boring." I mean, there are no hard and fast rules here. Sometimes the filmmaker will want to keep a theatrical-style trailer less than two minutes and we set that as a goal. But it's really ultimately determined by what I can do with the material. If it's strong, interesting stuff it might end up a few seconds over — but it will *feel* two like minutes. If the material is not that compelling, two minutes may feel too long.

By the time I finished my feature trailer career, a trailer for a studio movie could not exceed ninety seconds. And I mean, not one second over! It was one of the many marketing parameters that cause all commercial entertainment trailers to end up looking pretty much the same.

Some of the doc trailers I see on Vimeo and YouTube mimic these clichés — the "whoosh" transitions, the "crash cuts" and the melodramatic build. Sometimes they do it very well and I'm not criticizing the approach, per se. But, while this sensationalized approach may speak strongly to an entertainment movie audience, it may actually generate negative reactions in a documentary audience. But, getting back to trailers...

DIFFERENT TYPES OF TRAILERS

You asked about the different types. Yes, I deal with several different categories. Remember, trailers are an unruly genre and putting strict labels on them is not an exact science. But, from my experience, I think some general categories can be distinguished.

The majority of projects I edit involve **fundraising trailers**. They are *the* crucial element in getting a project up and running and they usually evolve over time as new footage is shot and new funding sources are found. Their length could be between three to eight minutes.

Work-in-progress trailers run longer so the viewer can see that you've got a viable, substantial project to offer. These could range from three to fourteen minutes.

A theatrical-style trailer is the one that will be used as your all-purpose "**calling card**" for the project. It's the one posted on YouTube and Vimeo and on the project's website. It's short — one-and-a-half to three minutes — energetic and dramatic and makes no obvious solicitation for funds (maybe a tasteful website link at the end.) Unlike the two types mentioned before, a theatrical trailer doesn't reveal the end of story. In an ideal world, it is edited from the completed feature. But a trailer of this type often has to be created (with various levels of success) at earlier stages of the project.

Teaser or sizzle trailers are mostly about generating advanced buzz for the project. They're sometimes cobbled together with rip-o-matic images from the Net with a voice over telling you how great the project will be once the viewer contributes funds to shoot it. It might include a "pedigree" montage of the filmmaker's past prestigious projects. A teaser is short (one to two minutes) unless the "past projects" are very prestigious and need screen time to be appreciated.

FEATURE TRAILERS

You've said that trailer editing is quite different from narrative editing. Can you explain some of the ways that one differs from the other?

I like to say that **they are two distinctly different "realities."** The trailer incorporates the same scenes as the full-length piece, the same truths and same emotions… but uses a **totally different "language"** to express them.

I often point out that while a feature may have emotional moments, a trailer is **one entire emotional moment** from beginning to end. It takes you immediately into an emotional space and holds you enthralled without a break and then drops you at the end.

But at the same time, it has specific information it has to convey: who the characters are, what the story is about, why the characters are doing what they're doing. Most importantly, it has to answer the question: **Why is this film important?** Why is it important to make this film now? Why should I want to see it? These things have to be clearly evident to the viewer — but they should never feel like "bullet points." They have to be imbedded in the trailer's emotional flow.

This brings us to **"the build,"** probably the most important element that distinguishes trailer editing from feature editing. A trailer must maintain a continuous forward momentum — and one that should pick up in emotional urgency as the trailer progresses thru its Acts I and II. The third act is often a wrap-up montage and a release of that tension. But sometimes it's a continuation of the build if you're planning a cliff-hanger ending.

THREE-ACT STRUCTURE

Trailers are usually quite short so I'm surprised to hear you talk about them having a three-act structure.

Dynamic, competent trailer editing is much more complicated to construct than most narrative filmmakers realize. A well-cut trailer is a very busy "world." There are lots of things going on simultaneously. At every moment there are multiple arcs going on: each character's arc, the main story arc, and the emotional arcs. And they're all intertwined. So that's a lot to juggle.

For me, the overall flow of the trailer works best when it's divided into a three-act structure. While narrative films are often divided into "chapters," trailers are not. I think the three-act format is a very functional way to design it and that's the structure you most often see. Personally, I enjoy the change of mood that each act brings. It seems more fulfilling to me, like you're getting a "three-course meal" in the three to seven minutes of the trailer's duration.

How would you describe each of the three acts of a trailer?

- In **Act I,** you're establishing the emotional mood of the trailer and introducing the characters and their milieu. It's the exposition phase where you're using dialogue bites and scenes setting up the story.
- **Act II** is the development phase — what happens to these people and events as they interact. This is usually the longest act. Sometimes the climax occurs at the end of it — if you're not planning on a cliff-hanger to finish the trailer.

- Act III can take several different modes. In most cases, it's the start of the **"end run"** — an intense emotional "build" that moves strongly toward a cliff-hanger climax ending. Or, if the climax occurred at the end of Act II, this can take the form of a wrap-up montage with a voice over stating why this film is important and why the viewer should see it (or contribute to its completion).
- To these three elements can be added an **Opening** — an intriguing, attention-getting first few seconds. And a **Coda** — a scene or a dialogue bite placed just before or just after the end title. If your trailer has a lighthearted theme, it will be the comic "end button."

Arranging your material into acts is a good way of organizing it, but it should **never jeopardize the trailer's flow and momentum**. It's something that has to be done carefully. There can be "hard" and "soft" three-act structures — that's something I demonstrate in my Trailer Clinics. There's also something about telling a story in three acts that's inherently satisfying to most people. I see a parallel to it in the sonata form used in classical music.

MUSIC FOR TRAILERS

That brings up music. You've told me that you consider your trailer cuts to be "musical." What exactly do you mean by that?

Music is the *life-blood of a trailer*. All theatrical movie trailers have wall-to-wall music. And documentary fundraising trailers do, too. That's mainly because the tension and flow in a trailer cannot be broken from beginning to end.

Each "act" should enter with a new music cue. Trailers that employ only one music cue really feel boring to me. Now, sometimes you're dealing with a cue that goes through different moods and changes. That can work very well.

I do not start cutting a trailer until I have a music cue to set the mood. The flow and emotional impact of a trailer are directly tied to its music. This is particularly so in the opening. Many times these cues will get replaced as the editing continues. Even if the first stage of editing requires assembling an audio sequence of dialogue bites to layout the story, I cut them together over a music bed.

In my seminars, I always tell filmmakers that the first thirty seconds of the trailer are the most important. Would you agree?

Absolutely! That's certainly the "One Big Truth" about fundraising trailers (laughs). It's probably the one thing everyone can agree upon. It's not so much a matter of the viewer's short attention span — trailers are usually short enough that people won't walk away. But grabbing their attention at the start of the trailer means you will have a much better chance of holding it for the duration.

I give a lot of thought and calculation in the first thirty seconds. But I believe the quest to hook your viewer's interest begins with *the first frame.*

We live in a media-saturated society. Viewers are now very sophisticated about "reading" images on a screen. Science tells us that the brain makes sense of data coming from the eyes by comparing it with past visual patterns stored in our memory. Therefore, if you open your trailer with a scene that "matches" a viewer's past experience, he or she will compare it with that past experience.

It works like this: The viewer of your trailer is going to see it within a context. Either by reading the text around it on your website or, if you're doing a presentation, you will introduce it beforehand. In both cases, the viewer will know the title of your project and something about the subject matter. So, don't start off with an image that confirms their expectation. For example, if your story is about the Brazilian rainforest, don't open the trailer with a wide aerial shot of the forest. That's exactly what they're expecting. Their instant reaction will be, "Hmm, another Brazilian rainforest story."

So, come up with something they don't expect. Maybe a tight close-up of an insect, the flutter of brilliant feathers of a parrot, maybe the rustle of an animal crunching through tropical leaves. Or maybe a mysterious audio bite that you pair with a totally unexpected image.

I often try to think up several completely different opening concepts and try them out. Solving these sorts of problems is really a trail-and-error process. If I can't solve them immediately, I go on to editing the body of the trailer. At some point a scene may jump out and say, "Hey, I'm your opening scene!"

If you've jolted your viewers in the first moment, the first frame, they'll remain more engaged with the rest of your trailer. You've thrown them a curve at the start and caught them off guard. They're now much more alert and intrigued to see what comes next.

When filmmakers come to you to discuss a trailer, what is the question they most often ask?

There are two, actually: What will it cost and how long will it take? (Laughs) I've had people call me and say, "Can you tell me what you charge for a trailer?" Before I can rely, I have to ask them a number of questions.

Would I be working from your finished piece with a color-corrected picture and final, EQ'd track stems? Or from the latest version of your rough cut? Or would I have to wade through hours of your original material? Is it Final Cut Pro or Avid? Is the trailer mainly for website placement or theatrical screenings? Does it have to meet NTSC broadcast standards? All these things impact the time required and cost of editing a trailer.

And there's the *scope of the trailer*. Will it be a one-minute teaser or a ten-minute work-in-progress?

Another thing I always do is *ask to see some material* before I commit to the project. A prospective client will describe his or her project to me on the phone, what they want to accomplish with a trailer, and how it's going to be used. Many times the project sounds wonderful, especially if they've shot lots of material. Even so, I require them to send me QuickTime files or DVDs of their material — which usually includes an existing trailer they want to improve. Most often, it's interesting stuff. Other times, for various reasons, the material is disappointing and I have to diplomatically tell them there really isn't anything there for me to work with.

Trailer editing is a creative process. It's not something you assemble and that's that. It's a plastic art form that needs to be shaped and re-shaped to achieve its best result. These steps are known as versions. I usually include five versions in my budget estimates. The filmmaker and I can go on forever with versions, but after five, they become an additional charge.

I believe it's always a good idea to *show each version to friends* or fellow film-makers. Many times they can identify weakness in the trailer that my client and I missed in our editing process.

Why did you create a trailer service specifically for the documentary community?

When I arrived on the documentary scene in 2006, I found that most of the fundraising trailers I saw really needed help. Many narrative filmmakers had no experience in constructing effective trailers.

Trailers had then become the most important element in getting a project taken seriously and properly funded. It seems now that before anyone will participate in a project, they want to see a video first. Even if you haven't shot anything yet, they still want to see what it might look like on screen.

Any last tips you might have for filmmakers cutting their own trailers?

I've been talking about how open-ended the trailer editing process is. But there is one "rule" of trailer editing that I completely adhere to: *Let the material lead you!* Yes, develop your concept and structure with great care and intelligence. Then begin assembling the sequence based on those ideas. But always — always — be alert to spontaneous ideas that pop up during the editing. Take time to try them out. Sometimes they don't work and some-times you get that "aha!" moment. You may labor long and hard in your edit bay trying to realize a concept that worked just great in your head. But if the material continues to fight you, it's saying, "This isn't what you're supposed to do." And when you do get it right, it's a sweet, sweet feeling!

And, oh yes, I have one last tip. Don't do a fade-out on a trailer that will be used on YouTube or Vimeo. On those sites, when the video playback stops it stays on the last frame. You want your website link or title to remain on the screen until the viewer clicks it off.

CHAPTER 7

LOADING THE BASES

—⚬⚬⚬—

Even if you're on the right track,
you'll get run over if you just sit there.

— Will Rogers

RULES OF THE GAME

You've polished your proposal and perfected your pitch. Before you step out of the bullpen, make sure you understand the rules of the game.

Rule #1: Know the Catcher Before You Pitch

The number one complaint from funders is that too many applications do not fit the foundation's guidelines. Don't try to throw a fastball past a seasoned funder. Carefully read the guidelines and criteria of each potential funding source. If your project doesn't fit, don't apply.

Before you pitch anyone, know who they are and how they can help. Film-makers need more than money — you need mentors, people who know wealthy people who want to be an associate producer while they sit in their paneled offices and you make the films.

Rule #2: Develop a Strategy

You can't invite a bunch of friends over, order pizza and beer, and send off a mass mailing of your proposal. It just doesn't work that way. You must have a specific strategy based on each individual funder. To develop this strategy you need to know where each individual funder is coming from. You must know what makes them tick. You must understand their objectives. Your proposal has to fulfill their needs, which means each proposal has to be specifically written for that funder.

My criteria are that a project must be unique and make a contribution to society. I know filmmakers have read my website when they write, "This film is unique and will make a contribution to society because..." You need to hang your hat on the funder's requirements.

Rule #3: Play the Field

Don't make the mistake of focusing all of your efforts on one funder or on one specific type of funding. Keep your options open. Learn everything you can about different financing opportunities that are available to independent filmmakers and romance every appropriate funding source you can find.

One of my grant-winning filmmakers told me she applied for five grants and won four. How did she do that? She spent her time reading the requirements, the number of people who apply, what type of films the organization had funded in the past, and then she decided which ones to devote her time to. She chose grants that she felt she had the best chance to win, and she wrote a special proposal to each one of them. It worked with me; I loved Rebecca Dreyfus' film *Stolen* from the two-page proposal she sent. She had me wanting to know more about the story and she became one of the top five finalists in the NYC film grant.

The judges looked at this concept of her investigation of the Vermeer stolen from the Gardner Museum in Boston and decided she would not win many grants. Her story was so engaging, they awarded her the grant. In addition to our grant, Rebecca sold the idea to *Court TV* and created a brilliant film.

Funders want to fund films that will be completed and distributed. This means they want to know that you are out there focusing on additional funding. I love it when I get an application that says, "Here is the list of organizations where we are applying." That tells me that they are not depending on my grant, they are investigating the field and they know where they have the most potential for funding. All funders and donors like to see that you are diligently applying for grants and personal donations.

Rule #4: There's No Crying in Baseball

Don't view a rejection as failure, rather see it as an opportunity to learn and improve. Follow up with each funder. Thank them for their consideration and ask for feedback. If the funder still shows interest in your project, ask if you can reapply in the future. If the funder is not interested in supporting this particular project, thank them for their time and keep the lines of communication open; they may be interested in funding future projects.

I give everyone a free consultation when they apply for the Roy W. Dean grants. Most filmmakers take advantage and set up appointments with me to discuss funding opportunities and what they can do to improve their proposal. Most state and federal funding organizations will give you feedback; you just have to be persistent to make an appointment, because it is worth it.

If you are not accumulating several rejections a month, you are not doing your job. Remember, even the best grantwriters end up with far more rejections than they do grants.

SCOUTING THE MAJORS: RESEARCHING FUNDERS

You know your funder is out there floating around somewhere in cyberspace but somehow you just keep missing each other. When you get tired of knocking on the front door, maybe it's time to try something different.

Try searching for films that are similar to yours. Find out who funded these films and research these funders. Research documentary film sites, online film and video magazines, and online video distributors. Netflix has a wonderful collection of films and often you can find funding names on the filmmaker's website.

Watch films and videos that are similar to yours and check out the list of funders in the credits. What businesses, individuals, and corporations do the producers thank? You've just found a list of sponsors who fund film projects like yours! Put these sponsors high on your list of potential funders and start researching their websites.

Is your film about a specific cause? Find nonprofit agencies that advance this cause and find out who their sponsors are. You've just found a list of funders who fund your subject! Research these sponsors and see if they fund media or film projects. These are people who might be willing to act as your sponsors or mentors, and may lead you to additional funding opportunities.

You've been surfing the net for years, but are you up on the latest search tools? Do you really know Boolean logic? Do you know how to access information that normal search engines can't reach? Do you know the difference between a spider, a crawler, and a MetaSearcher? If not, take an afternoon and brush up on your surfing skills. UC Berkeley offers an award-winning Internet tutorial located at *http://www.lib.berkeley.edu/TeachingLib/Guides.*

The Internet has revolutionized the way we access information, but please don't forget about your local library. Your library has an entire collection devoted to foundations and grants, including some of those expensive databases. Take the time to pay a personal visit to your library and meet the grants and foundations librarian. She can show you valuable trade secrets on how to search different databases and give you pointers on how to find other possible donors for your film. Your local librarian may turn out to be one of the most helpful people on your film crew!

In fact I recommend finding a librarian who loves your film and giving her/him a researcher credit on the film in exchange for helping you. Believe me, they can find things in a matter of minutes that might take you hours.

ORGANIZING YOUR SEARCH

Some people are good at finding information — they're so good they accumulate file cabinets and desk drawers full of computer printouts, newspaper articles, and magazine clippings. You know how it is: You can't get to it today, but you may want to read it someday, so it's added to the stack of papers precariously perched on the corner of your desk.

This is not information, it's clutter. Anything unfinished, unused, unresolved, or disorganized bogs us down and can keep us from moving forward. You will need to keep a list of potential funders and the type of films they fund so you can keep track of your contacts. Please don't let the list get away from you. It's tempting to start compiling a pie-in-the-sky list of potential funders for future projects, but try to keep your eyes on your current goal.

The key to being a successful researcher is not to accumulate piles of information that you may need someday, but to know how to find the information you need when you need it.

There are all kinds of complicated databases and fancy tracking systems designed to organize your business contacts. Your objective, however, is to get your film made, not learn how to use some complicated color-coded database. A simple list is all you need. It should include the funder's name; mailing, Web and email address; your contact person; and a place for notes.

We always keep links to hot funding sites on the *www.fromtheheartproductions.com* front page. Look under financing information for new articles on financing.

Bobby Mardis, Carole Dean, Carey Feldman, Barbara Trent. L.A. Dean Grant Awards

Barbara Trent, (Academy Award winner, Panama Deception), Carole Dean, Robert Townsend. Roy W. Dean Awards, L.A.

CHAPTER 8

WINNING THE MIND GAME

ATTRACTING SUCCESS

Faith and belief fund films. The journey starts upstairs in your head. You must be ready to throw away any preconceived ideas about the funding process. The economic forecasters were right. Times have changed — with the Internet and social media, this gives you even more ways to connect with donors and investors. You just have to learn to go outside the box and look for it. That is what this book is about, adopting new ways of thinking when it comes to funding your film. It is about recreating some of the old methods and accepting new ones.

The most important thing I know from nineteen years of giving grants and watching filmmakers finish films is that those *who believe* they will get the money are the ones who *finish their films*. Those who say, "I think I will have a hard time financing my film" often don't finish the film. That's why I know your mind and your belief system are paramount to the funding process.

Let me share some things I have learned. Hearing stories of other people's success lets us know that the potential exists. You know people who have raised tons of money for their film. You know the potential is there, don't say, "Well, it was five years ago." Just know they did it and so can you. The potential exists for you to fund you film, *it's simply a matter of releasing this potential.*

RELEASING A POTENTIAL

This is what I want to cover first, releasing a potential that already exists. In fact, once you understand the real meaning of manifesting it becomes much easier. The dictionary's description of manifesting is: Not hidden, clearly defined, easy to see and understand. So, clarity is the key to manifesting; a clear, concise vision is what works.

As Wayne Dwyer said, "You can believe it when you can see it." I want you to know that clearly defining your goal is a major key to manifesting. Let's pretend there is a *big field of infinite possibilities*, as Chopra says. Anything is possible. And we need to realize *what you think about* and *what you say* are paramount to *what you receive*.

You know other filmmakers have found money for their films. *So your job is to see this potential working for you in your life.* For example, an artist has something concrete to look at, either a model or a picture. He knows it exists and he wants to replicate it. He sees his potential and he is releasing it on canvas. A writer has an idea and she manifests it as a book or screenplay. At that moment, she gives that idea physical form.

FIRST LAW IN MANIFESTING

Both the painter and the writer are manifesting something from their mind into this physical reality. This is the first law in manifesting. It is changing a form of something. You are not creating something out of nothing; what you want to create already exists. A piece of coal by itself is cold and black. Yet it can burn; it contains the potential of heat. When ignited, that heat is released. The potential was always there, just like your film is there inside you waiting for you to release it. Once you clearly see what you want to manifest you start the process of releasing it.

So, take something that you fully believe you can do and put that on your goal list. Something that you feel you can create. Manifesting uses natural laws because it is an active state. You need to see what you want, visualize it, see it, and feel it. What would you feel like if you had achieved this goal? Move into that feeling now. Experience it. Is it pride? Is it success? Is it pure joy? Save that feeling and write it down. Emotions heighten manifesting, and the more emotions the faster the rewards. Shakespeare wrote, "My words go up; my thoughts remain below, words without thoughts never to heaven go!" Shakespeare knew the laws of manifestation require you to see your vision and that *sending thought with emotion manifests*.

My neighbor in New Zealand has lived by this principle. He was a Brit who wanted to be a farmer and his vision was a large spread in the South Pacific. He now lives on ten thousand acres of land with over fifteen thousand sheep. He calls it imaginology. See it, believe it, and receive it. These are the elements of manifesting. *You did this as a child*. I am sure some of you have created just what you visualized; I think we all have.

When Matt Damon was writing the screenplay for *Good Will Hunting*, he constructed the restaurant scene in his mind. He saw every nook and cranny of it. He gave it a name and then transferred his thoughts to paper with his words. The story goes that during the production he walked on the set and when he saw they had built the restaurant exactly as he envisioned, the moment was so profound that he cried.

I want you to be that visual; I want you to clearly see your goal as completed. Your job is to believe that you have achieved it, to keep seeing the complete product. *See your goal as if it exists now*, as if it is part of your life.

How do we manifest? Words are our manifestos. Your pitch and your proposal bring your film to life. Your words can create your future. I believe each of us is manifesting daily; the trick is to manifest what we want and stop manifesting what we don't want.

HOW DO YOU DO THIS?

Focus on your goal, see it completed, and believe it. That's your right-brain work. Visually see it and send up those emotions of joy, success, confidence, and pride to the universe. Always thank the universe for the smallest gift each day, thank them. Then create your action list for your left brain and *do what's on the list*.

First you create your intention — then you put your attention on this intention. This creates your reality. Let negative statements roll off you like water rolls off a duck. Don't take that negativity into your conscience.

When people say, "You can't raise a hundred thousand dollars, no way!" you just smile and let that negativity pass you by and let it make you even more resolute that *your intention already exists.* Your job is *to release the potential* and you are doing that through your visualizations, your faith and your attention to your "to do" list.

DAYDREAMING IS IN!

Fred Alan Wolf is a beloved physicist and I quote him extensively in my book, *The Art of Manifesting.* Fred says that when you are daydreaming, "it's like a handshake across time that happens." You actually go into the future and create your reality. What you daydream often happens to you.

Growing up in Dallas, Texas, I loved to be outdoors and only ran into the house for dire emergencies. My favorite time was when dinner was over. Normally, I ran out of the house as fast as I could because that was my daydreaming time. We had a slanted roof and I would climb on that roof and watch the planes taking off and I put myself on the plane. I saw the clothes I wore; usually they were French and right out of the current *Vogue* magazine. Sometimes I saw myself landing in New York City and checking into the Plaza Hotel. Sometimes I was on my way to New York to buy an Oscar de la Renta spring coat. I often went to Saks Fifth Avenue and was waited on hand and foot while deciding my new wardrobe. In all my dreams, money was no object. Sometimes I would be on a flight to India and I saw myself riding elephants or I was in Africa watching the wildebeests migrate across the Great Serengeti. Later in life, I actually did all of these things and *I know that daydreaming works.*

When I read the *Dreaming Universe* by physicist Fred Alan Wolf I jumped with joy when he said that he too had similar experiences. He said that when he went into this quiet place and imagined things happening, later in life they would happen almost exactly as he visualized them. Yes, that's manifesting. He knows it works, and so do I. It's important you use this wonderful right-brain imagery to support financing and creating your film.

To wrap this up:

1. Use your mind to fund your film.

2. See the completed film, believe it exists, and know that your job is to release it into this dimension.

3. Daydreaming is in! Please put it on your calendar "ten minutes a day." Devote this to feeling the emotions of success, joy and achievement while you watch your film playing on a giant screen.

CHAPTER 9

THE FEATURE FILM GAME

By Tom Malloy,
Actor/Producer/Writer

Tom Malloy is a prolific writer, he mentors filmmakers, he produces, he raises millions to make films and he wrote a brilliant book, Bankroll, *now in its second edition.*

Tom wrote and produced The Attic, *a thriller directed by Mary Lambert (director of* Pet Sematary *and* Pet Sematary II*). Then he wrote and produced* The Alphabet Killer, *a psychological thriller directed by Rob Schmidt (director of* Wrong Turn*). Then he wrote and produced* Love N' Dancing, *a dance film/romantic comedy directed by Rob Iscove (director of* She's All That*).*

Most recently, Tom produced the self-help documentary film The Inner Weigh, *featuring Bob Proctor (*The Secret*), which has been called a revolutionary film in the weight loss industry, as well as the TV pilot* The Fuzz, *directed by Art Wolff (director of the* Seinfeld *pilot). Tom is also a nationally-known motivational speaker. His message of "Making Positive Choices" has reached over 100,000 students.*

Tom can be reached at www.TomMalloy.com www.bankrollthebook.com and Tom-Malloy@gmail.

I asked Tom to tell us how he raises money for his films, and what he thinks are the most important parts of the financing process. Here are the topics he chose and his advice.

FINDING VESTED INVESTORS

This is about finding investors that have a reason to invest in a new film, not the standard, let-me-make-money investor. Because historically, independent films do not make much money, and it's a very tough business. It's the "nobody knows anything" concept that completely applies. Half of the country thought *Avatar* would fail before its release.

So, if you can find an investor for your film on a reason other than "let me make my money back," then that is a way to close. Now, that reason might be, "I have a thirteen-year-old daughter who wants a small role." Great. "I have a nephew who wants to be mentored because he eventually wants to be a director." Great. "I want to hang out on set and look like a big shot and mingle with movie stars." Great. These are all examples of vested interest reasons.

I encourage you to take your script and analyze it and think, "Who wants to invest in this?" Is it a World War II story? There are World War II veterans or kids of World War II veterans who have become very successful and might want to invest in your film. You can always find some kind of vested interest. If your screenplay is so strange and far out, then attack it a different way — try to find someone who wants their daughter to play a role or wants their son to be mentored. This is what you have to offer them. Understand this: to any investor outside the film industry, which is where I tell people always to look for investors, you are the conduit to let them into the film industry because you're making films. This is going to be your full-time job, if it's not already.

You are bringing these people into a world they have no other way to access. They can't pick up a camera and be in Hollywood, it's not going to happen. They need someone who has access. That alone is invaluable, and you have to realize how valuable that is and give that to the potential investor.

CLOSING THE DEAL

Closing is an art; selling is different from closing. Selling is pitching and getting someone excited. I know some people who are fantastic at selling but really not that good at closing. Closing is an icing that you put on the cake. When you close a deal it's a jump in the pool for the investor, it's an extra step that they must take. Closing is an art because it involves qualifying investors to know if they can invest. Closing is integral from the entire aspect of selling. Every single thing should move towards the close. There is an old sales saying: ABC, Always Be Closing. And you have to have that mindset, meaning if the person you're pitching is excited and they are thinking, "Wow, this is a great investment." Okay, that's all good and most people would just walk away from there and those are the people who are not good closers.

I on the other hand would say, "Okay, so what's the next step?" "When can we get this done?" "Can I get you the investment documents?" Start trying to put finite timing on things. So your language has to be geared towards closing investors. Pull out your iPhone or Blackberry and look at the calendar. But be saying actively, "I want to know when we can move forward."

I read a lot of sales books and I recommend that for any producer. You will get to a point when talking to the investor that you will finish what you're saying and there will be silence. You have to be comfortable with that silence. An inexperienced or inept sales person would interrupt the silence and they would say, "Oh, one more thing…" and there is no silence. That is a huge mistake because the silence is to allow the investor time to consider the deal. They are moving it around in their head and ultimately getting to some questions. If you sit there and keep interrupting, you'll most likely lose the deal.

I give my pitch and when it's over I'll shut my mouth and I don't care if five minutes goes by. There will be silence; I will not make a peep. I cannot stress enough how important this is to close.

THE SCRIPT

How do you tell that it's a killer script? There is an instinct that you'll develop over time. There are certain scripts that I love, I mean obviously they are rare, but when I love it I get behind it. I can tell that if I love it, a certain amount of people will love it, too. I've read so many scripts that

I can judge the quality, and I highly encourage you to do that so that you can develop your own instinct. Let's talk about developing that instinct.

I'm a successful screenwriter, I've written fifteen scripts, and so far eleven of them have been optioned, sold, or made into films. I'm in the Writers Guild and have made a lot of money in writing. Before I did that, I read fifty of the greatest screenplays of all time. You can find a ton of scripts online. Download these scripts and read some of the public domain scripts, too. Look for the top ten highest grossing films.

Great scripts can make your career. If you're putting all your time and effort behind a good script, it's not going to be as productive and may ultimately lead to failure. Let's say you have a script of your own or you've optioned it, go to Craig's List, Los Angeles, which is the only place you're going to find this. Say you want coverage on screenplays; you'll get back a ton of emails saying, yes, I will do coverage for x amount of dollars.

Now you want to find someone to do coverage for $30 to $80. Send it out to two or three people and see what you get back. If you send it to three people, it costs $100 to $200 and if all three say, "Amazing," then you know you have a killer script. And eventually, you'll get a coverage person that you trust and then you only have to pay one person.

My coverage guy passes on everything, that's exactly what you want yours to do because he knows that if he keeps recommending screenplays, I have to read those screenplays and I have to take my time and if he keeps recommending screenplays that I don't like, he's got about three of those and then I find a new coverage guy. The bottom line is there are ways to search for readers and develop a relationship with them.

What's the best way to get your 100-page script into two pages?

Well, there is an art to writing a synopsis as well as writing screenplays. You may not be the writer of the screenplay but you may have to write the synopsis. The best way is to remember that a synopsis is telling the story and ending in a question. The key is to write an overview of the three-act structure of the screenplay without giving the climax away. Here is what happens, here is the main character, this is the conflict, and here they are trying to achieve this resolution, but we're not going to give you this outcome in the synopsis.

Do you recommend writing or hiring someone for the business plan?

I think that you could get into a business plan debacle by reading these business plans and I've seen people spend thousands and thousands of dollars on them. They create these legal type business plans that are really hybrids of private placement memorandums and they lose the flashiness. My business plan is a pitch packet and that's the best way to do it, worry about the investment documents later when the investor is in that mindset. I would say it's okay to hire somebody to create the artwork and the layout and the design. But you are going to supply most of the information.

I highly suggest reading my book *Bankroll* which includes a business plan. I change the business plan according to what's worked and what's sold. My business plans are active and they are out there, and I'm responding to investors on what I feel needs to be in the business plan.

When do you hire an attorney to do the PPM?

I'm not a fan of the Private Placement Memorandum (PPM); I'm a fan of a pitch packet in an operating agreement. Now, for an operating agreement you're going to need an attorney. I say get some boiler plate, maybe from another film, someone who paid an attorney for it and tailor it to your film.

The lawyer is probably doing the same thing and may also be charging you for developing it. Then I give it to the lawyer so he/she can check it for me. You are talking about one or two hours work which cost you $300 to $700 versus creating from scratch, which can cost you $10,000.

How do you find good actors for scale?

Have a killer script. Failing a killer script, another thing that actors look for is a director. I know of two big-name actors that signed on to my film, *The Alphabet Killer*, prior to reading the script because of Rob Schmidt, our director. His last film, *Wrong Turn*, and his film before that, *Crime and Punishment in Suburbia*, were both very good films.

What did you do to find vested investors?

I used approaches such as the finder's fee approach or the six degrees of separation where I reached out to people and ask them if they knew people who had money. But at the same time if I take a look at my movie, and say it's a movie about Broadway singers, I'm sure that I can go to people who have invested in theatre and they have a vested interest in seeing these people succeed. I have been talking to a lot of New York art patrons.

Reach out to people and say if you find me a high net worth individual (HNI), I will give you an associate producer credit and a 5% finder's fee. Let them find it for you because you can reach so many people this way.

When I meet these people, I do not show up with the operating agreement. I show up with my business plan/pitch packet. Then if they go to the next step and they want to see the investment document, that is a big thing. I've given tons of business plans out; my closing ratio as far as the amount of business packages given out to people is about 1%. I'll give them out to anybody because they are not private placement memorandums, so it is not an offering.

When it's going to the next step and they want to see the investment documents, that ratio shoots up to 30%. Because it's real to them and they are talking about investing, not just blue sky. That's usually the document that they have to give to the lawyer.

How do you keep up the communication when the potential investor goes quiet?

I would say continue to make communication maybe once a week, at the most only let two weeks go by. You want to persistently stay on top of that person. I know because I'm a ridiculously busy person. How tough is it to get back to people? There are people I thanked for staying on top of me!

There are studies that have shown that there is a certain amount of closing on the first or second calls on a client and then it drops off. Then it continues to drop some on the third, fourth, fifth, and sixth call, but then on the seventh, eighth, and ninth it starts to go back up again. So, what I always say is "go until no." Keep going until somebody says stop — stop emailing me, stop calling me, and leave me alone, I'm not interested.

What's the best incentive to get the first money in?

The best incentive is a combination. Perhaps say, "It's a million-dollar film and I'm looking for $100,000." I say that I will pay that person back first so that they would be out. Basically I would be looking for 1.1. And then I'd let them know that they would be getting an executive producer credit and a percentage. Then they also get another ten producer points, perhaps.

I double their percentage for what they are investing. That executive producer credit will not be given out until someone invests $250,000. They like this. Their only risk is that the film doesn't even get financed. Once the film is financed they are out and they are paid back and then they still retain their percentage of the film. And maybe they will be paid back, like $120,000, so that they've got their 20% on the investment and it will be within a certain time period. So they would be pretty happy.

How do I use the 5% finder's fee?

There are security laws that bar you from just randomly getting finders everywhere. But the loophole I use is that I create associate producers. I can hire whomever I want as an associate producer or co-producer and I can pay a fee. That fee will be the 5% of the investment that they closed. I can do any business decision I want that's defined in the operating agreement. If you know John is looking for an investor for $500,000, 5% of that will be $25,000. I would just hire John as an associate producer of the film or co-producer of the film and pay him the $25,000.

I highly recommend the finder's fee approach. Ask your friends by saying, "If you find me a high net worth individual, you'll get 5% of their investment and an associate producer or co-producer credit."

Can you start shooting with only part of the budget?

The answer is yes. You are thrusting yourself into what I call the dangerous approach. You have to raise money while you're shooting. But something magical does happen, I cannot deny that there is no better time to get the money than when you are actually shooting. When they come on set, they see the lights, the actors and the camera, it's like the party they are not invited to and suddenly they want to pay to join in.

It's an incredibly powerful situation; you've got a gun to your head. Your mind is just functioning at this incredible rate. We call it the "crack high" in the independent film business. It's like you are actively producing. There is something amazing about that and you will find a way to get it done. Do I suggest this method? No, it ages you inside and you will get gray hair from it. But does it work? Yes.

What important tips can I give to filmmakers?

I have a ton of special tips. One, always be pitching, ABP. I've told you always be closing, ABC. But always be pitching. Literally, you meet somebody in the bar and they ask, "What do you do?" "I am a filmmaker, I'm producing a film and we are looking to raise 'x' amount of dollars..."

Literally, always be saying, "If you know anybody that would invest, I could give you a 5% finder's fee and an associate producer credit just for making the introduction." And then realize once that's said you can say, "We are looking to raise millions and there will be $50,000 in your pocket." Always be pitching. Somebody popped up on a Facebook chat the other day, "Hey, I haven't talked to you in a long time," and I said, "Listen I'm looking for investors for a film." You should always be in the mindset that you're attracting money.

Another tip, read books on the law of attraction. *The Art of Manifesting* is a fantastic one. Read this book and others where they talk about manifesting your dreams and using the law of attraction. I am a huge fan of self-help books. Why? Because they work.

Don't look for producers working in the business because they have their own personal agenda. I don't blame them because they have to pay their rent. It truly pays to stay outside the film industry. Find the guy who made $100 million creating paper napkins that has no way to be in the movie business and you are his way to become the film producer.

MAKE FILMS

Now, what do I mean by this? Always be actively making movies. You know, how many people do I know who say, "Yeah, we're making this $2 million film and we've raised $500,000 but we are not there yet." Come on, make the movie for $500,000 or try to make another film or make two films for $250,000, but just make movies. We are in a day and age where the technology is super inexpensive, and actors and crew are working on the cheap because there is a lack of projects.

You have an opportunity now to even take $100,000 and make a great movie that looks like it will cost $2 to $3 million. That was impossible even three years ago. I'm telling you it's possible now, so make movies. If you can afford it, attend the Cannes Film Festival, if not attend the American Film Market. Learn the business of sales and foreign sales and foreign distribution. Cannes is ten times to me the value of AFM, but Cannes is extremely expensive. FM is a lot cheaper and it's in Santa Monica in November. Get out there and make relationships. This business is all about relationships.

Always be working. I can go to a party tonight and I can guarantee you that it will be an industry function and my mindset will be who I meet that can help me can advance my career and my livelihood. I'm never just out there to party and have a great time; work is always in the back of my mind.

You are raising money for the film. Always consider this is work. I think the problem is that so many people outside the film business think that it's all fun and games and you have to remember that at the end of the day it's a business. It's the film business and you need to treat it as such.

I would equate the craftsmanship and the skill necessary to make a film with any other job in the world. It is a fine skill and it's a fine craft, and it's also a business. Treat it as such, have that mindset and try to enjoy the journey. You are doing something — if you're making a movie and even if you are living on your last five dollars you are doing something that everybody else dreams of doing, but you are actually doing it!

Rochester, NY. MEGAN PAIGE (Eliza Dushku) is a driven police investigator whose commitment to the job borders on obsession. The only other aspect of her life that receives any attention is her significant other KENNETH SHINE (Cary Elwes), who just so happens to be a lieutenant with the RPD (and jockeying for the same promotion as Meg). They're currently working on one of their worst cases yet, the murder / rape of a ten-year-old girl named CARLA CASTILLO ... and when Megan puts it together that she was murdered in Churchville, Megan becomes convinced that they are dealing with a serial killer. She becomes so caught up in her work that she begins to have hallucinations ... and a bloody Carla begins to haunt her regularly.

When Megan cannot crack the case (and worse, her boss CAPTAIN GULLIK-SON [Tom Noonan] pulls her off of it), it pushes her over the edge and Megan suffers a nervous breakdown. She's diagnosed with an adult onset of paranoid schizophrenia that finds her in a psychiatric hospital instead of her precinct and to top it off, she breaks off her engagement with Kenneth. TWO YEARS LATER: Megan regains work for the department, but now in the shadow of her former capacity (she's a records clerk) and also in the shadow of her former fiancee — Kenneth has been promoted to the head of the department. At least she's got a support group for mental illness survivors and wheelchair-bound friend RICHARD LEDGE (Timothy Hutton).

When another girl, WENDY WALSH is abducted, raped and murdered in Webster, Megan is convinced that the killer has resurfaced and her old fire is reheated. Against his better judgment, Kenneth allows Megan to ride along with investigator STEVEN HARPER (Tom Malloy) after she badgers him, but only in an advisory capacity. However soon after she is in the thick of things, her old symptoms start coming back, namely in the form of hallucinations of *both* dead girls now. And it's worse; she's beginning to manifest embarrassing physical traits as well in the form of involuntary movements and ticks (a condition called Akathisia), which causes her to stop taking her meds (thus making her hallucinations worse).

Ledge tells her that she's flirting with disaster but knows better than to try to talk her out of anything. Megan knows that the case is in danger of going cold with few leads, no suspects, and a serial killer on the loose. Can she catch him in time? Or will the "Alphabet Killer" go free?

CHAPTER 10

THE ROAR OF CROWDFUNDING

Interview with Danea Ringelmann,
co-founder of IndieGoGo

Crowdfunding is an exciting and effective way to raise money for your film. This interview with Danea tells you how it works.

What is IndieGoGo?

IndieGoGo (IGG) is the largest open funding platform in the world. It helps anybody in the world raise money from individuals. Since launching in 2008, we have distributed millions of dollars in 170 countries to over 30,000 campaigns.

Crowdfunding is many people supporting one big idea with funds. It's a new way of getting funding for your ideas. Instead of being limited by maxing out credit cards, waiting for bank loans, or filling out grant applications, crowdfunding is a fast and engaging way to raise money.

The idea of asking friends and family for money goes back for generations, but the reason crowdfunding is so successful today is because of the latest trends. It's never been so easy to communicate to others through Twitter, Facebook, etc., or to pay for something through credit cards or PayPal. Now you have access 24/7/365 across the world — and all in one efficient platform.

IGG's crowdfunding platform moves people beyond the traditional D.I.Y. (*Do It Yourself*) fundraising to a D.I.W.O. (*Do It with Others*) model. It starts with your network of friends and family and quickly expands across the globe. When done right, the results can be fast and furious.

CROWDFUNDING FOR CASH

How do you raise money with crowdfunding?

The important thing with crowdfunding is to have a clear call to action. That call to action is money. How much do you need, by when, for what, and what do people get in return? Some additional benefits include validation for your idea, marketing, and promotion, plus all the email addresses and data you can get from the process.

Who uses IndieGoGo?

Anybody in the world can use us for absolutely, positively, any campaign. We see the world of campaigns breaking down into three major areas — creative, entrepreneurial, and cause. This can be raising money for music, theatre, a new food or cosmetics company, to do a liver transplant or build a school. IGG is the largest open funding platform in the world where any idea is accepted.

Danae, what percentage of films hit their goals?

We allow you to keep the money, whether you reach your goal or not. We don't even talk about who reached their goal, so I don't know that number. What's important is that people are raising money. Thousands of campaigns are receiving money and accomplishing their goals. The most important things include being proactive, having a good pitch, and finding an audience that cares. The campaigns that find the biggest challenges are the ones that believe you just post it and funders will come. A successful funding campaign will take effort, and the more effort you put into it, the more IGG will support you.

How do you measure success?

We believe success comes in many ways. You don't necessarily need to raise 100% of your budget all at once, because we know making a film and raising money can take a long time. We know that you can raise more money over time as you build and grow your audience, which is why we enable multiple campaigns. And we enable you to keep your money, because we know that even if you don't quite reach your goal, it doesn't mean you're going to stop and give up on your project. You can always raise another round of money through your next campaign. You can keep working and growing your audience, so that in six months you can come back and do another even more successful campaign.

TIPS FOR SUCCESS

What tips do you give filmmakers for crowdfunding?

We tell people the three keys to success are having a great pitch, being proactive and having community support. A great pitch means really personalizing your story. Tell us why you're working on this project, what the impact of your project will be on the community, or how it impacts others.

You do not pitch your actual project; *you pitch the reason why you are the right person*, why you are actually working on this project, and why this film is so important. We know that people contribute to people; not just ideas, but people. So, if all you do is show your idea and you don't show who you are, you probably won't have as much success.

The second thing in being proactive is that it requires you to get out there and share with the people who want to see your project the most. You need to identify your influencers. Those are bloggers or organizations or forum leaders or Facebook group leaders, or just people in general who have an affinity with your project. *It's finding places where they discuss items* or topics that are *relevant to your project*. Because when you actually get your project into the conversation, it's much more organic and relevant for the people who are having these discussions. The interest that you'll build through that will be greater than if you try to spam everybody about your project, which we don't recommend.

Danae, to prove your point, Jilann Spitzmiller and Hank Rogerson are raising money on IndieGoGo for their film, *Still Dreaming*, a film about aging actors doing a Shakespearean play. By Hank blogging on a Shakespeare site they received a $7,500 donation from someone they never met.

Yes, this really works. The third way is having a community. Most projects are validated when they launch a campaign by family and friends of family or followers, people who already know the person. And that's really critical in getting momentum to your campaign, so that you can raise money from strangers later in the campaign.

How do you handle payment?

If they raise money on PayPal, they get the money instantly. If they raise money via credit cards, they get the money at the end of the campaign.

A filmmaker told me they were chosen to get on IndieGoGo's mailing list. They hit their goal because of this. What are the criteria to get on your mailing list?

We focus on being a democratic platform and giving everybody the same tools to succeed, and that's the reason we do not curate and why anyone can post. We also reward projects that do a good job of engaging their community and being active with their campaign, by featuring them. And the way we measure that is every campaign gets a GoGo Factor, which is an algorithm that is constantly updated every day. It's basically a measurement of how active a campaign is, based on internal factors. It is based on what the campaign earner is doing, how much they're updating and how many announcements they make, plus how active the community is in their campaign. How many comments they're leaving, how many shares the community is doing, how many re-Tweets and Facebook posts and contributions are happening, all add up in our IndieGoGo factor. The campaign with the highest numbers is featured in our newsletter, on our homepage, in the press releases that we do, and elsewhere. A key element is that it's all in their hands.

Getting rewards is directly related to the amount of time the filmmaker puts into the campaign. Do you have a place on your site where we can see some of the most successful campaigns?

Go to IndieGoGo.com and click on browse, and then click on successes on the left.

AVERAGE CONTRIBUTIONS

What is the average contribution?

The smallest contribution has been a dollar. The largest contribution was $10,000, and the average contribution on IndieGoGo is $79.

Would you like to tell us some of your top success stories?

A great example of a successful film campaign is *Wish Me Away* which is a documentary about Chely Wright, who is the first country music star to ever come out of the closet publicly. They raised about $25,000 in just a few weeks from Chely Wright's fans. *Wish Me Away* is a great campaign, because the documentary filmmakers went right to the people who cared the most. Those are the music fans of Chely Wright. Within a few weeks they raised over $22,000, from ninety-nine people. And they launched a new campaign to continue the fundraising to pay for postproduction.

Do you help people raise money for things other than docs and features?

Yes, there is a female filmmaker from Texas who's also going to South by Southwest. She was making a little film called *My Sucky Teen Romance*, which is a campy, vampire teen-teeny-bopper film. She's seventeen, and she's been making films since she was thirteen. She raised $9,000 in one campaign, because she kept it personal and made a pitch clip of herself. She was literally in a closet with her stuffed animals in the background.

She did a good job of keeping her fans updated and engaged throughout the life of the campaign. When it was time for postproduction, she created a new campaign and raised more money. She showcased her trailer she made with the money from the first round of fundraising. Next she shared it with Harry Knowles of *Ain't It Cool News* who is a fan of hers. Harry is kind of a legend in Hollywood for breaking news about film-related stuff. He has a specific audience that loves the type of films Emily Hagins makes. She did a good job of keeping him engaged. He blogged about her campaign and within a few weeks she raised over $6,000 to fund her postproduction. Now, she's going to South by Southwest with her film.

CROWDFUNDING FOR FEATURES

Is it legal for people making films-for-profit to raise money on IndieGoGo?

Yes. They can raise money because they're not giving any ownership. There's no profit participation enabled on IGG, because the money raised is a contribution, in exchange for perks. There's no ownership transfer, so it is legal.

Can teen filmmakers apply?

You have to be at least thirteen to use IGG. When you apply, you enter your date of birth and verify who you are. We send the funds to a bank account you specify. If a young person doesn't have a bank account, they can put it in their parent's account.

What do you think are the reasons IndieGoGo has grown so quickly?

Crowdfunding or raising money this way has existed since the beginning of time. Crowdfunding is the pooling of funds from people who are most passionate about a project, and the difference is today we have better tools. It's easier to send the funds when you can click a button on PayPal versus pulling out a checkbook, or putting cash in an envelope and mailing it.

All you need to do is keep it personal and tell your own story. We can assure your communication with your funders is seamless. We enhance the entire process and make it much more efficient and easy for more people to get involved, which is why we say, we help people raise more money from more people faster.

Our rapid growth is because this works. It's people sharing their stories with other people. Everywhere in the world, people want to get involved with cool ideas. We've just made it easy for those two sides of the coin to come together.

I believe that online crowdfunding helps filmmakers create a market for their completed films.

Right, a key benefit is market validation. When people vote with their money, they're validating your idea and saying, "I really want to see this film. Tell me when it's coming out." You can't get better data than this. It actually helps attract other interested parties such as investors and angels, and even banks and distributors can be impressed with your results.

Distributors want to know the demographics of your audience.

Yes, you can show them you have an audience and you can give them demographics. Now that *My Sucky Teen Romance* is going to South by Southwest, they have a following by a community that's been with them since the beginning of the film. These people will be there to re-Tweet their success at the convention.

A fourth benefit is the participation that you create around your film. Historically, filmmakers have gone into a darkroom, made their amazing film, told nobody about it throughout the entire process. And then they come out from behind the curtain saying, "Voilà, here's my film, come see it." Well, probably the reason they were so dependent on distributors is because no one knew about their film.

When you use production as a promotional tool and share your stories, dailies, and blogs on your film, then you enable people to step into a "film world," which is incredibly exciting and sexy.

From the Heart Productions is honored to be a fiscal sponsor for IndieGoGo films. We recommend documentary, short and low-budget indie filmmakers consider a crowdfunding opportunity. By connecting online with a fiscal sponsor you give your donor a tax deduction. Additionally, your donor knows that your film is being monitored and supported by people who can guide the production to completion.

CREATING A SUCCESSFUL CAMPAIGN, OUTLINED BY CAROLE DEAN

This is the preproduction work that goes into a successful funding campaign. I want you to see it as just like preproduction on your film, the better your research and development, the better your film. Pretend the date you launch your fundraising campaign is identical to your shoot date. Everything must be in place for success. Since From the Heart (FTH) and IndieGoGo (IGG) are partners, I will use IGG's information because I am familiar with it, and you can compare this information to other crowdfunding companies.

It is important to approach crowdfunding with the understanding that you are building your fan base as well as financing your film. This way, you know the time you put into preproduction will be returned to you in many ways. You are growing and moving into the interactive Web world where you will be supported by millions of people. Gone are the days where you make your movie alone; now you have immediate feedback, good or bad, from day one.

Marc Rosenbush says to put your ideas out there before you even commit to making a film! He thinks you should put it online to see if it has legs. If people like the concept, and you find there is a market for your film, then make it. Otherwise, you should reconsider.

Fasten your seat belts; it's going to be a bumpy night! You may be tossing this book out the window before this chapter is over, so have some patience. There is a lot to do. Just chill out and know that you will find crew and friends to help, because you can't do this alone.

To create a successful campaign means lots of things must be completed before you launch. The main purposes of your campaign are:
    Determine the potential success of your idea
    Raise money and resources
    Attract a following
    Find markets for your film

On the IGG launch page are questions that are paramount to financing. These are the decisions you need to make before you launch.

How long will you run this campaign? Most successful campaigns are sixty to seventy days. That's a beginning number for you to consider, if you do all your preproduction work before you launch.

IGG has a technical call every Friday to help with questions. From the Heart (FTH) also has monthly teleconference with crowdfunding advice, where we share ideas and success stories, and overcome obstacles. FTH also has private mentoring sessions to help you find your niche markets. When searching for a crowdfunding organization, look for these benefits.

You want to work with a company that has online information to support your campaign with important statistics. Most crowdfunding companies have a widget to embed on your website and Facebook page. Be sure this is available and easy to embed. This widget tells you the idea of the film from the photo and log line; it has your goal, the number of days left to reach the goal, and the amount raised to date. It should be everywhere. All of this is important feedback for donors during the campaign.

What does it cost? Remember, you pay the crowdfunding company a fee, and then on top of that, you pay the credit card fee. PayPal and Amazon are about 3%. Check for the current rates. You may pay more, if you don't hit your goal. IGG has waived that fee for fiscal sponsors like FTH to work with you. You get a tax deduction for your donors, plus you get paid whether or not you hit your goal! You pay one fee for the fiscal sponsor and IGG together. You may want to add this fee into your budget and raise it online.

Does your film have a foreign market? If so, IGG works in 140 countries; look for a crowdfunder with global markets. You want your film to go global and that information can benefit you with a distributor.

NETWORKING FOR CROWDFUNDING

Does your website have Search Engine Optimization (SEO)? This means that if someone googles your name or your film's name, you're in the top three listings. Consider how you can move up to the higher ranks. You need this to draw large amounts of traffic to your site.

Get all your email contacts on one mailing list with a professional organization like *www.constantcontact.com* or *www.ratepoint.com*. You need to be able to send information quickly and efficiently to your core audience and be able to add new names automatically.

Does your website have an "opt in" box? That's a must. You need to be collecting names every time someone comes to your site. Give them a free gift to get their email. These new names can be connected automatically to your mailing list.

Where are your "peeps"? Marc Rosenbush says, "Find your niche markets through Facebook and the Internet." Both have done a marvelous job putting your potential customers (peeps) in clusters. You want to outline the sub-markets that fit your film. Ask yourself these questions: What is the subject of my film? What is my main character famous for? What are his/her hobbies? What audiences do they have on Facebook? How can I tap into these people?

Who is composing your music? What is her/his audience? Who is your director? What fans do they have? Break out the story you are telling. Does it have Vietnam veterans? Does your character play tennis? Look at each segment of your film to find potential niche markets. Make a long list.

Now, search Facebook and the Internet using the keywords for your niche markets. Once you begin to find websites, look for an opt in box. Are they collecting names? Google them on www.alexa.com or www.quantcast.com and see how big they are. Put your list in order by size of members. You want the largest organizations to be a fan of your film and get donations.

Make a list of these potential partners for your film and decide what you have to offer. You want to connect with their members and maximize your marketing. You want to get your newsletters to them and you want to drive them to your Facebook page to "like" your film. You want to eventually get them to your crowdfunding place to donate to you. But first, win them over with information about who you are and the subject of your film.

MONEY

You need to decide the amount of money you want to raise. Remember, don't tell them your full budget. Normal people would be in shock to know your film may cost $300,000. They may feel their $25 donation is too little. Set a reasonable goal you believe is achievable. Jilann Spitzmiller sat down and went over her list of friends and family and gave each an amount that she thought they might donate. That's one way. You need to reach your goal; it's an emotionally important milestone for you and the film. You may want one larger donor to wait until the last to come in with the amount you need to put you over the top. Remember, most people do several campaigns. You can come back for more money in another campaign. Check your IGG and Kickstarter sites for success stories. What amount of money did they ask for and how long was their campaign?

Ask where does this money go? If you are using IGG and FTH as a fiscal sponsor, the fiscal sponsor gets the funds and disburses to you. Ask how often you get paid, how much do they hold for their fees, and what is the net amount you make for your efforts. Be very clear on this before you make a decision.

How much you need is a question you must answer. You can do a budget for a trailer, a shoot, some postproduction, or for your music. All of these items may fall into the $10 to $20,000 level. Whatever it is you want to raise, you need to share this with your donors, and explain to them exactly what you need the money for. This is your heartfelt "ask" that goes in your pitch for the trailer on your crowdfunding site. So pick the reason that you think will touch them the most for your first campaign.

I believe if you touch my heart, I reach for my pocketbook. I think we communicate through the heart chakra. Speak from your heart directly to theirs.

CROWDFUNDING TRAILER

This is a totally new type of trailer. It's wide open. I like trailers with the producer or the creator of the project telling me what they want the money for, why they are making the film, how much it means, and what they will do with the money. You will find many people look at your trailer but don't watch it to the end. You should have statistics to tell you how many see all of it; IGG has this information. I think you will be shocked to learn that 80% will not watch all of it. I believe this happens with all trailers, and now we have the statistics to verify this.

Please put your "ask" up front. I may not stay around until the end. Tell me from the beginning why you are committing three years of your life to this project. I want to "feel" your passion and instantly bond with you, so I can hit that donate button and get on with my emails!

Sell me quickly is the concept for a good crowdfunding trailer. Don't put anything important at the end. Yes, I would like to see a bit of the movie and your character, but remember, from the first edition of this book in 2003, I said, "People give money to people, not to films." Crowdfunding has verified that statement. You are the one they give money to, not the character in the film, or the subject matter your film covers. It's all about you. Get up there and tell me how important this film is, why you are making it, and how I can help. That's what brings in the cash.

ARE YOU READY TO RECEIVE?

"The time has come," the Walrus said, "to talk of many things." You must now look inside and ask some serious questions about your relationship to money. Ask yourself, why should people give me money? Can I really finish this film? Why should they trust me? What if??? There are a million of those "what if" questions. Get them all out. Walk and talk to yourself and get very clear on any confusion you have about attracting or receiving money. Now is the time, not when your campaign is running, and something is blocking it. That "something" may be you.

On my site *www.fromtheheartproductions.com* are free videos and interviews about manifesting. Please listen to them. Something may touch you and open your mind to receive the goodness waiting for you. We are magnificent beings that came into the world with a natural ability to manifest our needs. Somehow, most people lost this talent. If you did, you can find it again. It's not gone, it's waiting for you to reignite it.

Clear your mind to receive. Visualize yourself watching your widget meter go up and up with your money coming in. Know that each time you are online looking for peeps or chatting with a group, that all of this is part of your manifesting. Sometimes you put your energies in one direction and the universe comes back to you with money from a totally different place. Just keep saying thanks to your guides, your angels, whoever you want, because someone is definitely working for you on the other side. You are never alone.

CREATE A TEAM AND GET MOVING

IGG says you are better off with four on your team. I know you are awake now! Where to find them? What about your best friend who loves to surf the Web? What about your director who loves people? You can attract what you need. Just don't panic.

Outline what you need to do to make it a great campaign and assign specific tasks to those who are most talented in that area. As an example, one woman wrote 200 personal emails asking for donations to her film and sent them all out on the first day of the launch. I like this idea. I think one-on-one personal requests work. Get your list out and start writing. Get your crew to do the same thing to their personal lists.

Someone has to find your Strategic Alliances (SA). Those are the large organizations that are most critical to your success. If your film's market is for fifty-five and older, the biggest SA for you is AARP. You really want to find a group of twenty SAs and contact them with some gift for their members. You want your SA to post your newsletters on line and to let you chat about your film. You will give them something special. Private screenings, a credit in the film, talk to the Director of Marketing and discuss his/her needs and give what's necessary to gain these members on your fan base.

One person needs to get on IGG and Kickstarter and find similar campaigns. Donate and see what you get for your donation. Then you can see a thank you email and get yours prepared and ready to go out. What is their lowest donation? What is their highest? Think about what you have to give for your donation that you may not even realize. Does anyone you know have a summer home in Maine? Can you get that for two weeks? Can you give that as a gift to someone? Does your mother or father have 120,000 miles of frequent flyer points?

Read what other people are giving and use your creativity and lateral thinking to come up with things that you can get for little or nothing. One filmmaker doing a feature in his home town used his town's business people to give donations. He used a coffee house in the film and they gave him free coffee for one of his gifts. His character was a bowler and he connected to the bowling alleys. One created posters for his film to drive people to his crowdfunding place to donate. He did quite well financially.

Have weekly meetings with your team to discuss what they found. You have a brilliant group of creatives around you; use all ideas. Be original, be unique. No one is putting any limits on you. It's a new field, so you can go wild with ideas.

LAUNCH DATE CHECK LIST

After reviewing all the things you need to do, you should give yourself at least sixty days before you launch.

Upload your names to a mailing list.

Find your peeps on Facebook and the Web.

Create a Twitter account.

Find and connect with Strategic Alliances.

Create personal emails to all your family and friends.

Be online chatting with groups that are aligned with your film.

Consider advertising online to get more people to "like" your film.

Read everything on IGG or Kickstarter to do with funding.

Take the weekly class with them and learn even more.

Call your astrologer to pick a date! (Just kidding).

Find a date that is not over a holiday to start. (You will find holiday weekends slow for donations)

Know you will do this again so the time invested will be returned manifold.

Be prepared to communicate with your lists on a weekly basis.

Prepare at least four newsletters with heartfelt stories for the campaign.

Consider having contests to reach milestones, like hitting $5,000.

Tell them about the characters in the film.

Tell them heart-touching stories about your film or the characters.

Statistics show you need to send at least seven emails to hit your maximum donations.

Jilann Spitzmiller teaches an excellent online workshop on crowdfunding including detailed insight on IndieGoGo and Kickstarter and I highly recommend it. Go to www.documentaryhowto.com. *Another person who is brilliant on Internet marketing is Marc Rosenbush and I highly recommend his work on niche marketing, see* www.internetmarketingforfilmmakers.com. *From the Heart has extensive information for fiscal sponsors on funding films and even more detailed information for crowdfunding on our site.*

CHAPTER 11

INTERNET MARKETING

—∞—

Interview with Peter Broderick
of Paradigm Consulting (www.PeterBroderick.com)

Peter, you're known for creating the term "hybrid distribution." You've been correct in predicting many of the new distribution forms. I know because Jahangir Golestan, Bill Woolery and I came to you for a consultation on the film *Bam 6.6* many years ago. Your advice was to use the Internet and focus on the American/Iranian market. You were way ahead in your thinking and you were spot on about the benefits of Internet marketing. Because you are always looking into the future for new trends, I want to know what changes we may see in film distribution over the next three to five years.

Well, I often get asked to look into the future but I don't have a crystal ball that can foresee things perfectly. I do think that some of the things that have been happening are going to continue to develop or evolve in ways that we can look forward to.

And what are those ways, Peter?

The basic idea of hybrid distribution is splitting up rights. Filmmakers team up with distributors for television, for retail DVD, and for educational distribution. When it makes sense, they work with a service deal company for theatrical. They also retain the right to sell directly from their web-sites: DVDs, downloads, and streams. They keep the rights to sell DVDs at screenings of their films. This way they maintain overall distribution control of their film, which is just as important as creative control.

More and more filmmakers are doing hybrid distribution. They're not using the pejorative term "self-distribution," which still lingers. Many people look down on the idea of self-distribution, assuming that it's a fallback strategy — if you've failed to find distribution, then you have to do it yourself.

I tell most of my clients that Plan A should be splitting up their rights. Plan B can be making an "all rights" deal. While sometimes an "all rights" deal makes sense, most filmmakers are going to be better off splitting up their rights.

Filmmakers should look for good partners. There's a key distinction between a partnership and the master/slave relationship, which is how some distribution deals work — the distributor has all of the control, while the filmmaker is powerless. When we approach distribution as partners, the chances of succeeding are much greater. The best partnerships are win/win in that both partners benefit. It's in your interest as a good partner to make sure that your partner is doing well and vice versa, rather than fighting over how big your slice of the pie is. Filmmakers should begin a relationship with a distributor with realistic expectations, hoping the company will be a good partner on this and future movies.

More and more filmmakers are learning the importance of being strategic. In consultations I help filmmakers design and implement distribution strategies. For some filmmakers, the idea of a strategy seems too grand. In the Old World of Distribution, filmmakers didn't have strategies, they just had reactions. But as distribution has become more complex, with more avenues and options, strategy becomes critical.

CREATING A DISTRIBUTION STRATEGY

What should a strategy include?

First of all you need a clear sense of your core audiences. Don't think in quadrants, the oversimplified studio perspective — older males, younger males, older females, and younger females. Be much more specific about which audiences are most likely to embrace your movie. You need to build the audience and communicate with them while you're making the film.

As part of developing a strategy, think about the possible versions of your film — a feature, an hour, an educational cut with additional materials. For consumers, there may be two versions of the DVD: a Limited Edition that is just the film and a Collector's Edition with lots of extras. You should also think about what ancillary products you can sell directly from the website — CDs, books, T-shirts, etc.

The eight standard avenues of domestic distribution — festivals, theatrical, semi-theatrical, VOD (as in cable VOD), television, retail DVD, educational and digital, which includes iTunes and Hulu — are complemented by two avenues of direct sales: selling DVDs (both from the filmmaker's website and at screenings) and selling downloads and streams from the filmmaker's website.

Overseas the primary avenue for most filmmakers is TV sales. Eventually digital rights overseas will become more valuable. Neither theatrical nor DVD sales are significant overseas.

When defining a strategy, there are important questions of sequence to consider: Where do we want to start? Are we going to do things in the traditional order of festivals and theatrical, then DVD, and then TV? Or are we going to mix it up?

The best strategies continually evolve. After each stage of their strategy, filmmakers evaluate what's working and what isn't working. Then they modify their strategy so that they will do even better in the next stage. If they keep learning as they go, they will identify more opportunities and avoid many obstacles. A step-by-step strategy customized to the film and its audiences is essential.

THEATRICAL DISTRIBUTION

Should filmmakers look for theatrical distribution?

In terms of revenue streams theatrical will continue to be tough. Traditional theatrical distribution will be increasingly dominated by Hollywood tent pole movies. It'll be much harder for independent docs and features to make major headway in movie theaters.

But there is an area of growing importance. It's what I call semi-theatrical, through which a film is shown in a series of single, special event screenings. If possible, there's a personal appearance by the filmmaker and a discussion or something else that makes the whole thing special. Semi-theatrical is going to become more and more important.

Television will remain difficult. There are a limited number of buyers. Too many of them seem to be focused on repeating past successes with the audience they've been reaching rather than diversifying their programming to attract new audiences. Internationally, acquisition prices are declining.

In terms of DVD, while some people are worried that the death of DVD is imminent, I believe we have a number of good years left. It's still very important. Filmmakers need to sell DVDs directly from their websites (where they can make a much higher margin) and through retail outlets (where they can reach a broader audience).

DIGITAL REVENUE

As DVD revenues decline, digital revenues will increase. There will be a shortfall at some point when DVD revenues will be down more than the streaming revenues will be up. But digital revenues should continue to grow.

When you say digital revenues you mean from streaming and downloading?

Downloading and streaming, yes. I know these terms are all confusing. People say Video On Demand. I think of VOD as three different things. There's cable VOD. If you subscribe to cable television, you can pay and watch a movie. That's different from watching something through online VOD (such as iTunes), where you can either stream or download (rent or purchase) the movie. And then there's free VOD which enables you, when you've missed a broadcast or cable show, to watch it during the next two to four weeks for free (via cable or online).

There are also free online services such as Hulu that give filmmakers a share of the ad revenues. Hulu's been doing well and now there's Hulu Plus. Ad-supported services will continue to grow as a source of revenue.

I read that most theatrical distribution for docs or indies earn small profits.

Breaking even theatrically is considered a success. Most films lose money in cinemas because their costs city-to-city are greater than their revenues. The conventional wisdom has been that theatrical distribution will generate valuable publicity and awareness that will benefit a film in other areas. The $5 million to $15 million movies are having a harder and harder time getting financed and seen, while $100 million sequels keep on coming. Studios are trying to create franchises. When a studio executive was asked if a $50 million film was too small for her company to get excited about, she admitted that it was.

INTERNET DISTRIBUTION

You consulted on a film called *Food Matters* and in your Distribution Bulletin you said the producers skipped film festivals and put the money into the Internet. Why did the filmmakers skip festivals?

There are some films that really don't need festivals at all. The number of people who are going to be influenced by festival laurels on a DVD box may be a very small percentage of potential viewers. When a film has a large and enthusiastic core audience like *The Secret* had, it isn't worth spending time thinking about festivals.

In the case of *Food Matters*, the audience for films about health, nutrition, and food is large. I've consulted on many food films. Deborah Garcia's *The Future of Food* was the first. I then consulted on *King Corn* and *The Real Truth About Farmer John*. Such films keep finding audiences. People are really interested in the subject and they want to continue learning about it. *Food Matters* skipped the festival circuit entirely. They started online because they didn't know anybody. They had never made a film before and didn't have contacts in the industry. So, they said, "Okay, we'll begin online. And if we succeed then we can show distributors there's an audience for our movie." They sold 60,000 in the first six months online, which is a phenomenal number.

They made a good decision.

They then went to distributors but most weren't interested. Some said, "Well, it's too late. You should have involved us earlier." The filmmakers only made a few distribution deals. They realized the Internet was a fabulous resource and put more energy into it. One of the smartest things they did was to make screenings of *Food Matters* free. Anybody who owned a copy of the movie was allowed to screen the movie publicly, whether or not they charged admission. The filmmakers believed that the more people saw their film, the more they would talk about it and the more DVDs would be sold.

I notice that they were selling health products that matched the concept of their film. Was that beneficial?

Absolutely. They have a clear idea of their audience. They have been getting feedback online and offline. They know who's responding to the movie and they're attracting that market to the website. Many of these viewers bought the film but were hungry for more (no pun intended), so the *Food Matters* people started to sell food films by other filmmakers. It is a win-win situation. Revenues from sales of these films are split with the *Food Matters* team.

DISTRIBUTION PITFALLS

What are some of the pitfalls that filmmakers encounter when planning distribution?

The first mistake that people make is applying to festivals too early. That Sundance deadline comes along and even though the movie's not finished too many filmmakers cannot resist the impulse to apply. A high percentage of filmmakers are taking their movies out too early. Another common mistake is to jump at a distribution deal too quickly. Someone calls and says, "We love your movie. We're going to take you to the moon." The filmmakers are so excited after getting no response for months. All of a sudden somebody loves them. They can become putty in the hands of the first distributor that expresses interest. I say, "Well, that's great, but have you talked to other filmmakers who have worked with that company?" When they reach out to other filmmakers, sometimes they find that they are still in a honeymoon period with their distributor. I tell them to ask whether the distributor has made any sales and whether the filmmaker has made any money. Due diligence is so important.

Another mistake that filmmakers make is trying to do everything themselves. When it comes to distribution, you need teammates with skills and experience and contacts. You shouldn't do it alone. You need a distribution team just like you needed a production team when you made the movie.

When you sell DVDs from your website, you'll need a fulfillment company that can run credit cards, ship DVDs, and handle customer service. Many documentaries should have an outreach coordinator who can reach out to organizations and institutions that might be interested in partnering in the film's distribution. Filmmakers may also want somebody to book their movie theatrically and someone who can organize a semi-theatrical tour of the film. Additionally, they may need a sales agent to sell their foreign rights. They also may seek the help of a producer's rep domestically.

If they are going to open theatrically, they will want a publicist who can do traditional entertainment publicity. They may also want someone to help them with social media, which encompasses everything from Twitter and Facebook to the film's web presence.

People need distribution teams. One of my roles is to recommend people who can be good teammates. If filmmakers try to do everything themselves, many things may fall through the cracks and opportunities will be lost.

I want to know when filmmakers should come to you for advice. When we came we had a rough cut. You watched it and then you talked to us. We took notes and we were thrilled with the information you gave us. Is that how you work today?

When I started consulting on distribution, I expected that most people would come to me when their films were finished. And many people still do. But more and more people are coming to me earlier, and sometimes before they've shot anything. I may spend an hour at the beginning with clients. Then I will consult with them further down the road when there is a cut of the film to watch. No client has ever come to me too early. But many potential clients have come to me too late. Part of my job is to help people maximize the possibilities for their films. The other part of my job is to help them avoid mistakes. Sometimes people contact me, but they've already made so many fatal mistakes that it's heartbreaking. I can't undo them. There's no putting the genie back in the bottle.

The sooner people begin working with me, the sooner they start thinking in strategic terms. The earlier they start thinking about their online presence and how to build their audience, the better.

I do like watching a film before it's locked. I ran a finishing fund, Next Wave Films. During that time I watched 2,500 movies in some stage of completion and learned to give filmmakers constructive feedback. I may not know what the ending should be, but I can tell you when it isn't working. I can also let you know if the movie begins too slowly or if its title is terrible.

Peter, all of us thank you for your information and I'm so glad you are here to keep us on track.

I try to help them find a balance between optimism and realism. That's a hard balance to strike. When they're wildly optimistic, it's important to add some realism; and when they're grimly realistic, I try to add some hope.

CHAPTER 12

RAISING FUNDS FROM INDIVIDUALS AND BUSINESSES

I have a confession to make. When I was running Studio Film I used to hide in a corner office so filmmakers couldn't find me. Of course my wonderful dad (who was defenseless against a filmmaker's passionate pitch) would give me up every single time!

Small businesses and corporations are tiny untapped goldmines for independent filmmakers. Local businesses and corporations always have managers (or dads) who are very accessible and easy to talk to. Be it my dad, or one of my employees, someone was always knocking on my door in the middle of the day with some filmmaker's proposal. It was usually only a one-page proposal, which was a blessing since business seemed to grind to a halt whenever this occurred. Customers could be lined up at the counter but it didn't matter.

Everyone in the office got wrapped up in the drama that was unfolding. You could practically hear the drum roll in the background. Would she say yes or no? Looking back now I realize this was probably a conspiracy since everyone knew the buck stopped with me. People everywhere (yes, even people in Hollywood) want to be involved in a film.

When I scanned these proposals I would look for the following things:

- ❖ The story synopsis (hopefully brief and to the point).
- ❖ Why the filmmaker was making the film.
- ❖ Exactly what the filmmaker needed and why.
- ❖ Who would benefit from the film.
- ❖ How much the donation would mean to the filmmaker.
- ❖ What the filmmaker would do for me. (Credit or what?)

If you have a fiscal sponsor, make sure to note this on all of your proposals. Your tax-deductible status will go a long way when looking for donations.

- Customize your proposal for each individual business you approach. When you make it personal the recipient feels special.
- Start by making a list of all the stores and restaurants near your location.
- Visit the managers of these businesses with your one-page customized proposal in your hand and the best smile you can muster. Don't forget to dress the part. Wear a Panasonic Film cap and have a Sony bag slung around your shoulder. Make sure they see you and think Spielberg.

Sometimes you have to leave your proposal with an employee. Pitch the employee the same way you would the manager. Be considerate to all of the employees. If they are anything like the wonderful people who worked with me at Studio Film, once they get caught up in your enthusiasm they are going to beg their manager to become involved in your film. Think of the employees as your support team. Mention how much your crew enjoys their pizza, or how impressed you were the last time they did some copy work for you. Talk about your film and give your pitch as though you are asking for a $10,000 grant.

Most managers can make the decision right there on the spot without going to a corporate supervisor. I did business at Kinko's for years before I asked who I could see about getting a discount. When the woman at the counter told me she could help me I was flabbergasted. I thought I would need to fill out reams of forms that would be sent off through the chain of command. All I had to do was explain that I represented a nonprofit organization that helped filmmakers and ask for a discount. It was that easy!

Most independents forget that all of the little miscellaneous budget items add up. You are going to be into Kinko's for about $800 and Office Depot for another $1,200. The caterer is going to hit you up for about $2,500 for lunches, and you are probably going to have to fork over about $800 a week for equipment rental. All of these little extras can easily add another $6,000–$10,000 to your bottom line.

Go through your shooting script and your budget and make a list of all the things that might be donated through local businesses and corporations. Are you going to need a rental car? What about office supplies? You know you're going to have to feed your crew and your new cameraman can put away three pizzas in one sitting!

Your list might include car rental agencies, cell phones, grocery stores, bagel shops, the local pizza parlor. List any business that advertises. Target small businesses like the little mom-and-pop coffee shop around the corner because it is often more productive than going to a large corporate business like Starbucks. Local business people want to support their community and they will be receptive to your needs.

A business in a bustling neighborhood may have a lot of healthy competition. If this is the case, then mention the discount offered by their competitor and ask if they can beat it.

> *The most popular labor-saving device is still money.*
> — Phyllis George

If you can't get it for free, do your homework and know what you can get it for. Dov S-S Simons of the Hollywood Film Institute says you can get a discount on everything in your production budget. According to Dov, "No one who knows anything in the industry pays the rate card price." Know what the going rate is and ask for a discount.

Studio Film's three-tier price index was installed on every employee's computer. Businesses do this. Every salesperson knows the lowest price they can quote. This is the rate you want, even if you just buy ten items. Once your name is linked in the computer with a special rate you will get that rate every time you make a purchase. I have made special arrangements with David Cohen of Edgewise. Filmmakers who enter my Roy W. Dean grants will receive a discount for all of Edgewise's products, including film, tape, and digital supplies. If you apply for my grant or if you are an emerging filmmaker and you would like to receive this discount, call my sweetheart, Phillip Loving at (800) 824-3130 and he will get you in the computer as a Roy W. Dean grant applicant or a student from this book.

Bobby Mardis (one of my favorite producers) once told me that he never takes anything personal when he is producing a film. He gets the local production book, goes down it from A to Z, and starts asking. He explains how much he can spend and what he needs. If a business manager can't accommodate him he thanks her, tells her he will try her again on a future production and he moves down the list and calls the next vendor. He keeps at it until he finds someone who will give him what he needs at the price he has budgeted.

When you contact Kinko's, Jim's Car Rentals, or the local bagel shop, begin by asking for a donation in exchange for a mention in your film's credits, a copy of the completed film on DVD or for product placement. If they can't accommodate you and they are the only game in town, ask them if they would be willing to give you a 25% discount if you promote their business on your website. Always ask for a donation first and save the request for a discounted price as your last resort.

Remember, most companies work on a 25-40% profit margin so when you ask for a 25% discount you are asking the company to donate most of their profits to the film. Let them put a sign in the lobby that mentions they are donating to your film. Tell them you will pose for pictures, or let them shoot pictures of the cast and crew during production to use in an ad for the local paper.

Turn it into a great PR opportunity for them. Sometimes just offering to give a local businessperson a copy of the finished videotape is all it takes to get a smile and a donation.

I suggest you go to AbelCine (NYC or L.A.) and get their prices for camera rentals and while you are there ask if you can take a picture with their latest camera. Of course you want to have your camera person with you so you can be pointing to the shot. Once you have this picture you can scan it into your computer and now you have a production shot to use as a public relations trade for services. Just put the name of the targeted company like "Nextel Supports Filmmakers" for the heading on the page, then your production picture and below that put in the details. "Nextel phones are being used in the National Marmots documentary."

You can create several of these for your intended donors and when you go to pitch Nextel, show them this donation advertisement and give it to them for display in their lobby. Don't forget to mention the credit at the end of the film. Visuals work every time.

Once you go over your budget carefully and list all the printing, copying, beverages, food, bottled water, coffee and bagels, cell phones, cars, airline tickets, restaurant charges, and so on, you will be amazed at how much you can save by finding resources through local businesses. Be sure to read Patti Ganguzza's information on branding for more information on free goods on my website (*www.FromTheHeartProductions.com*) under financing information.

You can also negotiate with your crew. Many producers look for a production assistant who has a truck or an SUV, and they arrange a flat weekly salary that includes the use of their vehicle.

Your P.A. should be one of your first employees as they can free you from time-consuming jobs, like local pickup and deliveries. They can even do your shopping, get the cleaning, or walk the dog. Your P.A. can do those time-consuming jobs that take you away from the focus of your film, while you work on the art of funding your film!

After producing 140 shows, working with countless filmmakers over the last 35 years, and raising over $2 million in goods and services for my Roy W. Dean film grants, I have learned some valuable lessons. Never forget that the film business is a business. Before you approach a business or an individual, make a list of all of the benefits they will receive from your proposed venture. If their benefits do not equal or outweigh your benefits, then you need to rethink your proposal.

Your contacts will be more responsive when they know you are concerned with their image and their profits. This is how you create long-term friends in our industry. Remember, this is just one of many films you will make and people stay in our industry.

RAISING FUNDS FROM INDIVIDUALS

For a feature you get all your money from people. Documentaries usually get 50% of their money from individuals. So learning how to approach individuals is paramount to the art of funding.

When filmmakers approach individuals, they are looking for either an investor or a donor. It is essential that you disclose exactly what you are looking for and that you are completely honest when you discuss your film's investment potential.

Have a good attorney on board before you approach an individual investor. Do not take one dime from an investor until you have presented the investor with an investment memorandum. Mark Litwak discusses the legal side of the producer/investor relationship later on in the chapter on financing independent films. It is essential that you heed Mark's words. There are laws that protect investors and these laws are very clear.

Contributions do not require paperwork. Just send your donor a letter of thanks and you or your fiscal sponsor sends them the information they need for their taxes and you're on your way to the bank! Of course approaching an individual donor will require a serious investment of your time. Please do not approach your family and friends and immediately ask them to donate toward your film. Remember, when you ask someone to donate or invest in your film, they are essentially investing in you. Give them time to see your tenacity and they will be there when you need that extra bit to tide you over.

Romancing individual funders requires as much skill as creating a great pitch or writing a strong proposal. You must sharpen your people skills and be prepared to spend some serious time dodging the moths that fly out of their purses. "Doing time" sounds like a line from a Scorsese movie, but that's exactly what it takes. You need to put time into building a relationship with any potential donor.

If you met someone at a party and proposed marriage over cocktails they would think you were crazy! To ask for money you have to win their interest, their trust, and their confidence first. Potential donors need to know you and they need to know your film. They need to know why this film has to be made and why you are the only one who can make it. They need to see how dedicated you are to the project. Get them interested in your film before you ever ask them for a thing. Invite them to production meetings, script sessions, and fundraising parties. Show them your Facebook page, your website and proposal, and ask them for advice.

A filmmaker told me a wonderful story about a wealthy donor he was courting. The donor told the filmmaker that her husband had taken a small business and turned it into a multimillion-dollar corporation. She told the story with great pride, and it was obvious that she loved and admired her husband very much, so the filmmaker asked her if he could film an interview with her husband. He taped the interview, did a little editing, and presented her with an hour of her husband's life story.

She immediately attached herself to the filmmaker because the filmmaker knew what was important to her. Do you think he got his donation? Of course he did! But he built a relationship with her before he even thought about asking.

Amanda Mazzanti, a woman who uses From the Heart as her fiscal sponsor, is the President of Digitalady, LLC (Digitalady.com), a company that brings awareness of and identity to the underrepresented. As a social media and networking professional, she has worked with mostly female and minority business owners, but recently branched out into collaborating with nonprofits, social entrepreneurs and media makers. Simultaneously, Amanda is diligently working on her passion project, *Seeds of Inspiration* (MayaNutsMovie.com), a feature documentary film. Her vision is that the film will empower women globally, spotlight rainforest conservation, and potentially end famine in some of the most impoverished regions of the world.

Amanda also markets her client's businesses by incorporating videos, known as webisodes, into their websites. Her newest product, Legacy Videos, serves a growing contingent of people and their families, who are terminally ill or deceased. Amanda compiles various video and print footage from their lives, interviews loved ones and sets it to their favorite music, thus compassionately creating a beautiful and vibrant synopsis of a life. Isn't this a great idea for a way to make money in your chosen field and support you while you make your heartfelt doc?

So, where do you find these wealthy philanthropists? The society section of the paper is a good start for rich, grant-giving philanthropists in your area. Think about the Foundation Center for research on the tax Form 990 that nonprofits use. They have to report the name of their donors and the amount donated. This can be a gold mine for you. Think of the topic of your film, then go online or to the Foundation Center and search for that type of nonprofit. Find some and look for the higher donors. Now you have a list to contact and ask them to mentor you.

Remember those old address books you stored in your closet after you bought your smartphone? Dust them off and start looking for names. Find people in there who could easily part with five grand or more and not miss it. You might be surprised at how many names you come up with. As the years go by people move up the ladder, so don't discount someone who was a sales manager back in 1993. She might be the head of the company today. I don't care if you haven't talked to her in years. Pull out that name, make that phone call, and tell her about the film you're making.

Reestablish your relationship. Tell her you are producing a film about a very important issue and you thought she would enjoy hearing about it. Perhaps she has good business sense. Ask her for some advice, but don't mention money. People will donate time to help you when they see that you are on an important quest. Get her involved, then send her a one or two-page proposal. Call her up and invite her to a production meeting or a fundraising party.

She may suspect that you are going to pop the money question and she may turn you down. That's okay; you just saved yourself some time. Other contacts will take you up on your offer, especially if you have asked for advice in their area of expertise. The key is you must get to know these people. You must understand who they are and what their needs are before you can ask for money. Remember, you need a lot more than money; you need support, especially from people who know people with money. You need people to give you house parties to fund your film; you want people to open their phone books to you and invite their friends to parties to support you. You need legal advice and you need accounting advice, and getting that free or deferred can be a great bonus to you and the film.

Take some time and brainstorm. Think about people you have worked with over the past ten years. What about your spouse's affiliations? Do you know someone who donates time to a public official? If so, ask if you can get an introduction. It may take weeks for you to come up with a list, but that's okay. Fundraising is an important part of the art of funding your film.

Most of the producers you meet in Hollywood will tell you that they "have several projects in various stages of production," which is a dead giveaway that they are out there looking for money.

If you are doing a film about a woman who has survived cancer, seek funding from cancer survivors, from family members of cancer victims, and from nonprofit cancer organizations. If you are doing a film about the plight of our oceans, whose name comes to mind? How about Ted Danson and the American Oceans Campaign?

Contact Mr. Danson, tell him about your project, and ask him for some advice. Go to the American Oceans Campaign website and research their sponsors. Remember Form 990 from the chapter on foundations and grants? This form also lists individuals who have donated to the foundation.

How do you get to know potential donors once you have found them? It may be as simple as picking up the phone and calling them. Give them your two-paragraph pitch but don't ask for money. Tell them that you are researching your subject and ask them about their organization. Look for people who can help you with information on your subject matter. You might ask them to support your film and send your newsletter to their members, thereby gaining names from your opt-in box on Facebook and your website.

Concerned citizens who have money usually know other concerned citizens who have money. Take the time to get to know each individual and listen to what they have to say about your subject. Once you have established a relationship, find a role for this person somewhere on your project.

Perhaps they could help throw a fundraising party, be the expert advisor on your subject, or act as your mentor. Investors and donors will pay special attention to your proposal if you have people like this on board.

You must be persistent. When I first started out in the film business, skeptics told me that no one in their right mind would buy short ends. I had to overcome some heavy opposition to get going, but I was determined. Capturing a market is like fishing with a net. If you work one market at a time it is much easier to capture the entire market when you land your first sale within that market.

I started out by making cold calls to film schools. I had to keep at it for over a month before I got my first order, but as soon as I took that order I hung up and called the film school down the road and told them their competitor just placed an order. Suddenly they were interested. My cold call sales ratio went from a 5% return to a 30% return because I was working within a tight industry where people know each other. I stayed with my idea of selling to one market (film schools) until I captured one fish in that market. Businesses and corporations are more open to a new idea when they discover their peers are.

Consider doing the same thing when you look for individuals to fund your film. If Mary Smith from Americans for Cleaner Oceans has agreed to act as your mentor, go to similar organizations within the community and make a list of their board members. Call each person and develop a relationship. Let them know that Mary Smith from Americans for Cleaner Oceans is working with you. These methods will provide you with advisors, mentors, and donors.

The rule of the industry is: *If you ask for money you get advice. If you ask for advice you get money.* What if you can't get them on the phone? What if your potential donor is as reclusive as Howard Hughes? Get to know his secretary or his personal assistant. This is how good sales people become successful sales people. Secretaries and personal assistants can get you through to the people you want to know, so take some time and create a rapport with these people. Get on a first-name basis with a potential donor's secretary. Chat about her vacation. Ask her about her children.

If you are professional and personable, and if you have a good pitch, you will get through to the person you want. A secretary's job is to protect her boss. If she believes that you will not embarrass her, and that you have something important to present, she will put your call through.

It's all in your approach. Sherrie Findhorn was one of my top sales people. Before Sherrie came to Studio Film she worked for the Yellow Pages. This is where she learned to smile on the phone. That's right, Sherrie told me that sales shot up when some executive put mirrors on every sales person's desk and asked them to smile when they made their cold calls. Try it! Especially on a day when you feel like biting the heads off nails. You will be treated better and it will lift your spirits.

Don't be afraid to go to the top of the ladder. I know these people are often hard to get to, but that just makes success that much sweeter! Who do you think wrote my first ad for Studio Film and Tape NYC back in 1970? The late Ira Eaker, co-founder of Back Stage! The first time I went to see Ira he asked to see my copy. I was so green back in those days I didn't even know what copy was, but Ira took the time to work out a great ad for me. I ran that ad for years. Ira and I remained good friends right up to his recent death. Sometimes the nicest people are at the top. They may be hidden away by a protective secretary, but if you believe in your project you can find a way in.

"Okay, Carole, so when do I get to ask the sixty-four thousand dollar question?" Be patient, grasshopper. Don't even think about asking for money until you have all your preproduction ducks in a row. Form your production company and put together a solid preproduction package while you're getting close to these potential donors and investors.

POPPING THE BIG QUESTION

You put together a strong preproduction package and you have taken the time to establish a good relationship with your potential donor. You know who they are, what their values are, and what is important to them. This "ask" has to have their interest at heart, it has to benefit them in some way, which could be a tax deduction or you may want to dedicate the film to their deceased mother or offer them an associate producer credit for a generous donation.

Now you are ready to ask! It's a good idea to take them out for dinner at a nice restaurant, look them right in the eye, and ask them if they will donate to your project. Say something like, "Would you be willing to donate $10,000 to my film?"

They have heard your pitch so many times they know it by heart, so don't pitch them again. Instead, give them a production update. Tell them about some of the grants you have applied for and tell them where you expect to get the rest of your financing. Be 100% honest in every statement you make.

They know all about the paperwork inside that preproduction package lying next to you on the table. You have discussed many of these things with them over the past year and they have given you advice along the way. Perhaps they even helped you with some of the paperwork. Don't remind them that you have a nonprofit fiscal sponsor and that their donation will be tax deductible. They know that. This is not a why don't you look it over and let me know later meeting, this is a look me in the eye and give me an answer meeting.

Remember, you are asking this person to invest in you. You already know they trust and respect you. You know they want to help you complete your film. You have invested a great deal of time to bring this person into your film and you would not be sitting across from them now if they did not have the same passion for your project that you have. Your chances of walking away with a check are going to be ten thousand times better than if you had just sent them a package in the mail and followed up with a phone call.

How much are you going to ask for? If you ask for too much you will probably walk away empty handed. Most donors do not like to admit that they can't afford to donate $70,000, but they might be able to swing $10,000. Do your homework and know how much they have donated in the past to causes like yours and make sure you approach them with a figure they can afford. Don't embarrass them by asking for too little — that's even worse than asking for too much!

Every one of us has a comfort zone and when we give donations we usually write checks for that same amount, from the Red Cross to saving the oceans. Find out what that person usually donates and ask for that amount. Sometimes the richest people will always go back to the same amount. One wealthy socialite always wrote $4,000 checks. By getting to know her, the filmmaker knew that was her comfort level, so that's what she asked for and that's what she got. Had she asked for $10,000 she would have been turned down, if she asked for $2,000 then she would have lost $2,000. Know the magic number.

The person who gives you this $4,000 will often give it to you again. They just need to be kept current on the film, and when you are coming down the home stretch they will be there with you for another donation.

Every person who donates to your film must be considered equal. It's like my dad who put in the same time with the $100 sale as he did with the $10,000 sale. Your many $50 donations can become $5,000 when they know you are serious and determined to make that film. Keep every name of all the donors and put them on your email list.

If you want to make that film, set a deadline and start working. I know that you work on your grant application right up to the deadline, then FedEx it overnight, because I'm the one that gets bombarded with a ton of applications the day before the deadline! Filmmakers always work best under pressure.

I want you to open your mind to all of the creative ways to raise money. The money is out there and it is mostly in the hands of individuals. You just have to approach fundraising with the same level of creativity that you use throughout the entire filmmaking process. Think of fundraising as another art form.

FUNDING PARTIES, INSTANT CASH

Pasta Party

Mindy Pomper entered my grant for her film *Save a Man to Fight*. It is a great story of the women in World War II who took over men's jobs so the men could go to the front lines. Her film includes women pilots who flew planes towing targets for the men to practice their shooting skills. Can you imagine? Yes, women were expendable and Mindy's film is cut with government propaganda films where women were told they had to wear rubber girdles to hold in that little tummy. Marching in the hot Texas sun with a rubber girdle; it's hard to believe what these women did for their country.

Mindy won my grant from her heart-felt pitch where she along with four other finalists pitched their films at Raleigh Studios to a packed house of filmmakers eager to learn how to win grants.

While Mindy was making her film she would get out her phone book, call all her friends and say, "I need some cash for production so I'm giving a dinner party. Please come and hear all about my film, many new things are happening and I have some footage you will really enjoy seeing." She would also say, "Bring a friend, it's a $40 donation for dinner."

She always had a full house and averaged $60 per guest. Mindy did this twice a year and took in a nice piece of change to keep her petty cash full. Plus she kept her friends up to date on the status of her film and she enlisted their ideas for funding.

Mindy was smart to fill the room with filmmakers and non-filmmakers. This way the filmmakers could entertain single guests so no one felt left out. I recommend you always have filmmakers as "shills" at your parties. Their specific job is to latch on to some potential funders and keep them meeting people and learning about the film so they are more apt to feel comfortable. Having someone answer questions gets them closer to the film. Plus, people love to talk to filmmakers. I sat down at a funding party to get off my feet. A retired man was next to me and I started talking about the trailer that was playing and how much work went into making it. I called his attention to lots of things, explaining how the filmmaker had traveled across the country to get all those shots with her cameraman and how long it took her to edit, etc. He ended up being the largest contributor that day. Things we take for granted can be very impressive to potential funders.

I believe that your initial $50 or $100 donation can turn into $300 or $500 once your donors see you moving forward. This only works when you stay close to them and they know how hard you work to make this film happen. Just tell them the good stuff; if they knew all the pitfalls of a filmmaker it would freak them out.

Staying in touch with every donor is paramount to the art of funding. Get everyone's email and be sure to create a special mailing list of these names. You want to keep in touch at least every two months with a Rah! Rah! email telling them the progress you have made. Give them the results of funding parties, grants you applied for, comments from anyone important in the filmmaking industry, and let them know what has happened since the last email.

You don't make the "ask" from this email list until you need something. Keep them up to date, and then when your coffers are running low, ask for what you need in the email telling them where you are and what process is next and let them know how much you need. Seldom do you want to tell your potential funders your short will cost $30,000 or your doc $300,000. They can't imagine where you will get all that funding. Handle it like you are feeding them an elephant, one bite at a time.

If you haven't already promised to put their names in the credits, do this when you need funds. The amounts you choose are up to you, but many filmmakers say $100 is a rolling credit, $500 is three names on a screen and $3,000 gives you a full screen credit. For larger donations you want to talk to them in person.

Faun Kime's Successful Party

Faun spent time and effort on this party and it paid off with great PR and a net donation of $10,000 for her film, *The Tomato Effect*.

Faun hired an assistant immediately because there is lots of work involved and your assistant's salary will pay off with donors, potential donors, and perhaps a second or third party.

My list of 44 things to do for a funding party is really built around this type of party. Creating your website so it will hold lots of logos is important. This is the quid pro quo that you trade for that weekend from Hilton or the organic winery for that free case of last year's award winner.

The donor's logos will be on your first page, so you want to hold logos on both sides to maximize the number of donors.

FUNDING EXTRAVAGANZA OUTLINE

1. You need to plan a date at least 60 to 75 days in advance.

2. Hire an assistant for $10 an hour plus a bonus based on how much you bring in, perhaps 10% of the income as their bonus; they will earn it.

3. Get your website up first. Contact my donors, *silkem@gmail.com* and *graphics@skullco.com* — they love to work with filmmakers.

4. Your website has to have your film's pitch and the first two paragraphs must fully explain the story of your film. Make them dynamite.

5. Design the site with a video of you on the first page talking about your film.

6. Your site has to give the meaning of the film quickly and succinctly.

7. You need a place for people to send donations with an address for mailing and PayPal for impulse money. People who surf the web don't want to call you, they want to click on buttons to send you money; make it easy.

8. You need to know who in politics or the sports world or the entertainment field will like your project. Then make a target list of these people because you need a local "star."

9. Start with your search for a local "star." Someone whose name is well known.

10. Set your date for the event based on their calendar so it is locked in.

11. Create personal invitation letters to other people who would know your "star" with an outline and pictures of your film. Follow up with phone calls to their offices.

12. If you have to reach athletes, see if you can find their managers and you can send packages either directly to them or to the managers. Each letter has to appeal to them for their personal support of your subject matter. You can offer then a thank you credit at the event and on the film. You want their support for the project (not money) first, and you want them to come to the event second. Once they see your passion and get to know you, then make the "ask."

13. Find a caterer who will give you a major discount using your website and mention on Facebook as your repayment for their reduction in price. Let them know you will feature them boldly on your website as "catered by" and you will put them in your program and give them credit on the film and mention them in any PR opportunities. This will work!

14. Give a down payment on your Visa card to seal the deal.

15. Look for more people of the same ilk as your known guest. For example, if this is the mayor's wife, like Faun had for her party, read the papers for socialites and contact them with your package and a personal letter inviting them to the party stating the mayor's wife is coming.

16. If this is an athlete, use the same practice: find any other athlete in the city who may be less known. Remember, athletes follow athletes,

politicians follow politicians, etc. Now you are 100 times more likely to get any of these people to come to your event because you have a name they want to meet. Send them your proposal; call back with a personal invitation.

17. Faun charged $75 and she said she would never charge an entrance fee again because she made most of her money on the silent auction so your job is to get them there.

18. Now the fun begins: You are inviting everyone in your phone book, your mother's phone book, your father's phone book, the kids you went to school with, and the man you worked for ten years ago who is now the manager.

19. You need a great invitation. You might want to use a photo that represents your film. Use a branded photo so people can see your vision. Using postcards with an invitation on one side can work.

20. Creating an invitation just for this event is another way.

21. You need to send out four times the amount of invitations to get your core amount. If you want 100 people, send out 400 invitations and you can expect to get about 150 or so RSVPs and you may have 100 people show up (these are Hollywood statistics).

22. At the same time you want to find donors who will give you things you can auction. Faun said that people sometimes ran the auction up to the full price because they wanted to get something for their donation.

23. Guide your donations toward women. Men say, "Honey, I think we should donate" and the women say, "Okay, but what can I get for it?" (Sorry, ladies, but that's true.)

24. Call hotels for rooms on the weekend when they are slow. You want to auction off two nights at the Hyatt or one night at the Hilton.

25. Each hotel has a PR person just for this reason, to give rooms away when you have something in return to offer them.

26. What's that? Demographics, demographics, demographics! My film audience, my party audience fits your demographics.

27. You have to do your demographics and know what your film fits; age 18 to 38 and median income of $80,000 is a good one. Hyatt and Hilton both want that group of people.

28. You call up the PR department and ask them to go on your website while you have them on the phone. You show them where you will put their logo and then begin to tell them what you want. You pitch them the two-minute short pitch that has everything in it.

29. They like the concept of the film, they say can't do two nights but can do one night, you say "Wonderful!"

30. It has to be an open-ended gift to be used in whatever time limit they give you.

31. Go after yoga lessons.

32. Wine by the case or six bottles at least.

33. Tango lessons. Who takes them? No one, but it sounds so romantic.

34. Bouquet of flowers.

35. Potted plants from a nursery.

36. Three hours in a limo, what woman would not like that?

37. A free tour of the opera house, etc. Be creative.

38. Go through the yellow pages and use your imagination. People love to be part of a movie and you're making a movie! You are a producer and they will be part of the funding for the film.

39. They will get a DVD of the finished film and be on your website as a donor.

40. Now you have a room and food, go after some free booze. That should be easy. Many liquor companies want to be in films and around filmmakers.

41. What about entertainment? You are in the entertainment industry, so who do you know that might be able to perform for ten to fifteen minutes for you? You might want some Latin dancers or some interesting musicians to play while people talk.

42. As the time draws closer, call your main person and tell them how things are progressing. Let them know that you have all these wonderful donors for silent auctions so people will go home with certificates for donating to your film, and "ask" them if they have any friends that you could invite? This is a big ASK. They should give you a few.

43. Send them packages first, then call them and say, "The mayor's wife suggested I invite you to this event as she/he is coming." Pitch it succinctly and focus on how much you need their support to make this film. When they say, "Okay", ask them if they can give you the name of any of their friends that might enjoy a great event like this because "Yolanda" is dancing or the local TV star is the host and it should be a fun evening.

44. When these people RSVP, ask for their friends' names and invite them too. The same with the names from your mother and father's phone books; call to see if they are coming and ask them for more names.

I know this is a lot of work but look what will you have at the end of the event:

- ❖ Tons of people who love you and your film
- ❖ A list of supporters for your emails
- ❖ Names for advice that may eventually bring you money
- ❖ A core group of donors for more parties and other films

YOUR FUNDRAISING TOOLBOX

The Funding Trailer

A trailer is one of the most valuable resources you can have in your fundraising toolbox. Barbara Leibovitz won the Roy W. Dean film grant with her promo for her film, *Salvaged Lives*. She was so confident she would win that she had her camera ordered and had me open the office at seven o'clock the next morning to get her raw stock! Less than a month later Barbara presented her uncut footage to the East Coast IFP where she secured more financing. This is what it takes to make a film. Visualizing is paramount to funding.

Film is a visual medium and it's hard to sell this kind of product on paper. Creating a five- to ten-minute promo trailer is one of your most important goals in the art of funding your film. Be sure to read my interview with Fernanda Rossi on story structure in your promo tape.

Win a Grant

Barbara knew winning the Roy W. Dean Film Grant would provide her with the needed equipment and professional services. Look for grants like this to support you in the beginning so you can get out there and start shooting. Winning a grant is like priming the pump; it will empower you as a filmmaker and start the ball rolling for more funds and donations. Potential investors and donors are more likely to fund a filmmaker who has already won a grant. Use the name of the donor on all of your grant applications and hire (or trade with) a public relations person to get the most you can from this first win.

P-a-r-t-y!

In *The Fundraising Houseparty*, author Morrie Warshawski tells filmmakers to find a wealthy supporter who shares their cause, and ask them if they would be willing to throw a fundraising party. If you find someone who is well connected, they will have an amazing house and an amazing guest list. Think about it. They will invite friends and associates who can write a $500 or $5,000 check without batting an eye! Pick up a copy of Morrie's book; he has perfected the fundraising houseparty down to the last detail, even the invitations (*www.warshawski.com*).

Shoot Your Donors!

During your fundraising party have several experienced camera people with digital cameras roam the room and conduct short interviews with possible donors. Edit it on your home computer and produce a short video that addresses your film's cause while highlighting these featured interviews. Offer a copy to guests for a $100 donation. Follow up with everyone who purchased a copy and ask them if they would like to do a more formal interview in exchange for a tax-deductible donation.

I interviewed my dad using an old mini-VHS camera. He told wonderful stories about playing in watermelon patches in Dallas and how the boys would drop a ripe melon on the ground, then dig their hands into it, enjoying every last bite. These tapes are priceless and I wouldn't trade them for the world. Think of ways to sell the concept of creating a family interview. It is a marvelous way to leave something for the grandchildren. You can set your own prices. You might charge $3,000 for an hour, $2,000 for thirty minutes. You are a professional film producer and you will be using the latest Hollywood equipment and techniques. Always sell the sizzle.

Give 'em Credit!

Have you ever noticed that some films seem to have more producers than cast? Producer credits are like money in the bank. An executive producer credit can be worth $50,000 or 50% of your budget while an associate producer might bring in $20,000. The numbers are based on your budget and the sky's the limit. Be creative and make up a title!

The next time you watch a film sit through the credits. When you come to the part that says, "The Producers wish to thank...", read the names and start adding. Each one of those names can be worth $1,000 or more. A full screen credit could be worth $3,000. A dedication to the memory of a sponsor's loved one could bring in $10,000 or more.

Finding and developing relationships with funders is hard work, but take heart. The hardest part is going after your first funder. Once you get that out of the way you will build your portfolio of funders and other funders will follow. Before long you will create your own network of funding sources. Remember, if you are honest and professional it will be a positive experience and your funders will be there for future projects.

Carole Dean. Barbara Leibovitz.

Mindy Pomper, Carole Dean.
Roy W. Dean Awards.

CHAPTER 13

ARCHIVAL FOOTAGE

A Conversation with Rosemary Rotondi

Raising money and saving money are the concepts of this book. If you are considering a researcher for your film, I believe it is important to know how a researcher can help you. While I was researching Rosemary's bio, I noticed Betsy Blankenbaker used her. I met Betsy in 2001 when she applied for my NYC grant for her brilliant film *Something to Cheer About*. We have been friends since. At that time Betsy submitted her film *New York in the Fifties* as her past work. I was impressed with her film and I still remember some of those archival photos she used. Here is my conversation with Betsy on her experiences with archival footage:

BETSY BLANKENBAKER'S EXPERIENCE

New York in the Fifties was my first film produced with archival footage and I needed a lot so I went to an expert. There is no one better than Rosemary (I've used her for several more films since). I would not have uncovered the incredible footage Rosemary found if I researched the footage on my own. Anyone who lived in New York City during that era said the film captures the look and feel of that period, which is the biggest compliment possible. I let her do her job and she delivered way beyond my expectations.

Do you think hiring Rosemary saved you money or enhanced your film?

As a filmmaker, you have a budget for the archivist and a budget for the footage. Rosemary did come in at her budget (with more than enough fantastic footage to choose from). I did spend more than I had budgeted for the footage, because I wanted all the footage she uncovered! Great stuff. The footage she found definitely enhanced the film.

Do you recommend filmmakers using archivists and if so, why?

It depends on your budget. If you don't have much money, there are great resources online now like Buyout Footage. I always search there first. An archivist already has a great relationship with the archival collections and will definitely find the best footage for your film (and save you hours and hours of searching). Ultimately, after hearing my needs for *New York in the Fifties*, Rosemary went out and found unbelievable footage. It made the film.

Rosemary Rotondi has been an archival film, photo and network news researcher for twenty-five years. Some recent projects include Charles Ferguson's documentary Inside Job, *Matt Wolf's* Teenage, *National Geographic Channel's* 9/11: The World's Fallen, *Crayton Robey's* Making the Boys, *Mark Mori's* Bettie Page Reveals All *and others. Here is my interview with Rosemary:*

How many years have you been finding footage and stills for films?

I have been a researcher for documentary filmmakers for twenty-five years. My credits list is available on *http://www.archivalfilmresearch.com.*

Many people say they saved money using an archivist. Have you found this to be true considering the amount of time most untrained people need?

Yes, this is absolutely true. A trained, professional researcher knows which worldwide archives, libraries, historical societies, and university archives to approach, how to create an all inclusive "game plan" for the research process. A skilled, professional researcher also has something no intern or inexperienced researcher has: preferred vendor relationships with many archives. An intern or inexperienced researcher will get a filmmaker the same exact footage from each archive that is on their pre-fabricated compilations reels. As a result many documentaries (all too often) use the same footage over and over again. This dilutes a documentary.

Please explain what you do for filmmakers and how you know what they need.

I ask each filmmaker to compose a visual needs list for me. We usually discuss the list a few times together either on the telephone, by email, or in person when possible. I ask to not use YouTube before contacting any researcher. Often that footage is not easily traceable, adding time to the research process. YouTube adds a lot of time to archives and to researchers trying to "match" footage that is likely not labeled in detail re: its original source. Best to give your experienced, skilled researcher your research list and then trust their vision.

ARCHIVAL FOOTAGE FOR LOW BUDGETS

Regarding payment, do you give them an idea of what you can do and suggest a budget?

Budget for archival film, photo and network news footage depends on territories the filmmaker(s) wants to license. A rate card is obtainable from each archive. And if filmmakers license over 30-60 seconds many archives are open to negotiating the rates. That is depending on territories (i.e., if a production wants ten years of rights or in perpetuity rights). As of 2011 some rates can range from $25 per second to $125 per second. Hollywood studio clips are usually the most expensive to license and require talent signing off on their image being used, so those with small to medium budgets may want to avoid using such footage.

Can you work with small budgets?

Depending on the documentary's theme and subject, usually all small and large budgets can use public domain footage and photographs, as well as photos and footage from other archives. Some archives are willing to work with small independent filmmakers. If a filmmaker cannot afford to have me to go down to Washington, D.C. to the National Archives or

Library of Congress, then I suggest friends I have in D.C. who are experienced with both organizations and we work together as a research team. The LOC has a wonderful print and photo archive on line and I use that for clients.

Most books say find an archivist in post. When do you suggest contacting an archivist?

As early as possible engage an experienced researcher in the creative process and collaborative process. Waiting until late into your process is not conducive to the best creative collaboration. Research requires digging and real time. Rates negotiation takes time too; archives and researchers have a unique relationship that requires respect. The more time, the better the research you will receive — and the more a researcher has time to percolate, throw out the research "net" and dig for you as a filmmaker — the better the results. Researchers are creative too.

Betsy Blankenbaker is a friend of mine and I see you did two films for her. Can you tell us about them?

I worked for Betsy on *New York in the Fifties*, based on Dan Wakefield's autobiography, and this remains one of the greatest creative experiences of my entire career. With Betsy she allowed me real time over a period off/ on of 18-24 months to conduct research for her. She respected me totally as her lead researcher and always gave me nurturing, positive feedback and guidance regarding the research I conducted for her. I conducted research for her as well on her Althea Gibson documentary and *Something to Cheer About*. We have one of those rare creative relationships whereby we are in tune with one another and are inspired by one another's standard of work. She is not only a great filmmaker but a great individual who knows how to inspire her creative team members.

Please tell us how filmmakers can contact you.

Filmmakers may contact me by calling (212) 989-2025, my home office line. My email address is *rotondiresearch@nyc.rr.com* and my website is *http:// www.archivalfilmresearch.com*. My Facebook page is *http://www.facebook.com/ pages/archival-film-and-photo-research/158108340903953*

Do you love what you do?

Yes, I love what I do 101% and feel blessed that I wake up each day excited by what I do for my living. I look around and realize often that I love what I do — and most people do not seem to be able to claim this. I feel blessed. With research I am always learning, learning, and learning. I feel honored finding footage and photos for my clients and contributing to and supporting their creative vision.

CHAPTER 14

FOUNDATIONS AND GRANTS

A foundation is a nonprofit organization that donates (or grants) money, equipment or other supplies to organizations and individuals. Foundations are also called charitable trusts, endowments, and public charities.

Private foundations are usually funded from one source, typically an individual, a family, or a corporation. Public foundations are built from multiple sources, including grants from private foundations, government agencies, and donations from private individuals. Foundations have a responsibility to uphold the principles of the foundation and make sure their funders' donations are being used for the intended purpose.

If you've searched for funding in the past you already know that many foundations will not grant money to individuals. Will these foundations make an exception? Sometimes, but it's rare. Donating funds to individuals is more complicated because the IRS requires nonprofits to obtain advance approval before distributing funds to individuals.

So, what's a starving artist to do? One option is to find a fiscal sponsor.

FISCAL SPONSORSHIP

Fiscal sponsors receive and administer funds and provide various levels of organizational support to individuals.

Another important step in the "Art of Film Funding" is to investigate the possibility of using a fiscal agent for your project. Fiscal sponsorship can give you access to funding opportunities and other resources available to 501(c) (3) nonprofit organizations. Private individuals will also be more likely to donate their hard-earned money if you have fiscal sponsorship because they can use the donation as a tax write-off.

A fiscal sponsorship is a relationship, and like all relationships it is important to find a good match. Each fiscal sponsor has different guidelines and goals. Most fiscal agents charge a fee. Just make sure you and your fiscal sponsor have a clear agreement in a contract regarding the management and disbursement of funds, what fees, if any, the fiscal agent will charge, and who will retain legal identity and control over your project. See *www. FromTheHeartProductions.com/fiscal.shtml*

Read their website and then talk to them with any unanswered questions. Don't be afraid to ask how long it takes from the time you give them a donation until you get your check back in the mail.

Features are often financed through fiscal sponsorship. From the Heart is working with Kyle Pagach, who is raising over $2 million. It's important to distinguish between a "donor" and an investor. By using a nonprofit you give your donor a letter stating "this is a donation." Being clear on this issue will prevent any miscommunications so they know they do not own any part of the film. I will let Kyle tell you how he is funding his film with From the Heart as his fiscal sponsor.

Making a Movie that Matters

In a recent interview, Rutgers University Head Football Coach Greg Schiano said, "There are two ways of doing things — the easy way and the hard way. The hard way is usually the right way." Now I'm pretty sure Coach Schiano has never worked in Hollywood, but his advice rings true in my business as much as his. Making movies is hard work. Making a movie that matters is even harder.

The first film I produced took over three-and-a-half years to finance and shoot. When it premiered at the 2004 Sundance Film Festival, my partners and I thought we had arrived, and in many ways we had. A couple of young, first-time film producers had found an original screenplay written by first-time directors and climbed the preverbal mountaintop by financing, producing, and selling a feature-length film on the biggest stage a small project will ever see — Sundance.

We had sold the film in over twenty countries, received numerous awards, and shown the movie at film festivals around the globe. Then one day, it was over. The phones stopped ringing and the congratulatory emails stopped showing up in my inbox. For all intents and purposes, my movie was just another title in the ever-expanding digital content sphere. Maybe a few people would see it each year, but probably not unless I gave them a copy or told them about it (it's called *Paranoia*: 1). You can rent it at *www.Netflix.com*.

That very rich experience and the empty feeling it left me with has brought me here. My current challenge is this: How can I produce a film that maintains a presence, and more importantly an audience, long after its initial run? I believe the answer lies in the story itself. Storytelling in its purest form has existed for thousands of years. Stories change, but the basic elements of good storytelling don't. If you have universal characters and themes, your story will be entertaining (good actors don't hurt either). Now, entertainment in its modern form has become a more temporary pleasure. In Shakespearean times, people would talk for months about a play they saw and wait months more for the next show. Today, we can just turn on our televisions or computers or go to the movies, where we laugh, we cry, we leave. We may discuss the film in the car on the ride home or at the water cooler the next day, but for the modern audience, most entertainment ends with the credits.

Now I would like to pose the question, What if there was a way to create dialogue long after a film has ended? What if the label "straight to DVD" wasn't seen as a filmmaker's purgatory, but an opportunity; an opportunity to distribute a film to a broad audience and use entertainment as a way of educating? This idea of creating content and characters that motivate a targeted, long term dialogue is what motivated me to make a movie like *Exit 131* (*www.exit131movie.com*). *Exit 131* is the fictional story of a small town football star, returning home in search of forgiveness for the death of a fifteen-year-old girl he knew in high school. The film explores the serious topics of underage drinking, drunk driving, and teen driver distractions from many angles, examining the effect the crash has had, not only on the family and friends of the victim, but those of the driver as well. *Exit 131* plans to continue the success of existing road safety industry educational content by expanding the format to include fiction as a way of educating and informing teens in high schools and colleges across North America. By creating educational materials that focus on the film's story and characters, we will be able to provide parents, school administrators, and teachers the opportunity to create an open dialogue with their children about the very serious topic of distracted driving, one that is built on mutual respect and openness, not preaching or finger pointing. But here's the cool part. They get to watch a movie while they are learning. Not some educational filmstrip or After School Special, but a real independent film of the highest quality with actors they know and respect.

With that in mind, our hope is that like-minded individuals and organizations will help us promote our WEAR A T-SHIRT… SAVE A LIFE! initiative by raising awareness within their community. Working with our friends at Original Retro Brand we have designed high-end, boutique quality T-shirts with various state license plate logos reading "NO PHONE", "DNT TXT," and "DZGN8D". The idea is to "crowdfund" the project by reaching out to the masses, more specifically people who care about teen road safety and distracted driving. The website *www.Kawziz.com* was created to give people a place where they can support initiatives like *Exit 131* by making small tax-deductible donations. In return donors receive a gift, in this case a boutique quality, state license plate T-shirt that allows them to spread their own personal message of road safety every time they wear it. We are also looking to create affiliates and co-fundraising opportunities with corporations, local businesses, and like-minded individuals and organizations. The idea that we can raise awareness with film has always been very appealing to me. But to raise awareness at the same we raise money to make a film — now that is twice the reward!

Check out my blog (*www.exit131movie.com/blog*) for a place where people interested in film, film finance, film production, film distribution, teen road safety, drunk driving, distracted driving and even fashion, can discuss *Exit 131* and projects like it.

FINDING THE GRANTOR TO MATCH YOUR FILM

The money to make your film is out there. Foundations have money and resources already set aside to give away to the right individual or organization. It's their job to give these resources away. Your job is to make sure your project matches their criteria and guidelines.

Choose a potential funder from the list in the Appendix and visit their website. Start with their mission statement, then go directly to their funding guidelines. When you find a funder that looks promising, dig in and explore their website from top to bottom. Learn everything you can about this funding source. When was the foundation established? Who established it and why? Find out who funds the foundation. As you research, jot down questions that come to mind.

If you've gotten this far and the foundation still feels like a good match, dig a little deeper. What causes have they funded in the past? You're probably not going to want to pitch your documentary about endangered marmots of the San Juan Wilderness to an organization that is an ardent supporter of the Independent Taxidermists of America. Knowing what type of organizations or individuals a particular funding source has embraced in the past will give you additional insight into the types of projects they fund.

IRS 501(c) (3) defines nonprofit, charitable, tax-exempt organizations. IRS Form 990 is used by tax-exempt organizations, non-exempt charitable trusts, and political organizations to provide the IRS with information required by section 6033. Why should you care? Because you can find out a lot about an organization by accessing their tax forms.

I know, it sounds positively sneaky, doesn't it? Don't worry, I'm not asking you to put on a cat suit and slip into their business office at night with a flashlight. These records are available to the public. If you're into snooping (and what great filmmaker isn't?), then you'll want to stay awake for this next part.

Form 990 discloses all kinds of juicy tidbits about an organization's finances, board members, and you guessed it, their philanthropic activities. Accessing this one form will tell you what kind of programs the organization supports and the names of all grant recipients for that fiscal year. It will also give you the name, address, and phone number of the operations officer (the person in charge of the grant you are applying for), and whether or not they accept unsolicited proposals.

You can access information on over 700,000 U.S. private and community foundations for free through the Foundation Center's Foundation Finder, located at *www.fdncenter.org*. If you don't have the name of a foundation, GrantSmart (*www.grantsmart.org*) offers a database of U.S. grant makers and foundations you can search using keywords.

Give it a try! Access the Foundation Finder, type in the name of the non-profit, and you will be given direct access to a PDF link containing this foundation's most current individual tax records.

It's astonishing to see how this one little tax form can provide a wealth of information about a foundation that you are interested in. The Foundation Center has a very slick diagram of a 990-PF that shows you exactly where the most important funding information is located. You can download it for free at *http://foundationcenter.org*.

Find a potential funding source for your film project and check out the operations officer. Who's on the Board? Who won last year's grant competition? How about the year before? Try to find websites of past winners and learn everything you can about their projects. Email them and congratulate them on their award and say something positive about their film. Tell them you are applying for the same grant and ask them if they have any suggestions, tips, or advice.

Remember to keep jotting down questions. You will need them later.

There are other foundations out there that will take a chance on an emerging filmmaker if the project and the filmmaker match the foundation's philosophy. If you are a first-time filmmaker, make sure the grant you are applying for supports emerging filmmakers. Perhaps you can increase your chances if you attach an experienced crew to your project. You would also increase your chances of winning a grant if you take a prior grant winner from the organization your film matches on board your crew. I know from giving grants that when I see a prior winner of my grants on the crew of a project it immediately instills confidence.

CONTACTING YOUR POTENTIAL GRANTOR

The next step in the "Art of Film Funding" is to find a foundation that looks promising. Now comes the part you've been waiting for! Take out your list of questions and choose the best one. You are going to call to the person who funds the grant. Place your call in "prime time" between 10 a.m. and 12 p.m., or between 2 and 4 p.m., and ask to speak directly with the operations officer in charge of the grant. If they don't answer, try again later. If you must, leave your name and number and the best time you can be reached, then make sure you're ready when they call back.

If you leave your cell phone number, keep your cell phone turned on and be ready with pen and paper handy. Don't worry, they will call you; it's their job. You did your homework. You know what the foundation is about and you know they support projects like yours, so they will be interested in what you have to say.

Individuals who work for nonprofits are passionate about their cause. They are overworked and underpaid. They believe the world needs more films on important issues and they want to help you get your film made.

Remember, this call is to connect with the decision maker for the grant you want to win. Your job is to touch them, remembering that we communicate through the heart chakra. This connection puts energy to your application; it is the voice behind the film. It's you and the film you want to convey to the funder through your passion so that later during the selection process, when they see your name on the application, they feel they know you.

Now what are you going to say when you get them on the phone? Remember that pitch you've been working on? You are going to tell them who you are and give them the concept of your film using that stunning under two-minute pitch that you have worked so hard on. Write down key points in case you get nervous and keep it with you so you are ready when the phone rings.

You know your pitch by heart. I know this and you know this, but you just might be a tad nervous so believe me, have your notes near. Your initial approach is critical so let's go over the steps:

You have the name of the person, the correct spelling and pronunciation. You have read this person's bio and you know about their past contributions.

Compliment them and thank them for their continuing efforts to help independent filmmakers.

You have read the website thoroughly and know what type of projects they fund.

You have an important question to ask that is not answered on the website.

You have your pitch in front of you.

You're organized.

You will not keep them on the phone long.

You will not take another call with them on the line.

You have researched prior winners and you know that your film fits within the scope of previously funded projects.

Get ready to take some notes!

Be relaxed and make the impression of a dedicated, passionate filmmaker who is determined to fund this film, with or without them.

I love it when filmmakers ask questions. Sometimes they ask how many applications we receive, or how many grants we fund per year. These are important questions and they are not answered on my website. I can hear them doing the math in their heads as they try to determine what their chances are.

Most filmmakers will pitch their project, then pause and wait for my response. This is good because it allows me time to process what they have just said. I usually reply with a question. They will typically have a quick answer that will lead to another question. This is what you want to achieve with this first call. You want to spark interest and draw the funder into the heart of your project.

Do not keep the funder on the phone too long, and do not over-pitch your film. Take a breath between sentences and allow the funder adequate time to respond. We know you are passionate about your film, but learn to listen to feedback and remember to come up for air!

I would have talked less and listened more
if I had my life to live over.
— Erma Bombeck

LISTENING IS AN ART

Listening is an art. My father, Roy W. Dean, was a wonderful listener. When Dad retired I asked him to move to Southern California and help me run Studio Film and Tape. I opened shop in 1968, and started selling short-ends. I noticed that there was always a lot of leftover film at the end of each feature film production and thought if I could get access to all this unused film I could sell it. I ignored all the skeptics, put on my mini-skirt and boots, marched over to Universal Studios and asked them for "those little ol' short ends that you really don't want." Before long I was buying up short-ends all over Hollywood, testing them and selling them for a profit.

I was thrilled when Dad sold his house in Dallas and moved to California in mid-life to start over again with me. He could have had any job in the office, but he chose to work at the front counter because he wanted to meet the filmmakers when they came in to buy film and sound stock. Dad never grew tired of listening to filmmakers describe their latest projects. He would literally end up spending hours with one filmmaker because he would ask the magic question that every filmmaker loves to hear: "So tell me, what you are shooting these days?"

Renee Ross and I got pretty good at anticipating the magic question. Dad would be up there at his post chatting away with some new filmmaker while Renee and I were busy working behind the scenes. Suddenly we could sense it. He was going to ask! Renee and I would stop, look at each other, then we would start waving our arms, trying to get Dad's attention. We'd shake our heads and mouth, "No! No!"

But it never did any good. Every time a new filmmaker came through the front door Renee and I knew that Dad was going to ask that magic question. We could be scrambling around, waiting on customers, pulling our hair out, and Dad would be up there at the counter listening intently as some filmmaker described his latest masterpiece.

I always try to remember Dad's patience when I have a "Starbucker" on the phone. Sometimes I will go outside, water my plants, prune my roses, come back in and fix a cup of hot tea while the filmmaker goes on like an Animaniac on crack.

Often when people go on like this it is because they are nervous. Calm yourself. Don't feel as though you need to fill every moment of silence with some profound statement. Develop the art of listening. When you let funders participate in the conversation they will be able to process what you are saying. They will formulate questions and will ultimately remember more about you and your project.

Back to your phone call: After you have delivered your perfect pitch, ask the funder if your project fits their criteria, then listen. Remember, your phone call serves two purposes: You are trying to find out if the funder will accept a proposal for the film you want to make, and you want to create a connection with this person. This is probably the first person that will read your application; it may be the only person who reads your application, so leave a good impression.

What do you say if the funder tells you that your film does not fit the foundation's criteria? Thank her for her time. Offer some sincere words of gratitude for the job she is doing and let her know you will contact her again when you have something that fits their criteria. Then go out and buy a nice Hallmark card and write a personal note thanking her once again for listening to your pitch. Remind her of the title of your film, and send along your best wishes for the future success of the foundation.

If she gives you the thumbs up, thank her for her time and confirm her address (oh, and please wait until you hang up to let out that scream). Go out and pick up a nice Hallmark card and write a brief note inside thanking her for the time she spent discussing your film about the endangered marmots of the San Juan Wilderness. Include a condensed version of your pitch and let her know that you will be applying for the grant. Sign your name and post it with a colorful endangered-species postage stamp.

Why send her a card? Because these film funders talk to each other. If you become a grant finalist with another foundation she will probably either hear about it or read about it. She will remember your card and think about you and your project in a good light.

You have now made two connections with the woman who will be handling your first application. Make a note on your list of potential funders and call her back in six to eight weeks with another important question that is not answered on the website. Send her a card for every occasion from Independence Day to National Marmot Day. Include a brief note about your film along with your condensed pitch and wish her a happy holiday.

Keep each potential funder close to your project by keeping them up to date on your progress and achievements. Let potential funders know if you win another grant, or if you have found an award-winning director for your project. Remember to keep track of each contact that you make. When you keep your funders involved in your progress they will be drawn deeper and deeper into your project. When your application crosses their desk they will remember you and your film. I know this from experience.

There is something special that happens when a funder picks up an application from a filmmaker who has kept her close to the project. Once a funder has been swept into your passion she is inwardly cheering for you. She is already connected to you and your film.

Keep all of your notes on each foundation organized and continue to look for questions that you can ask. When the next month rolls around, pick up the phone and make your second call.

Filmmaker Jilann Spitzmiller told me that she keeps a file of granting organizations by the deadline of their grants. This way she knows when she has to have the application ready. Jilann always called me to ask questions about the grant and she has won two of our grants, so it works!

Decide how many organizations you will research each day, then make a commitment to sit down and put in your quota every day. Give up those Netflix downloads and use that time to search the Web. Filmmakers often go back and use the same funders for subsequent projects. Just know that while your initial search may be time consuming, it can also lead to future funding.

Work your way through the list of funders included in this book. As you work, add funders you find along the way. Look on the From the Heart website for updated funding lists and for interviews with winners of the grants to find where and how they funded their films. You will have to kiss a lot of frogs to find a prince (or princess), but once you've found one it's worth it.

CHAPTER 15

TENACITY PAYS OFF

Interview with Jilann Spitzmiller
of Philomath Films

Philomath Films is headed by Jilann Spitzmiller and Hank Rogerson and is a film company that embraces characters and narratives on the fringe that have relevance for us all. In taking us outside of our normal assumptions and experiences, Philomath offers up projects that stretch the mind, entertain the spirit and reach straight for the heart. Their celebrated documentary feature, *Shakespeare Behind Bars*, embraces the cinema vérité narrative style that the company is known for; giving us an unflinching gaze into the dark areas of the human psyche and showing us that there is always the possibility of change. Philomath Films productions have won numerous awards including Audience Award at AFI Fest, Best of Show at Bend Film, and many Best Documentary Awards. Their work has debuted at festivals such as Sundance, SXSW, and Edinburgh, and has been broadcast around the world. They are three-time recipients of ITVS funding and two-time recipients of Sundance Institute funding. They were finalists and recipients of the Roy W. Dean Grant in 1999 and 2003, respectively. Jilann and Hank have a passion for helping other documentary filmmakers move forward in their craft and careers. To that end, they've established DocuMentors (*www.documentaryhowto.com*), which provides tools, tutorials and resources for documentary filmmakers of all levels.

What advice can you give producers who want their film on PBS?

We've been extremely fortunate to have been funded by ITVS three times — twice for the documentaries *Homeland* and *Shakespeare Behind Bars* — and once for a multimedia website, Circle of Stories, which plays at pbs.org. My husband and filmmaking partner, Hank Rogerson, and I have done all of the grant writing and producing together.

I think it's important to first understand the connection between ITVS and PBS. ITVS is funded by the Corporation for Public Broadcasting and is the largest funding service for independent programming on U.S. public television. If you are funded by ITVS, there is a very good chance your film will air on public television, but it is not guaranteed. It may run on national PBS or may be offered by ITVS to PBS affiliates if national PBS doesn't pick it up. It is best to check out their website (*www.itvs.org*) for yourself, as things change.

I think we have been successful with ITVS funding for a few reasons. Number one, we keep in mind the ITVS mission, which is to enrich the cultural landscape providing voice to underrepresented communities. That's partly our own mission as a film company, so it's a good fit. ITVS is also very interested in reaching diverse audiences through many different platforms and it's good to brainstorm how your project can accomplish this.

As for the grant writing itself, we have worked very hard on how we present our materials for the application. We've really developed concise and descriptive writing skills. You must be able to communicate your vision and story with detail and vitality. You've also got to have a dynamite work-in-progress tape that keeps people wanting to see more.

We are tenacious. We applied for funding five times on our last project, *Shakespeare Behind Bars*, until it was finally funded. Each time we were rejected, we got feedback on our proposal and reworked it according to ITVS readers' advice. After the third time applying, our proposal did not change much. What changed were the different reader groups that saw our proposal, and finally we hit pay dirt with the right reader group. They liked the film and recommended it for funding. Unfortunately, ITVS no longer provides reader feedback in the first application round as they once did.

Sometimes your proposal might be strong but you are unlucky with the composition of the reader group. Funding by committee can be subjective.

What is the proposal process for ITVS?

From our experience, the three-phase application process is pretty arduous and can take up to five months. In the first phase you submit a fairly summarized proposal and work-in-progress tape. The second phase is just submitting more copies of your work-in-progress. The third phase is more involved, where you submit a longer proposal and more detailed budget information. There is also an unspoken fourth phase, which is if you are considered for funding. Then you may need to negotiate the final funding amount and submit even further documentation supporting your ability to finish the film with the proposed amount of funding.

Jilann is a judge for the Roy W. Dean LA June 30 grants. She is a brilliant source of information on documentaries. Here are more grant-winning tips from our interview.

What tips can you give us on creating the proposal for ITVS?

It is important to be able to describe how the film will look — the visual description, the style, who the characters are, what's interesting about them. How do the characters relate or contrast to each other and generally, what's the overall content or theme of the film. If you are doing something innovative in your storytelling style, be sure to describe that in a way that's clear and evocative.

Also, speak directly to the question of "why are you the right person to make this film." Convince them that you know this subject intimately and that you have the insight to make a compelling, outstanding film.

Your work-in-progress videotape is also essential and must quickly and effectively showcase your story, characters, and your filmmaking ability. Sometimes we've spent several weeks or months just editing a sample tape until it strikes the right balance. It's helpful to screen it for a variety of people to see what they are getting from it before you submit it for funding.

From reading thousands of applications for grants, I want to see the film from the written word and very few submissions are visual.

You might assume when writing an application that you need to write about the themes, but you also need to write about what the film will look like, what the story structure is, what style you will use in your camera work, what type of sound, etc. All of these things need to be in this proposal. People are sitting in a room, perhaps at a desk, reading piles of applications and if you don't make your film come alive immediately in language on the page, you will not make an impact on these readers who have the power to fund your film.

You aim for a visual description of the film, even if you are doing a documentary and you don't know how the film will play out?

Exactly. Even though documentaries are unpredictable in terms of what they will eventually look like or what story they will tell, you still need to consult your own personal crystal ball and predict what you think the outcomes will be. That also makes you a better filmmaker because it makes you question your idea and your characters and your content, and it helps you see where there may be weak, unrealistic or dull spots.

WINNING SUNDANCE GRANTS

How did you win the two Sundance grants?

Sundance was our first funder with *Shakespeare Behind Bars*. They came in with $15,000 seed money for R&D before the film had any footage, which is unusual these days. We then applied for a second round of money and we received $60,000, so we got their maximum grant at that time of $75,000.

After we received the initial $15,000 for our idea, we submitted a second proposal for the production money. By then we knew more about our characters, what their story arcs might be, and we had more teeth to put into the proposal. Once you start shooting you can add some details of scenes. I always do this; I even add direct quotes from characters to make it emotionally compelling. You might as well be writing a short story. You have to put an immense amount of stock into the craft of writing your proposal.

BBC LICENSE FEE

What did BBC ask for when they licensed the film?

After the award of Sundance's grants, BBC gave us 25% of our budget in return for a licensing period of 18 months for exclusive TV broadcasting in the U.K. We actually cut a slightly different version for them according to their particular needs. After we finished the film to our liking, we then tailored it for them with their guidance.

ITVS was the last major funder to come into the project. We were actually weighing an offer between ITVS and HBO. The ITVS offer was more money so we went with them. They are a last-money-in funder; usually they will come in at the end of the film. If you have no funder and are going to ITVS, you have to know if the maximum grant they give will cover your budget. ITVS wants to know you will definitely finish the film and that they can offer it to PBS and try to get a national broadcast.

We also won the Roy W. Dean Film Grant for *Shakespeare*, which helped us with a lot of in-kind services during production, post and distribution. The grant offers some interesting services like marketing help and a free screening in a beautiful screening room in L.A. We used this for an important press screening prior to our theatrical release of the film. We also applied to this one three or four times before we got it! Don't take no for an answer!

ITVS contracts for domestic TV only, so do you also negotiate sales to domestic DVD, schools and other markets?

Yes, they license for domestic broadcast for four to six years and allow you to sell the other distribution avenues of your film. ITVS asks for approval of any sale agreements so they can verify that the ITVS name is on the product. They need to keep their name in front of audiences and they want to check your agreement to be sure the sale does not infringe on ITVS's rights. You can negotiate with them for a theatrical window and the street date of your DVD and a date for your educational sales. Many films made for ITVS do very well in educational markets, churches, and libraries. You have a lot of opportunities for income through distribution.

Each time you make a sale arrangement, do you also return money to ITVS for the initial investment?

Yes, ITVS is our only funder that is getting a return on their money. They basically share your net profits in proportion to the amount of their funding.

It is important to know that ITVS puts a lot more into the film besides money. They devote staff time to getting your film out to the viewing audience. They put a lot into your outreach. They may build a website for the film and they have an in-house publicity person. There are many benefits to their funding beyond the financial assistance. Also know from your end as a producer, you'll spend additional time working with ITVS staff and creating deliverables for them, so it's important to factor that time and money into your final submitted ITVS budget.

In terms of other distribution for *Shakespeare Behind Bars*, it aired on Sundance Channel and Starz/Encore for eighteen months concurrently. It also had a sizeable theatrical run in the U.S. and continues to play at special and educational screenings around the world.

What is your next film?

We are currently in production on a documentary called *Still Dreaming* which follows a group of retired entertainers as they rekindle their acting careers by mounting *A Midsummer Night's Dream*.

How will you distribute this film?

At this point, early in the distribution process, we're looking into all options and are excited about the new Transmedia and cross platform possibilities. One thing we're really interested in is the fact that we can reach our niche audience now through the Internet. We've been working on this since the development phase of the film and it is something that will benefit all avenues of our distribution. It's helped us in the short term with crowdfunding as well.

ITVS-WINNING DOCUMENTARY PROPOSAL

Shakespeare Behind Bars
a documentary film

—— ✸ ——

SYNOPSIS

Shakespeare Behind Bars is a documentary in postproduction about a diverse all-male Shakespeare company working within the confines of the U.S. prison system. The film follows twenty inmates for one year as they rehearse and perform a full production of a Shakespeare play at the Luther Luckett Correctional Complex in LaGrange, Kentucky. Five of these men are followed in-depth. In this prison atmosphere, theater is changing their lives, as the words of Shakespeare act as a catalyst for these inmates to examine their past with remarkable candor. They are all individuals who have committed the most heinous crimes, and are now confronting and performing those crimes on stage. In this process, we see these unlikely men testing the power of truth, change, and forgiveness.

TREATMENT

The film *Shakespeare Behind Bars* opens on two men in a wide, golden field learning a speech from Shakespeare's *The Tempest*. The camera begins in close as they work on the piece, bringing passion to the famous line, "We are such stuff as dreams are made on." As their energy builds, the camera pulls further and further back to reveal the larger picture — these men are behind many barriers of barbed wire and metal. An armed guard watches them through binoculars from a tower nearby. But for a moment in time, these two inmates are transported from the bars of prison to the place where creativity and dreams reside (see WIP tape, start).

Shakespeare Behind Bars, the film, is about this journey — how the words of Shakespeare act as a vehicle to transport this group of incarcerated men to a potentially better place in their hearts and minds. In this unusual prison theatre program, they have the support and encouragement needed in order to examine their darkest selves, and to shed light on how they might find healing and redemption.

The film will be structured around the creative journey of one year in the life of this group that calls themselves "Shakespeare Behind Bars." This is their seventh year, and the troupe will be performing *The Tempest*, Shakespeare's last play. Combining several genres, *The Tempest* has elements of romance, tragedy, and comedy. The play focuses on Forgiveness as the main theme, and also explores the ideas of Isolation, Nature vs. Nurture, and the Father-Daughter relationship. The inmates will cast themselves according to their own crimes and backgrounds, and what they are willing to take on emotionally. They will work intensely with volunteer director Curt Tofteland. Curt is part director, part therapist, part mentor, part father to these men. Whenever they can, the inmates rehearse on their own during Curt's absence. And just as in Shakespeare's day, men play all the female roles.

The film begins in the fall at the start of rehearsals as the men cast themselves and progresses as they rehearse and develop their characters throughout the year. The viewer is a fly on the wall at cast read-through where the men grapple with the text, and have intense one-on-one discussions with Curt who constantly pushes them to find their personal experience within each part. The film will focus on certain key, pivotal scenes of *The Tempest* and revisit them in both rehearsal and performance footage. Through the actors' journeys, viewers will vicariously examine and understand the timeless language, characters and themes of Shakespeare, which can sometimes seem daunting to audiences.

At the heart of the film are the conflicts that the men struggle with inside themselves. As the year progresses, the parallels between themselves and their characters is enlightening and sometimes uncanny. Our audience will first be introduced to these men simply as actors. Their past acts will be revealed gradually over the course of the film to build dramatic tension. Each interview will go deeper into the reasons why they committed their crime, their feelings about their actions, where they are emotionally in the current moment, and how the words of Shakespeare are helping them to process these complicated issues. (See character descriptions below.)

Shakespeare Behind Bars will not glorify these men or excuse their crimes, but rather attempt to take a more humane look at them. The objective of *Shakespeare Behind Bars* is to give audiences a close-up, visceral experience — a unique look at prisons and the incarcerated. To go beyond political rhetoric about crime and the need for more prisons. To shed light on a program that costs the taxpayer nothing, and to profile dedicated individuals who are tackling the shortcomings of the American prison system.

By following these men through this creative process, the film explores the universal themes of redemption, transformation, and forgiveness. It will raise questions for the viewer such as: Should we rehabilitate criminals? How does art transform the human conscience? Who deserves forgiveness? The inmates' interviews address these probing questions and provide revealing answers. Because of the unlikely setting of prison, these themes and issues are given a fresh, new angle, and will provide a broad and varied appeal for many communities across the U.S.

THE CONTEXT

The statistics on the U.S. prison system are jarring, and title cards interspersed throughout the film will help put this particular prison program in context. Since 1980, the prison population in America has quadrupled, while the violent crime rate has stayed about the same. Today more than 60% of those in prison are there for non-violent crimes, and in the past twenty years social programs for education, drug rehabilitation, job training, Head Start, affordable housing, and legal aid have been cut to help fund 700 new prisons nationwide. At the current rate, by 2020, approximately 60% of black males between the ages of 18-34 will be behind bars; 12 million people will be incarcerated nationwide.

Also adding insight will be the prison's progressive and genial warden, Larry Chandler (see WIP, 04:30). He personally believes in trying to rehabilitate prisoners in a political climate that is largely about throwing away the key. He talks about how politics dictate the way in which the prison system is run, and how this interferes with effective reform. "I guess I'm just a warden who hates prisons," he laughs. "More than anything, the day they come in, you ought to start preparing them for the day they leave." Statistics support his view, as 97% of the Luther Luckett population will be released to walk the streets again. Warden Chandler runs a reform-minded institution, which concentrates on education in hopes of making the inmates better members of society. The Shakespeare Behind Bars Program is a part of the overall attempt by Luther Luckett to reform its population through education, therapy and job training, and new members of the Shakespeare Program must have a clean prison record, and be sponsored into the group by a veteran member. Since the program began in 1995, of the twenty inmates who have participated in the Shakespeare company and then been released, only two have returned to jail. This 10% recidivism is far below the national average of 41%. This information will be presented on title cards.

THE CHARACTERS

The characters in *Shakespeare Behind Bars* are not your ordinary, stereotypical prisoners. These guys are "the best of the best," or so they say at Luther Luckett. Luther Luckett is the most rehabilitatively focused prison in the Kentucky system. It has the most educational and therapeutic programs, and prisoners here are expected to partake, or they get transferred to a prison with less to offer. And within this general population at Luther Luckett, one has to have a clean record to join the Shakespeare group. As a result, at first glance, most of the men in this program do not seem to be hardened criminals. But their past actions all have a deep darkness that haunts them.

Leonard Ford (Caucasian) says that he and the group are "ready to go" with the new season after their summer hiatus. "We're all people trying to achieve something unique for ourselves and take advantage of this process," he says as we see him and the others playing theater games (see WIP, 10:00). He underscores that this is no ordinary acting troupe — that they will likely have to deal with someone getting sent to solitary confinement or getting transferred, and will have to recast roles midstream. Leonard is the intellectual of the group, and his work in rehearsals and his interviews provide the film with thought-provoking moments from a philosophical mind confined behind bars with plenty of time to contemplate. Leonard believes that *Shakespeare Behind Bars* is subversive — "It subverts society's desire to separate me from humanity." In 1995, Leonard was married with four kids and working as a computer programmer. He was highly respected within his church community and even ran for the office of mayor. Today, he is serving a fifty-year sentence for sexual abuse of minors. At the start of the film, after seven years in prison, he evades questions about his crime. But Leonard says he looks forward to working on *The Tempest* and its theme of isolation — it takes place on a deserted island — and playing the role of the villain, Antonio. "He's a villain who does not get what he deserves, and that's unique." In years past, Leonard has always played the villain, and although he tried to avoid doing so this year, he ended up with the role when another cast member got transferred in the first week of rehearsals.

Over the course of the film, Leonard's role of villain takes on literal meaning within the walls of Luther Luckett. "I pray to God it doesn't get much lower than this," says Leonard in January, dressed in a green jump suit, his hands shackled (see WIP, 33:50). "Antonio is fun to play, but not one to mimic in real life." In an ironic self-fulfilling prophecy, Leonard has become the cast member sent to "the Hole," or solitary confinement. "A prison within a prison." On day twenty-one of a ninety-day stint in the Hole (for allegedly messing with the prison's computer system), he is a stark example of the effectiveness of isolation. He appears shell-shocked and his interview is raw. For the first time, Leonard admits to his crime of sexually abusing seven girls. He has spent a lot of time in the Hole rehearsing his lines to blank walls, and thinking about mercy. As he makes his bed, washes his hands, eats his lunch alone, we hear a cacophony of delirious inmates shouting obscenities at each other from their solitary cells. "It seems that those who need mercy the most are those who deserve it the least." Even though he has been rehearsing in solitary, Leonard will never get the chance to play the role of Antonio. Two weeks later he is shipped to another prison in Kentucky. "Antonio" has to be recast, and ultimately, this new actor, Rick Sherroan, also gets thrown in the Hole just days before the performances. The group must recruit a new inmate who has no acting experience but who admirably learns blocking and lines in only four days.

Sammie Byron (African American/Hispanic) is a leader and mentor in the group, and has been in the Shakespeare program for seven years. This year, as he prepares for possible parole in August, he will take a smaller role in the play and will help coach less experienced members of the troupe. At the beginning of the rehearsal process, he performs the famous St. Crispian's speech from *Henry V* to inspire the new guys (see WIP, 13:00). Sammie is a survivor of physical and sexual abuse who had created a seemingly stable adult life with a wife and a successful business. He threw it all away, however, when he strangled his mistress almost twenty years ago. He is now serving his twentieth year of a life sentence. As one of the original members of the program, Sammie feels Shakespeare has been a vehicle for him and the guys. "In rehearsals we deal with our own personal pains and what it is we need to change our behavior...it changes lives. It's changed me." Sammie tells us that while playing Othello two years ago, he experienced a breakthrough when forced to strangle Desdemona, his wife, on stage. (Stills from that production will be used to help illustrate this event.) In reliving his crime, he was able to examine the reasons it occurred and then began taking steps to change himself through therapy and job training at the prison. *The Tempest* provides Sammie with an opportunity to further explore forgiving himself, as he works towards his parole hearing a few months after the performance of the play.

Over the course of the film, we see Sammie preparing to be set free after twenty years in prison, while at the same time coping with the fact that he may never get out. "My emotional state — that's what worries me the most about getting out," he says. "'Cause I don't want to make the same mistakes I made in the past." Although Sammie is nervous about leaving prison, everyone else in the group is confident that he will make parole and do well in the transition to life on the outside. They look to him as a mentor, not only regarding Shakespeare, but also as someone who has truly grown and changed in prison.

Hal Cobb (Caucasian, homosexual) is hoping for insight and forgiveness regarding his crime, and he lobbied hard to play the lead role. "There is a part of me that wants to play Prospero, and there is a part of me that wants to run" (see WIP, 06:45). He knows too well that he will have to confront his demons by playing a controlling and plotting vengeful type, who in the end chooses forgiveness. He speaks about only knowing numbness while growing up, and never being allowed to communicate his real feelings. Hal grew up in a fundamentalist family, went to Bible college, became a preacher, got married and had a daughter. But he felt he was living a lie and going to hell because he was a closeted homosexual. One morning he electrocuted his pregnant wife in the bathtub by knocking a hair dryer into the water (see WIP, 55:15). After passing his wife's death off as an accident, he moved to Los Angeles with their small daughter and began studying acting. Ten years later he confessed his crime in a twelve-step program, and his roommate turned him in. In the eight years he has been in prison, he has not seen his daughter because she requested they not communicate. She is now nineteen. Hal will play Prospero in *The Tempest*, who, along with his daughter, has been banished to an island for twelve years. He hopes that playing Prospero will bring him closer to his own daughter and closer to gaining her forgiveness. "Resolution can't come without communication, and not talking is what got me here... my hope is for one day to find forgiveness, and I hope this play will help me do that."

Throughout the year, Hal dedicates an enormous amount of time and energy to the play. He researches his role and the theme of forgiveness in the prison library, and constantly coaches others on their parts. Eventually, as the months pass, he realizes that this is all just a distraction from "the true work" he needs to do. "It's difficult to reverse forty-six years of suppressing," he says as we see him receiving his daily medication of Zoloft. "I feel like if I really allow myself to feel all my shame and anger, I may never surface." By performance time, Hal realizes the only forgiveness he can ever expect is his own.

"Red" Herriford (African American/Caucasian) will play Prospero's naïve and virginal daughter. Red is currently at Luther Luckett for armed robbery, and has severe learning disabilities. As a consequence, he has always played smaller roles in the Shakespeare group, but this year, he is stepping up to play the much larger part of Miranda, the fifteen-year-old female ingénue. But it is not a role he chose willingly. He feels that Hal and others "put the role on him" because of his size and looks. Then, despite himself, one day in rehearsal he connects deeply with his character when he realizes that, like Miranda, he was told at age fifteen of his true lineage — that the father he had never known was white. The parallel with his chosen character shocks him, and opens him to exploring his own pain, confusion, and anger regarding his past. "It's hard to explain. This part here is just perfectly, truly for me... these virtues, and these feelings I'm having." Red struggles to articulate in front of the other men who at once support him and tease him for identifying with a young woman's pain (see WIP, 18:00).

Over the course of rehearsals, Red is constantly irritated by others and what he takes as their criticism. As he exits rehearsal one day, he says to Sammie that he is frustrated with Hal because he is so controlling, "just like my own father. Always in power." This father-child dynamic continues to play itself out for the rest of the film, and is another example in the film of the striking parallels between the characters in the play and the inmates.

Richard Hughes (Native American/Hispanic) believes that he "will never be redeemed by his Creator." A former Marine scout sniper, he killed forty-eight people in Lebanon, and another twelve in Desert Storm. But he is not proud of this since he feels it "sucked all the humanness out of me," as he became "a robot performing someone else's mission." One night five years ago he killed another man, execution style, who had threatened his fiancé. Brought up in a climate of violence by his father who was also in the military, Richard sees incarceration as his vision quest. Reconnecting with his Native American heritage, he regularly holds Cherokee ceremonies on the prison yard, and he is learning the Cherokee language, both of which we filmed. Richard is a "newbie" in the theater group, being sponsored by one of the group's old-timers. He sees Shakespeare Behind Bars as a possible tool to help him regain a sense of the humanity within himself. It's also a way to keep the boredom of prison life at bay.

In the early spring, Richard reaches a major personal milestone with his character, Sebastian, when he realizes that he has always been a "Sebastian" — a follower who did everything to please others (see WIP, 43:45). "My character is me — I've been a Sebastian all my life." He has the epiphany as he realizes for the first time that he did not have to kill his victim, that he did have a choice. An in-depth discussion in rehearsal occurs concerning this. Another member named Gene Vaughn offers that when one begins to take responsibility for their own actions, it is then that they start to heal and change. "I've been trying to rationalize what I did," Richard responds. "But each time I tried to justify the murder, a little voice said maybe it ain't quite right." He continues to work through this revelation until the performances.

Curt Tofteland is a life-long Shakespearean actor and director who has been coming to Luther Luckett to work with adult male inmates in the Shakespeare Behind Bars program since 1995. The film will touch upon

Curt's journey, as a person coming in from the outside, trying to help repair lives devastated by acts of self-destruction. Although he works with professional actors most of the year, he says that working with this group of inmates is far more rewarding because of their courage and dedication. Curt also thinks Shakespeare would have appreciated this motley acting company of convicts. "People in the theater back in Elizabethan times were thought of as pickpockets, thieves, rapists, and murderers." Curt believes in seeing these men for who they are today, not for who they were, and not as defined solely by the crime they have committed. For Curt, his key direction for these guys is: "Tell the truth."

DRAMATIC STRUCTURE

The film will follow a three-act structure and will largely play out like a character piece. What supplies much of the dramatic tension will be the pace at which information is revealed about each of our characters. We will learn about each main character's crime at different points in the film, beginning with Sammie in Act One, followed by Leonard, Richard and Red in Act Two, and finally Hal in Act Three. As the viewer gets to know them as actors, they will begin to wonder what these seemingly charming and interesting men could possibly have done. Then, as the viewer learns about each dark past, they will have to wrestle with the conflicts presented by appearance versus truth, character versus action, past versus present, vengeance versus forgiveness. As Prospero learns to forgive those who wronged him in the play, the viewer will go on the same journey, deciding whether or not to forgive these felons in the film.

Act One of the film will set up our main characters and their inner conflicts, as well as the external conflicts they are dealing with, such as going up for parole after twenty years in prison, in Sammie Byron's case, or trying to reconcile with family, as with Hal Cobb. It will lay out the main themes of *The Tempest*, and give a clear idea of how the Shakespeare program is run and directed by Curt. For the viewer, the text of Shakespeare becomes more accessible, as we see Curt breaking it down, and the guys beginning to learn and understand it. We'll get a solid sense of place at Luther Luckett, as the film crew was allowed unfettered access to daily life in the prison. And as rehearsals begin to take off, we will see how the words and characters of Shakespeare are beginning to open the men up, exposing emotions and issues that need to be resolved.

Act Two will provide for further character development as rehearsals progress, and as interviews deepen. In this act, more of prison life is shown as a backdrop to these interview sequences — such as inmates receiving their daily meds, doing laundry, in the cafeteria chow line, or seeing their families during weekly visiting hours. In rehearsals, a general sense of ennui has taken hold as the guys are at different levels of commitment with the play, and the performances seem like a long way off. Key events of this act will be Leonard getting thrown in the Hole and Richard's epiphany.

Act Two continues to build toward the performances and the tension and nerves in the group are starting to rise, as evident in vérité scenes in rehearsal. Sammie steps back as the group's leader in order to let someone else take charge, but at this point they are a "ship without a captain." Both in rehearsals and on the yard, guys are critical of each other, and arguing as their egos clash. Some of these men are learning to use communication skills for the first time, and understanding how to take and give criticism, as well as how to work in a group. As Red says, "This is what happens when you put together a cast of convicts. It ain't Mary Poppins theatre." This is illustrated perfectly when the cast loses their Antonio once again, as Rick gets thrown in the Hole for selling drugs. In a humorous scene that breaks some of the tension, we see the men, about twenty of them this time, rehearsing on the recreation yard without Curt's supervision. They choreograph the play's banquet scene into a free-form break dancing sequence, and create a rap song from Shakespeare's text.

Act Three. Finally, May arrives and it's performance time (see WIP, 1 hr.). With two cameras catching all the action, we see Sammie speaking his lines to the wall, Hal and Red holding hands, Richard checking entrances and exits with the "new" Antonio, Ray, and Curt shouting orders to anyone who will listen. The men huddle up and with a "1-2-3 Shakespeare!" the play begins. The first performance is for the prison population and will briefly cover parts of some scenes from the first half of *The Tempest*. These will be scenes that are already familiar to the viewer, since we can recognize them from the rehearsal process (such as the scene where Red connected with his character, Miranda, for the first time.) This performance footage will be intercut with audience cutaways and backstage footage, such as the guys coming backstage to apologize to each other for missing lines, or high-fiving another cast member for a job well done.

The rest of *The Tempest* will be briefly covered in footage from the second performance, which is done for friends and family. Once again, key scenes and lines will be highlighted, such as Prospero's line "The rarer act is in virtue/than in vengeance" (see WIP, 1 hr. 9 min.). These moments will also be intercut with backstage shots — Hal adjusting Red's costumes, Sammie looking out at his family. The play comes to a close and the men have an opportunity to speak to their families. For Hal, none of his family comes, but a former member of his church shows up to support him. Sammie is overcome with grief, unsure whether this is his last play at Luther Luckett. The energy is high, the emotions are deep, but the moment is brief, as the men must get back to their dorms to be counted. In a slow dissolve sequence, we see the men exit the visiting room for a final time as the lights go out.

Epilogue: It is the fall of 2003, and Sammie Byron did not get parole in August. He was given six more years. But in a bizarre turn of events, he will be getting out of Luther Luckett for a short period of time, as he and the inmates are going "on tour" with *The Tempest* (see WIP, 1 hr. 10 min.). Transporting prisoners is an enormous security risk, so the men will be shackled and wearing orange jumpsuits as they are given the opportunity to see the outside. A familiar face rejoins the cast as Leonard Ford has come back to Luther Luckett, and for the first time he will not play a villain. He will replace one of the fairies.

The second prison they visit is a woman's prison where the reception is electric. The women get charged up by the performance, and it's Gospel meets Shakespeare. It's a high note after a year of soul searching and hard work. The Epilogue will be used to tie up story arcs with title cards over footage. Over the course of the year and the film, we will see men changed — enriched, challenged, awakened, and fulfilled. In a time of ever-shrinking funding for the arts, this documentary demonstrates to general public television audiences the universal idea that a creative process offers everyone the opportunity to change.

SHAKESPEARE BEHIND BARS ON PUBLIC TELEVISION
Public television and this program will be a perfect match up for several reasons. This film will raise vital issues regarding the role of rehabilitation in the criminal justice and U.S. prison system — issues that deserve more

public discourse and consideration as we continue as a society to put more and more people behind bars as a "solution" to crime. As prisons become severely overcrowded and more privatized into commercial corporations, the questions regarding how much rehabilitation should exist and what works deserve further examination. In addition, the film raises the larger question of the relevance of art in society, and whether or not the arts can be a path to growth and a source of healing.

Public television, and specifically the participation of ITVS, affords a project such as this an important element of public outreach, which will result in viable public dialogue on these issues. This film would not have the same impact on a commercial cable channel. A public television broadcast offers far greater opportunities to promote follow-up discussion groups, both in communities and on the World Wide Web. For these reasons, the filmmakers would like this film to be accessible to the widest possible audience, not just those who are able to subscribe to pay TV.

COMMUNITIES WHO WILL BENEFIT FROM THIS PROGRAM

This film will appeal to and serve citizens in a wide range of disciplines, such as those interested in public policy; the criminal justice system; the arts; theatre; education; and psychology. These categories touch people in all geographical and cultural corners of the U.S. In addition, prison issues are relevant in any community, due to the prevalence of prisons nationwide. In terms of racial and social communities, the cast of characters in the film is quite diverse, but their stories are universal in nature. In addition, anyone who is interested in the psychological healing process — whether to address grief, anger, or abuse, among other issues — can draw inspiration from this film. This film also has a valuable educational aspect, potentially demystifying Shakespeare for viewers.

Most specifically, this film can inspire dialog for the incarcerated, as well as those working with or who are touched by the criminal justice system, including victims and law enforcement. This Shakespeare program can serve as a model to others who would like to explore healing through the arts. And the focus on incarcerated men gives voice to people who have been largely forgotten by society.

Convicts are often stereotyped, stigmatized and disenfranchised even though they may be striving to change, or have successfully put their past behind them.

FILMMAKER'S RELATIONSHIP TO SUBJECT/COMMUNITY

Director Hank Rogerson has been an actor for over ten years and has been involved in Shakespeare and other theatre programs throughout his career. While directing the film, he was able to understand the inmate's journeys as actors, and could bring to light those internal processes of discovery that happen when studying a part. For example, Hank asked Red about playing the role of fifteen-year-old Miranda, and how he would physicalize the part. He asked Red, "How would a fifteen-year-old girl stand?" It's something that Red hasn't thought of yet, and the moment is poignant and revealing as Red envisions the delicateness and innocence of the body language of his character (see WIP, 18:00).

SHOOTING FORMAT, STYLE, APPROACH

Shakespeare Behind Bars is shot in 16x9 on DV cam, in a cinema vérité style — straightforward and intimate, revealing the emotional journeys that the inmates are taking. Complete access within the prison itself has yielded a variety of footage of life inside the wire and will provide for textured montages of prison life. We filmed our main characters in a wide variety of activities, in order to avoid too many "talking heads," and this vérité footage will be woven together with interview clips.

Transitions between scenes will consist of anonymous, close-up shots of prison life, which convey the tedium and repetition of daily life. And the film will use the visual theme of reflection — in mirrors, windows or puddles — to underscore the inmates' own process of self-reflection in the Shakespeare program. The film will have some titles to give background on the inmates, the prison, and the prison system in the U.S. The film's opening theme song will be a polished version of a rap called "Honor" that the inmates created using text from *The Tempest* (see WIP, 1 hr. 08 min.). The soundtrack will have ensemble instrumental music, as well as rap and hip-hop themes, echoing the music created by the inmates for the play. The sound design will incorporate the natural sounds of prison —

steel doors, P.A. calls for count, crickets mixing with the electric buzz of floodlights.

The editing will reflect the moods of the scenes themselves, whether it is a heated scene in rehearsal, or a slow scene of a man praying in his cell. We will also experiment with the convention of time, using slow motion, freeze frame, and time-lapse.

LENGTH CONSIDERATIONS

In cutting this film to 56:40 for public television, we may find that five characters are too many to follow. At this point, however, we cannot say which of the five we would be eliminating. This will be revealed through the editing process.

Note: You can find all of Philomath Films' winning ITVS and Sundance applications in the Members area of DocuMentors at *www.documentary-howto.com*

CHAPTER 16

TRANSMEDIA PROPOSAL

By *Sara Maamouri and Jesse Deeter*
(Who Killed the Electric Car?)

A transmedia documentary
directed and produced by Jessie Deeter
produced and edited by Sara Maamouri

Principal contact: Sara Maamouri
Mailing Address: 117 Holladay Ave.
San Francisco, CA 94110
Mobile: 510-418-7171
burned@saramaamouri.com
www.burned-documentary.org

INDEX

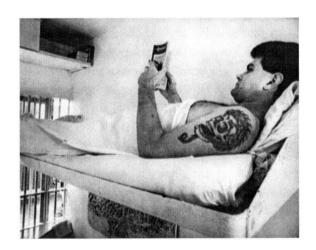

1. Abstract

Burned is a transmedia film project that tells the story of a man who was wrongly executed for the arson deaths of his three children. Using an interactive web platform as well as a mobile/tablet application, the project will allow viewers to see the story told as well as engage with its complex elements: the criminal case, the fire investigation as well as this man's letters from death row.

2. Project Background and Rationale

> *"[There has not been] a single case—not one—in which it is clear*
> *that a person was executed for a crime he did not commit.*
> *If such an event had occurred in recent years,*
> *we would not have to hunt for it;*
> *the innocent's name would be shouted from the rooftops."*
>
> — *Antonin Scalia, U.S. Supreme Court Justice*

Cameron Todd Willingham was twenty-four years old when he was found guilty of starting a house fire that killed his three young children. But twelve years later, an arson expert's review of the case determined there was no proof of an intentionally set fire. The evidence that led to Willingham's conviction was based on faulty practices and handed-down lore; the review, based instead on science-based arson investigation techniques, showed no evidence of arson. When this new information was presented to the governor of Texas, it was ignored. Willingham was executed in 2004 for what has been proven to be an accidental fire.

This young man's story is vitally important for two reasons: first, his is the first instance in modern American history where, "There can no longer be any doubt that an innocent person has been executed," according to Innocence Project Co-Director Barry Scheck. Second, forensics expert Gerald Hurst says that the Willingham case is one of hundreds of arson cases in the state of Texas alone that should be reviewed using modern scientific methods rather than the "junk science" previously used to convict them.

In order to fully leverage the evolving media environment, where the viewer is no longer content to be a passive observer of a film, *Burned* is designed as a dynamic transmedia experience. This approach will deepen audiences' understanding of the Willingham case by allowing viewers to interactively respond to the aspects of Willingham's story that appeal to them most, in the order that they want to digest the information. Through this closer look at the Willingham case, viewers can gain a better understanding of our justice system and criminal investigation practices. *Burned* will feature a web documentary and a singular digital outreach portal with interactive media as well as professionally produced content that can be accessed through multiple two-way communication streams on multiple devices. The project is built around the belief that strong, compelling storytelling has the power to transform passive viewers into energized, involved citizens.

The Death Penalty

The United States stands nearly alone as an industrialized democracy that is still putting people to death. The group of nations still executing its own citizens is shrinking, and its membership is stark. In 1998, 93% of the world's executions were carried out by just five countries: China, Iran, Saudi Arabia, Pakistan and the United States of America.

Politically, both progressives and conservatives carry voices calling for the abolition of the death penalty. Roy Brown, state senator and 2008 Republican nominee for governor of Montana, stated, "I believe that life is precious from the womb to a natural death." Richard Viguerie, considered by some to be the father of the modern conservative movement, wrote in an article for Sojurners magazine, "(D)eath row inmates have been exonerated by DNA evidence, raising the prospect that prosecutors and juries made mistakes in cases without scientific evidence and in cases that predate the science." Even mainstream conservative columnist George Will refuses to support the death penalty, specifically because of the specter of fallibility.

The Capital Case and Investigatory Practices in *Burned*

One of the issues that *Burned* addresses is the shifting nature of arson investigation in the U.S. and its impact on the Willingham case. In some arson cases, a fire is considered accidental until the fire investigator completes an analysis and deems the fire to be deliberately set. But this is not universal.

The default in cities like Chicago is if the cause of a fire is unknown, it is called arson. This practice gives the initial fire investigator tremendous power: the power to blame, to persuade, and ultimately, to kill. At the time of the Willingham case, the practice of arson investigation relied almost entirely on anecdotal observation and on-the-job experience. Tragically, arson investigation standards were only just starting to evolve at the time of Willingham's trial, bringing investigatory techniques up to date to rely upon scientific method analysis. Sadly, Willingham's defense team did not bring these new standards into the courtroom. While subsequent scientific evaluation found no causes of arson in the Willingham case, this information was ignored by the Texas Board of Pardons and Paroles and Governor Rick Perry.

Other films have been made about Willingham, including our own director and producer Jessie Deeter's collaboration with PBS Frontline to produce *Death by Fire*. However, films about the death penalty tend to attract audiences that are pre-disposed to be anti-death penalty and turn off some potential audiences before they even tune in. The transmedia nature of *Burned* is our response to these predispositions. *Burned* will empower communities, schools and institutions to come to their own conclusions by getting inside the justice system through this one case. With multiple entry points into the story, we will draw audiences in to act as members of the jury, reviewing the court case, the forensic investigation, the science of fire or Willingham's personal story as told through his letters from death row. Our project will also draw a broader and younger audience than the typical documentary would: Watching films is typically a more passive experience, while our dynamic approach encourages the viewers to return time and time again for more information. By producing an interactive film project with innovative technologies, we hope to target young people who might be entering law enforcement, fire academies and law schools.

This ambitious project allows us to place narrative innovation at the service of civil justice.

3. Project Description
Cameron Todd Willingham's story is complex, which makes it ideal for the multiplatform storytelling style we have chosen. We have designed this

project to provide an immersive experience that will transport audiences to the shell of a home with a burnt Christmas tree in the living room, a courtroom in Corsicana, Texas, or a lonely cell on death row. Our goal is to create spaces both online and offline that introduce audiences to the intricacies of death penalty trials and the science of fire in an entertaining way, and encourage them to grapple with one of the most complex social issues we Americans face today.

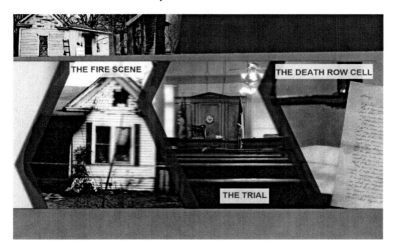

We envision one central website (a dynamic, curated, interactive platform) where most online activities and content will happen, link, intersect, and cross-fertilize. Upon first entering the site, the viewer will be given the choice to watch a three- to five-minute video that will introduce the story by describing the events from the fire up until Willingham's arrest. Alternately, they can choose to skip this and will be given a text summery and explanation of the site. Upon reaching the end of this introduction, the viewer will reach a home page where there will be the choice to create a log in or continue as a guest (similar to the motel lobby base in the web documentary Prison Valley *http://prisonvalley.arte.tv/*).

There, they can choose to enter one of three main areas, as follows:

1.   The Trial:

A virtual courtroom where the audience will be invited to be part of a jury and see how the Willingham trial actually unfolded. Visually, the courtroom consists of a quadrant split screen, with a still 2D image of the **Witness Stand** on the left where the testimonial videos will play, an **Evidence Locker** on the upper right which will list evidence viewed, the **Trial Minutes** on the lower right — a typed up document representing the actual Willingham trial minutes, which will serve as a way to navigate the evidence that is available.

This section will work in a number of ways: To begin with, there will be several **live events** scheduled in conjunction with law schools and high school social studies classes, as well as with pro- and anti-death penalty organizations. Working alongside the teachers, professors and members of these organizations, we will organize and invite groups of twelve to become virtual juries. Each jury member will log in on their own computers at a designated time and fill out a "Jury Selection" questionnaire. Once they complete the questionnaire, their data is gathered and they are passed on to the virtual trial.

Over the Witness Stand area, they will begin to view the trial: a series of two- to five-minute videos will present the evidence in the Willingham case as told in interviews with the witnesses who testified in the case, the prosecutor, the defense attorney and Willingham's family and friends. As each video segment is viewed, the title of that segment will show up in the Evidence Locker and will be highlighted in the Trial Minutes.

The juries will be in closed, moderated live chat rooms to discuss the evidence. They will then get to vote on whether or not they believe Willingham was guilty. After their decision, they will be shown analysis of the evidence that they originally saw, provided by various experts. They can reconsider their previous decision as they are given another opportunity to vote. The overall live trial experience will last approximately 45 minutes, depending on the deliberation time by each virtual jury.

We will track the results of these votes, which will be available to our partners and will show the various elements that may have affected the juries' ultimate decision, such as gender, geographical location, education level, what pieces of evidence they viewed, etc. The data gathered, as well as the transcriptions of the "jury's" deliberations, will all be available in the live archives.

During the timeframe of the live events as well as after the events are over, we will offer a **single-player version** of the jury. At any given time after the launch, if an individual comes to the site without an official live event invitation, they can go through the jury selection and trial process. This experience will include sections of dialogue from the live sessions as well as some created by our legal advising committee. The jurist will then be able to vote at the end of the trial and see demographic information about people who voted in a similar manner.

In addition to this single-player version, we are looking to open up the live event for participants to set up their own live virtual trials by inviting their friends or finding other interested participants, possibly through a Facebook integration.

We are developing the platform for **The Trial** with consultants who have extensive experience with customization for transmedia platforms.

The Trial will include:
- a number of two- to five-minute videos to present evidence and analysis
- an evidence locker that will allow the "jury" to review what evidence they have seen so far
- a progress bar that tracks what percentage of overall media has been viewed
- a Bailiff button that allows live juries to get help

2. The Fire Scene:

Here the audience can play the part of the fire investigator. They are led through a 3D-modeled recreation of the scene of the Willingham fire, using the actual fire investigators' video walk-through as well as fire scene photos. The user's journey can go anywhere from five to twenty minutes, depending on the individual user's choices.

Throughout the house, pop-up tags will show up for various burn patterns that audiences can click on to see and hear the original fire investigators' analysis and conclusions and then debunk them with the help of video footage of Fire Expert Gerald Hurst.

In addition, several of the most crucial elements used to determine that this fire was an arson (such as the pour patterns) will be analyzed using actual fire re-creations that we will be filming with our partner Tory Belleci of Discovery Channel's *Mythbusters*.

The Fire Scene will also be developed in a more detailed and longer playing version as a mobile and tablet application.

3. **The Death Row Cell:**

A lonely cell on death row, created using stock video footage from the jail that we stylize and loop to create a back drop, onto which we will overlay the actual of letters written by Willingham. We see the letters with the words animating as they are spoken, and hear the words as an actor's voice reads them.

In this segment, there will be a number of letters that would be available right away. After viewing those letters, the user will have the option to write a letter as a pen pal, asking the questions you would want answered about the case, the trial, life on death row, etc. This will then unlock more letters, sorted by theme or by timeline. Until they are unlocked, the themes and timeline will be visible but greyed out, to give the user an idea of how much material is still available.

Additionally, the user can unlock certain areas by completing more of The Trial or The Fire Scene. Throughout the period leading to the launch and during the live events, we will also use the Twitter feed to release excerpts of Willingham's letters, in order to help the users better understand Willingham's perspective. By divvying the letters into these bite-size pieces, it makes the letters more accesible to users and gives us a way to build Willigham as a person in their mind.

These three areas are all interconnected. In any one of these areas, at different times, the audience will be prompted to make a choice to follow through with one idea, to leave the area they are in, in order to learn more about a topic that may interest them in one of the other areas.

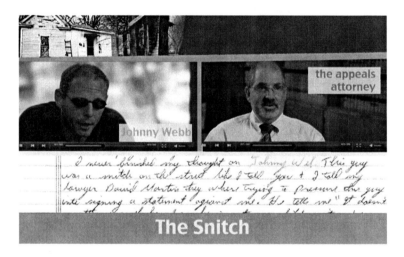

For example, in the trial, one of the elements used as evidence to convict Willingham was the testimony of Johnny Webb, a jailhouse snitch, who claimed that Willingham confessed to him. In The Trial section, we will hear from Webb in an exclusive interview. Later in the analysis of the trial, audiences will be given the option to "Learn more about Jail House Snitches" from legal experts discussing the use of jailhouse snitch testimony as it poses special challenges to fairness and accuracy in criminal trials. If the audience wants to learn still more about Johnny Webb, they can then select that option, which will take them to The Death Row Cell where they can hear Willingham's letters that talk about Webb and his interaction with him.

We feature multiple points of entry, thus engaging audiences that might be drawn to this story for different reasons, whether it's the logical appeal of analyzing the trial, the intellectual curiosity of understanding the science of fire or the emotional draw of hearing the alternately hopeful, angry and incredibly sad voice of Cameron Todd Willingham. *Burned* will allow the audience to engage and interact with the film as well as learn more about the issues at hand: statistics and facts about the death penalty, scientific analysis of fire scenes and more.

4. Community Engagement Overview

Target audience

There is already an extensive base of social justice in places across the United States, as well as civil liberty organizations actively working towards the abolition of the death penalty. While we hope to engage a wide general-public audience, the target audience for continued discussion and elevation of *Burned* would be comprised of criminal justice and fire investigation professionals.

The legal community in the United States is already engaged in a conversation about the death penalty. In the Bay Area, the lawyers that we've come in contact with are particularly interested in *Burned* because a large majority of them recognize problems within the judicial system when it comes to the death penalty. They see *Burned* as a valuable tool to open up the topic with the rest of the country. *Burned* can be highly effective in law schools nationwide, where examining the death penalty is often its own course, if not an entire section. At Boalt Hall UC Berkeley, for example, a Death Penalty Clinic was created because of the complexity of death penalty litigation and the importance of our legal system's greatest punishment.

The death penalty is a topic that draws diametrically opposed reactions. We aim to engage both sides of the argument, as well as the even larger pool of undecided or neutral viewers, by creating a visually compelling project that recounts the horror of what happens when an average person, considered a societal misfit, falls into a perfect storm of bad evidence, rigid opinion and flawed justice. We believe our project can help incite civil discourse surrounding the death penalty by providing education on the nature of fire and the evolution of fire investigation, and help a nation of people come to a common place of discussion.

We have crafted a robust community engagement plan that aims to:

1. Engage the traditional documentary viewer interested in exploring new worlds and broadening their personal understanding of the U.S. legal system and the death penalty;

2. Attract new, young and diverse audiences to an educational media event;

3. Utilize new technologies to make Willingham's story relevant to a technically-savvy audience and create a digital portal for audiences to interact with the content;

4. Provide avenues for audiences to engage with the legal system and consider the impact of this case on their lives through the effective use of community partnerships; and

5. Help organizational partners integrate the film and web-based content into their ongoing educational work beyond the broadcast.

A number of key elements will weave the effort together. The components of the multi-platform project will include:

- One digital outreach portal that will offer an interactive space that will serve as a centralized destination for the project — this space will contain the three interconnected areas mentioned above (courthouse, fire scene and death row cell)

- In addition, the online portal will include forums, civic engagement tools, educational resources;

- A mobile / tablet application that would run a more extensive version of the Fire Scene;

- Targeted marketing campaign to reach our core audience;

- User-friendly materials that will help our target audience use the films as ongoing tools for education;

- The **Impact Dashboard** — Thanks to our affiliation with BAVC, we will be early adopters of the Impact dashboard and provide the data tracked to our partner organizations. This toolkit would help track and map engagement activities that develop out of the screenings and online efforts;

- Evaluation process that documents the techniques used to engage the target audiences for future multi-platform projects.

In addition, we will be leveraging social sites to create more opportunities for "real-time" engagement and further promote the project, making it accessible to our partner organizations:

Short video podcasts culled from the film and interviews with the producers, scholars and characters that can be streamed or downloaded via mobile devices and the website. These two- to five-minute videos and podcasts will be released in the months leading up to the launch as a way to build anticipation and cultivate unique visitors to the website, but also to extend the reach of the content into communities who expect customized media content.

A customized Facebook page that will serve to drive traffic to the digital portal, promote events and community screenings, create a base to energize and engage *Burned* fans and offer opportunities for audiences to discuss the media and engage in real-time conversation. The producers will communicate with audiences and participants through this page beginning in the production phase of the projects.

An ongoing Twitter feed (live now @Burned_themovie) that is releasing interesting facts and statistics related to the death penalty, news related to the Willingham case or death penalty law as well as production updates from the *Burned* team. During the months leading up to the launch of the site and the live events, we will also be tweeting excerpts of Willingham's letter to tease the content and build a sense of his time spent on Death Row. There will also be an official hashtag for the experience and discussions to engage the audience into bookclub-like discussions.

Campaign Materials

As a service to the partner organizations, *Burned* will develop and disseminate user-friendly materials that will support community and educational use of the project. The materials will be available for download from our digital outreach portal and will include Resource and Discussion Guides, House Meeting Kits and high school curriculum. We will also work with law schools to determine how best to support use of the project for Death Penalty Clinics, such as the one that exists at UC Berkeley.

Campaign Evaluation

We plan to incorporate the **Impact Dashboard**, a tool that will enable our partner organizations to develop measurable outcomes and assess them before and after the *Burned* launch. We will develop an audience survey for community screenings to measure the reach and impact that the film has on target groups – such as young adults, diverse populations, etc. To assess the effectiveness of the web components, we will employ Google Analytics to track the number of individual impressions and click-thrus to the digital outreach portal. The results will be shared with the field as a case study of transmedia interactive campaigns.

5. Producing Team

Jessie Deeter - Director/Producer

Jessie Deeter is a Piedmont, California-based documentary producer, director and journalist. She was the Producer of *Who Killed the Electric Car?*, which premiered at Sundance and was released by Sony Pictures Classics in 2006. Jessie also directed, produced, shot and wrote the hour-long documentary *Taking Guns from Boys*, about disarming Liberia after a bloody civil war. The full film aired on PBS affiliate KQED in 2007 FRONTLINE/World in 2005. Jessie directed and produced the Frontline documentary about Todd Willingham, *Death By Fire*, which aired on PBS in 2010.

Sara Maamouri - Producer/Editor

Sara is a documentary filmmaker and editor based in San Francisco. She began her career working for several Frontline documentaries as well as the Academy Award–nominated *Promises* and *The Future of Food*. Recent projects include ITVS-LINCS awardee, *The Music's Gonna Get You Through*, directed by Gabrielle Mullem and premiered in Spring 2010. She most recently edited the Cyprus documentary *In This Waiting*, a feature-length film which tells the stories of seven Cypriots of either Turkish or Greek origin, who have lost loved ones in the civil war in 1974 and are just now beginning to learn of their fates. *In This Waiting* premiered at Thessaloniki Documentary Festival in March 2011.

Thaddeus Wadleigh - Director of Photography

Thaddeus was awarded Best Cinematography for the feature film, *Loco Love*, shot in 24P HD for HDFEST 2003. He has photographed in both HD and film projects for Universal, Tri Star, Warner Brothers, MTV, Artisan, HBO, VH-1, TNN, Spike TV, Trio, Bravo, and many others. He was the Director of Photography for *Who Killed the Electric Car?*

Chris A. Peterson - Consulting Editor

Chris specializes in independent film and original television projects, and has completed theatrical and broadcast releases for Sony, Universal, NBC, HBO, Cinemax, PBS, BBC, Bravo, Sundance, Fox, Discovery and the History Channel. Recent credits include independent feature *Miss Nobody*, starring Leslie Bibb and Adam Goldberg, and *Who Killed the Electric Car?*

Sarah Gibson - Consulting Producer

Sarah is an award-winning producer whose notable credits include two Sundance Film Festival Competition features; *I.O.U.S.A* in 2008 and *Small Town Gay Bar* in 2006 with Executive Producer Kevin Smith. *I.O.U.S.A*, featuring Warren Buffet and Alan Greenspan was distributed theatrically in August 2008. She is currently producing Ondi Timoner's feature documentary, *Cool It!*

Lisa Long - Transmedia Expert

Lisa Long is the co-founder and a director of Six to Start, an award-winning transmedia company based in London, UK. Six to Start counts among its clients the BBC, Channel 4, Penguin, and Muse. Lisa has worked on games across a variety of custom platforms as well as games that take advantage of existing social networking technology such as Facebook and Twitter. In addition to her duties at Six to Start, Lisa serves as a consultant for d-media, a UK network bringing together the film and digital industries to further development of digital storytelling platforms.

Arshad Tayyeb - Multimedia Software Developer

Arshad Tayyeb is currently a lead software developer at doubleTwist, and a software industry veteran. He has worked on software that has shipped to millions of users at Netscape, AOL, Gracenote, Sony, Medialets, and doubleTwist, and helped developers around the world. He has been writing iOS applications since 2007, and is a consultant for iOS and Mac technologies. Has helped companies develop and ship multimedia and web-integrated applications.

Scott San Filippo - Multimedia Software Developer

Scott San Filippo is an innovative information architect and software developer who led several pioneering technical projects in the digital entertainment industry at Electronic Arts, Liquid Audio, and Gracenote. Scott is now a technical consultant for several digital media and traditional companies, helping them with their mobile and web strategies and development.

Shimrit Berman - Graphic Designer

Shimrit Berman is a web and multimedia developer and designer based in Berkeley, California. With extensive experience in print journalism, television and radio, and strong background in graphic design and web programming, she always traveled in the intersecting area of the two worlds. Upon her graduation from the masters program of the Journalism department in UC Berkeley where she focused in online media, she began collabrating with film directors, writers, musicians, photographers and entrepreneurs, devising and developing online environments for their needs and goals, using a variety of platforms and applications. Among her projects are websites for the documentary films *City of Borders*, *Arresting Ana* and *Pizzo*, as well as current website development for Alan Squire Publishing, founded by bestselling writer James Patterson.

Scott Kravitz - Animator

6. Partnerships and Advisors

Burned has partnered with the following organizations (Letters of Support are available upon request):

- **BAVC – Media & Social Change Consultants:** The Bay Area Video Coalition (BAVC) inspires social change by enabling the sharing of diverse stories through art, education and technology.

BAVC's vision is to support diverse groups of independent media makers obtain the skills they need to tell, distribute, and preserve their own stories and the stories of their communities through existing and emerging media formats and outlets. As Mediamaker Fellow for 2011, Producer Sara Maamouri is working with BAVC to develop *Burned*.

- **Voice of Witness** – A division of McSweeney's Books, founded by Dave Eggers. Dave Eggers and Lola Vollen are on our advisory board and are consulting with us during the development and launch phase of *Burned* and have ideas about engaging online communities to create awareness about our project.

- **Discovery Channel's** *Mythbusters* – We have met with Tory Belleci of *Mythbusters* and are developing a partnership, using the scientific analysis from *Burned* to develop a stand-alone episode about the Willingham fire, which we are pitching to The Science Channel and The Discovery Channel. The fire footage we acquire for this episode will then serve in the Fire Scene segment of *Burned*.

- **Death Penalty Focus** – is one of the largest nonprofit advocacy organizations in the nation dedicated to the abolition of capital punishment through public education; grassroots and political organizing; original research; media outreach; local, state and nationwide coalition building; and the education of religious, legislative and civic leaders about the death penalty and its alternatives.

- **Wildfire Post-Production Studios** – Wildfire is offering to support *Burned* by providing free post-production services (Color correction, Online & Sound mixing) and other finishing work at their studios in Los Angeles.

- **UC Berkeley Boalt Hall Death Penalty Clinic** – The program staff are advising us on the structure of the legal aspects of our project, to make sure the trial section is accurate, authentic and informative. In addition, students enrolled with the clinic will participate in live jury events.

7. Project Timeline

We have been developing *Burned* for seventeen months, and we are now fundraising aggressively. We have completed 90% of filming but are still planning to film fire scene experiments to use in the Fire Scene section.

Over the next eleven months we aim to hit the following deadlines: (Please note: Many of these steps overlap)

1. Sept. 1st, 2011:   Story Research & Development
2. Sept. 1st - Dec. 20th: Story and Video Segment Editing
                              Content evaluation with our consultants
3. Oct. 15th - Nov. 11th: Rough platform design
4. Nov. 14th - Feb. 24th: Site and Application architecture and design
5. Technical Design and Development (Site and Application) - 3-6 months
6. Jan. 2nd - Feb. 6th   Animation & Graphic
7. Feb. 6th - 17th   Video Online (sound and color correction)
8. Feb. 20th - Mar. 2nd   Overall Platform Integration Testing
9. March 9th begins   Live Launch

During this timeframe, we estimate the following expenses:
1. 2 iOS developers or an agency for 3 months - Estimate: $100,000
2. 2 Web developers or an agency for 3-6 months - $50-100k
3. 1 Graphic Designer for 1-2 months - $30,000
4. 1 Animator for 1-2 months - $15,000
5. Composer and Sound mixing - $25,000
6. Editing costs (Editor, Assistant Editor) - $50,000

These expenses do not include the film finishing costs, which will be provided to us at no charge courtesy of Wildfire Post-Production Studios (Color correction, sound mixing and online). With full funding, we would plan to launch a fully functioning version of the website and tablet application in the Spring of 2012, which we hope to time in conjunction with a digital launch at SXSW 2012.

8. Requested Funds

With the funding we are requesting, we would focus on building the website version of our project which can stand alone, with the three main components cited in Project Description.

1 web developer for 3 months	$45,000
1 graphic designer for 1 month	$20,000
1 producer / project lead for 4 months	$15,000
1 film editor for 4 months	$10,000
1 animation / graphics	$7,000
1 assistant editor part-time for 4 months	$2,000
TOTAL REQUESTED	**$99,000**

CHAPTER 17

MUSIC CLEARANCES AND LICENSES

By Maureen Ryan,
author of *Producer to Producer*

This information is from Maureen Ryan's book, Producer to Producer, *courtesy of Maureen Ryan and Michael Wiese Publications.*

PLAN FOR SUCCESS

You may ask, "What do music licenses have to do with raising money for your film?" The reason it is so important is it is one of the ways you protect your film's investors. Once you have raised the money and shot your film, you need to make sure you properly obtain all of your music licenses so your film is available to be sold and distributed.

Too often filmmakers aren't diligent about their music clearances. The film premieres at a film festival and they get approached by a company to distribute it (!), but now they have a big problem. They never cleared the music rights for the film, and the interested company can't purchase it until the film's soundtrack is properly licensed.

So it is crucial to plan for your success. Get all the proper clearances, so when you are approached by a distributor you are willing, ready, and able to take the deal! You owe it to everyone who worked on the film and everyone who funded it.

CREATING A MUSIC SOUNDTRACK

A music soundtrack is usually comprised of music that was previously produced and is commercially available and/or music composed specifically for the film by a composer. Either way, you'll need to obtain the music rights.

Music rights consist of two kinds of rights for each piece of music — the Master Recording License and the Synchronization (Sync) License. A *master recording license* refers to the rights for the performance of a piece of music — e.g., Bruce Springsteen's recording of "Santa Claus Is Coming to Town." These rights are usually obtained through the record label that made the recording — in this example — Columbia Records, a subsidiary of Sony Music. The *synchronization (sync) license* pertains to the rights for the song itself and is usually held by a publishing company that represents the person(s) who wrote the song. The writers of the song "Santa Claus Is Coming to Town" are J. Fred Coots and Haven Gillespie. The publishing companies are EMI Feist Catalog, Inc. and Haven Gillespie Music.

To negotiate the master recording license, contact the record company and ask for the licensing department. Doing an Internet search is a good way to track down this information. If you have a CD of the song, you can get the information from the cover. To find out who the publisher is for the sync license you can search the websites of the two major publishing groups — www.BMI.com and www.ASCAP.com. As the producer, you need to contact each company — Columbia Records, EMI Feist, and Haven Gillespie — and request the rights you require for your project. This process is often called *clearing the rights* to a song.

WHAT RIGHTS DO YOU NEED?

Once you have the contact information for your music, you'll need to figure out what rights you require for your film and how long you need the license. Here are the rights generally available for any piece of music:
    U.S. theatrical
    U.S. network television
    U.S. cable television
    U.S. DVD
    U.S. VOD (Video on Demand)

International theatrical
International network television
International cable television
International DVD
International VOD (Video on Demand)
Internet/Web
Film festivals
Educational

For international rights, they can be sold per region or per country, i.e., UK/Ireland, Spain, France, etc. If you can afford it, the best rights level to ask for is all of the above. That is usually referred to as "all media worldwide." The other consideration is the length of time you own the rights. The longest time period is usually referred to as "in perpetuity." If you can afford "all media worldwide, in perpetuity" it's perfect, you are covered for every scenario forever.

There is one other designation you'll need to ask for, which is either an "exclusive" or "non-exclusive" license. Usually non-exclusive is enough for a film soundtrack and it allows the rights owners to license the same song to others for other purposes. Exclusive would mean the publisher and the recording artist couldn't license to other entities. Decide what you need before you contact publishers and record labels.

Depending on the artist, the song, the record label, and the publisher, you may not be able to afford all the rights you want or need. That's when negotiation comes into play. The publisher may be willing to give you the sync license for all media worldwide, in perpetuity for a reasonable sum, but you can't afford the rights for the specific performance on the record. In regards to the Bruce Springsteen example, you might be able to obtain an affordable price for the sync license, but Springsteen's record label will require a fee that is well beyond what you can afford to pay. You could decide to record your own version of the song with a singer that would be an affordable alternate. Then you would do a "buyout" with that vocalist so you had the rights for all media worldwide, in perpetuity. Or you may decide you have to have the Springsteen's version, but can only afford the film festival rights for two years. If you decide to license for film festivals only, you might be taking a big gamble.

If the film does well at film festivals and a company wants to distribute your film, you may not be able to afford all the rights you will need to accept the deal. The amount of money paid to you for the distribution rights for your film may not be enough to acquire the necessary rights for the song. Then you'll have to face a hard decision to turn down the distribution deal, re-record the song by a different artist, or replace the song with a different one on the soundtrack. You would need to make sure that the distribution company would still want your film if you had a different song on the soundtrack.

My advice is to not take that gamble. Always plan for the success of your film and make sure to lock down all the rights you need for all markets, domestic and internationally. If you cannot afford to do that when you are finishing your film and want to take it out to film festivals only as the first step, then negotiate the future purchase price for all rights while you lock down the film-festival rights only. That way you will know how much the additional rights will cost in the future and it won't suddenly increase if your film becomes successful afterwards. You'll know what your music licensing costs will be and you will know what you need to get for a distribution fee if you go to sell the film, in order to cover the music licensing costs.

PUTTING IN THE LICENSE REQUEST

Now that you know what rights to acquire, you need to decide when to ask for them in your pre/production/post timeline. If the song is sung or heard as diegetic sound in the film, then you need to obtain the rights before you shoot the scene during production.

For example, if you have a scene with a character singing a lullaby to her baby before the child falls asleep, you'll need to obtain the sync rights for the song from the publisher. You'll also need to ask the actor to sign a master recording rights license for her recording of the song. If a band is performing a song on a stage in a scene in which people are dancing to the tune, you'll need to obtain both the master recording rights to the performance and the sync rights for the song the band performs. This needs to happen before you film the scene. If you don't secure the rights for all the territories you need, then you run the enormous risk of not being able to use any of the footage you shot for that scene in your final cut.

The only way to remedy this kind of problem in the edit room would be to get the rights to another song with the same beat to match the cadence of the actors who are dancing and the musicians who are performing. Then you would need to cut it into the soundtrack and then edit the footage in a way that would never show any of the musicians or singers in close up. It is incredibly difficult, perhaps impossible, and a huge waste of time and energy in postproduction. It would be much smarter to get the rights before you plan to shoot the performance of the song on-camera.

The use of other music for your film's soundtrack that is seen being played in a scene should be acquired when you are fairly certain you will need it in the final cut. You want to contact the record labels and publishers early enough so there is enough time to get an answer before you have locked picture. If you find that you can't afford the rights, you have time to replace it with another piece of music. You also don't want to waste time on negotiating for rights to music that ends up on the cutting room floor, so you need to figure out what music has a good chance of ending up in the final soundtrack and begin contacting the appropriate entities for the rights. Lastly, if you have several recordings that are on the same record label, it may help you to negotiate a better deal by waiting until you have the list of everything on that one label before sending in your request.

The timing on getting rights is tricky because it can take many months to successfully negotiate a license. Start at least three to five months ahead of time for major record labels. They have more requests and bureaucracy so you need a longer lead time.

MUSIC RIGHTS REQUEST LETTER FORMAT

Finding out who owns the master recording rights and the sync rights to any given piece of music can require a bit of detective work. If you have the CD that the recording is from, you should be able to get the name of the record label and the publisher from the printed material that comes with the CD packaging.

If you downloaded the music or don't know where the song came from you can use the Internet to do the research. The first place to start is the major performing rights society websites — *www.BMI.com* (Broadcast Music, Inc.), *www.ASCAP.com* (American Society of Composers, Authors and Publishers) and *www.SESAC.com* (Society of European Stage Authors & Composers) — they collect the fees and distribute the royalties to the songwriters and publishers. They each have fairly powerful search engines that allow you to type in the name of the song and give you the publishing information and often the name of the album it was released on. From there you can find the contact information for the sync and master recording rights. Remember to search each publishing website because they are separate organizations, and usually a song is only registered under one of the groups.

If you still need more information, do an Internet search for the name of the song and/or the artist. You can look up the discography for the title of the album and the record label. From there you can search for the label's contact info on the Web. Once you have the contact info for the publisher and the record label, call them and ask for the music rights person. You will be given the name and number for that person or an email address. Often the phone number is connected to an answering machine that will give you a list of all the information they require before processing your rights request. Usually the request needs to be in writing and sent via fax or email. Send the following information:

1. Title of recording/composition.
2. Album title.
3. Artist/band/orchestra name.
4. Usage you require, e.g., background music under pictures, sung by the lead character. Also describe what is seen on the screen when the music is heard, e.g., someone being shot or a family driving in a car on a highway.
5. Short description of your film.
6. Time length of usage, specify minutes and seconds and if it is repeated later in the film, state the time length for the additional usage.
7. What territories you are requesting, e.g., all media worldwide in perpetuity.
8. State if it is for exclusive or non-exclusive use.
9. What you can afford to pay for the rights (or gratis) and if you have already made deals for the same amount of money to other publishers/record labels.

NEGOTIATING THE MUSIC RIGHTS

The record label or the publisher own the rights and they want to get as much money as possible for them and you want to pay as little as possible. Therein lies the negotiation process. Use the sales skills that you perfected throughout the making of your film. Your film will give exposure to the songwriter or performer by being included on the film's soundtrack. There will be film festivals, DVDs, maybe a television or Internet sale, etc. Added exposure is not an incentive for a well-known musical artist, but for an up-and-coming band or singer it should be of some value.

To increase your chances of a successful negotiation try to find a mutual friend or contact who can bring your request directly to the artist or songwriter. Getting in direct contact can help make a much stronger case for your request. If you go through the label or the manager, you could get a "no" without the artist even knowing about it because the manager deemed the monetary offer too small. But if you can send the artist a copy of your film with a beautiful handwritten note from the director explaining why the song is brilliant and essential to the film, you might get a wholly different answer. This happened on a film I produced several years ago. We got a quick "no" from the manager but then sent a copy of the film and letter to the artist directly. He really liked the project and gave us the rights for an affordable sum. Writer/director/producer Paul Cotter (*Bomber*, *Estes Avenue*) has some advice regarding music soundtracks for low-budget films:

> "If you've got a tight budget, it's great to be flexible about the music and who you get on the soundtrack. The basic rule I follow is 'like attracts like.' If you've got no money, find bands that have no money. You're then on a level playing field and they're usually cool, understand your predicament, and are willing to play along. Just be honest and upfront with them, which is something you should be with everybody (honesty goes a long, long way in low-budget filmmaking). Also, they need the publicity you can give them. Don't go for Lionel Ritchie. He's loaded and doesn't have time for riffraff like us."

MOST FAVORED NATION

The term *most favored nation* (MFN) refers to the concept of paying every-one the same amount of money for the same thing. It comes from inter-national trade agreements where each country signed to an agreement has the same terms as every other country. Music rights negotiation uses the concept of most favored nation as well. It is the industry practice to pay the same amount for the sync rights to the publisher as you do for the master recording rights to the record label. And usually you will pay the same amount for each of the rights per song. So if you are paying $500 for sync rights and $500 for master recording rights for one song, you will do that same deal for all of the other songs on the soundtrack. The only exception would be for a song by a very famous band, which would be a vastly higher number and would not be part of the MFN pricing system.

The best strategy for negotiating rights would be to go to the entity (pub-lisher or label) you think will give you the best deal first. If the song is a well-known composition being sung by an unknown performer, go to the record label first to make a deal. Once you have an affordable negotiated rate in writing, then you go to the publisher for that song. Let them know that you already got the master recording license for X amount and ask if they would be willing to give you the sync rights for the same amount. You'll use most favored nation when you are negotiating for the rights to several recordings. Let's say you have seven pieces of music you wish to clear — start with the five songs that will be the easiest and most affordable first. Then go to the last two and let them know that you have already negotiated the rights to most of your soundtrack and that the publishers and labels have agreed to X amount for the rights. Ask them to take the same deal for their song(s).

If they agree to it, be ready to send out the paperwork for signature. If not, you may have to agree to a higher amount for the last two songs to make the deal. If this happens, because it was all done on a MFN basis, you'll have to pay the higher amount to the first five publisher/labels, as well. It's like the tide in the ocean — it raises or lowers all boats equally.

If the higher amount for each composition proves to be too expensive, you may decide to replace the expensive songs for those that will accept the lower amount you negotiated for the first five compositions and complete your soundtrack with different music.

CHAPTER 18

FINANCING INDEPENDENT FILMS

A Conversation with
Entertainment Attorney Mark Litwak

Mark Litwak has been a donor for my Roy W. Dean Film and Video Grants for over fifteen years, and is a great patron of the art of filmmaking. Top filmmakers quote Mark on a daily basis. I sincerely believe his books are a good investment, whether you are new at filmmaking or a seasoned veteran. You will avoid problems and save money if you have a solid grasp of the legalities of the film industry. Visit Mark's website at *www.marklitwak. com*, where you can find more about his books and read many brilliant articles.

Mark, in your articles you talk about several ways to finance films. Which would you say is the most common and why?

There are several ways to finance films including by territory pre-sales, investors, studio funds or some combination. Many documentaries are funded with grants and donations.

The popularity of each financing method varies over time. At one time, a lot of pre-sales were being used to finance production, but right now it is very hard to do presales because there is a glut of completed films on the market, and buyers often prefer to license a completed film than take a chance on a project to be produced. Most first-time filmmakers do not have the track record and ability to attract the name actors necessary to make pre-sales.

FINANCING FEATURES

Nowadays filmmakers mostly rely upon equity investments for financing and production incentives such as tax breaks and refunds from various states and countries that help subsidize the making of a film. Puerto Rico offers a 40% rebate. Hawaii and Louisiana also have very generous incentives for investors. A listing of state, federal, and international incentives can be found at *www.marklitwak.com/resources/domestic_programs.html*.

Is Canada still subsidizing productions?

Yes, Canada provides incentives and so do many other countries. In addition to the incentives offered, at times there is a favorable exchange rate when converting U.S. dollars to Canadian dollars, which can be an added attraction. Likewise, in some countries in Eastern Europe production expenses are so low that the net effect is similar to shooting in a country offering a generous incentive.

Do foreign countries offer incentives?

New Zealand and Australia and many other countries have very popular programs to encourage production. The rules are subject to change so one must always check before assuming an incentive is available. Some incentives are capped to a certain dollar amount so that financing is essentially offered on a first come, first served basis, and if that year's funds have been exhausted you cannot obtain the incentive.

Mark, how early in production do you believe filmmakers should see an attorney?

It depends on the experience of the filmmaker and whether there are legal issues that need to be resolved. For a first timer pretty early, for an experienced filmmaker, he or she may not need help for a while. There are some filmmakers who may have a legal education and lots of practical experience, who may never need help from an attorney.

RELEASES AND COPYRIGHT

I know of cases where filmmakers did not get the appropriate releases and paperwork and ended up spending more on attorneys later in the production than they would have if they had consulted with one early in production.

That's often the case. Sometimes filmmakers produce a film and cannot obtain distribution for it because they did not properly secure their copyright. I know of a producer who did not get a release from an actor, and then lost touch with that actor, and could not locate him. This caused problems when it came time to demonstrate to the distributor that the filmmaker had rights to the actor's work.

In some instances if you are raising money from third parties, you need to see an attorney before you accept funds to make sure you are complying with the law. If the person giving you the money is doing so because they are making an investment, their interest is considered a security, unless the investor is actively involved in producing the film. And if securities are involved, then you need to comply with state and federal securities laws. You may need to make certain disclosures, which is usually done via a private placement memorandum (PPM). This document discloses all the risks of the investment to potential investors before you accept their money.

If someone wants to give you money as a gift, that is, with no expectations or obligations attached, mazel tov! Take the gift and thank them — you don't have to comply with the laws that govern investments, although gifts are sometimes taxable, and the gift giver may want to obtain a tax deduction.

In documentaries there are often donations of money or in-kind services. There may be gifts from family or friends or charitable contributions. In order for the person making the gift to receive a tax deduction they may want to give the money to a 501(c)(3) corporation, a type of nonprofit entity. If you don't have your own 501(c)(3) corporation, you can arrange with an existing one to serve as an umbrella organization for you. This enables the gift giver to receive a tax deduction and allows the filmmaker to make their film.

PRIVATE PLACEMENT MEMORANDUMS (PPM)

When filmmakers bring their film ideas to you, do you help them with the investment package?

Yes, we can prepare a private placement memorandum (PPM) and related documents.

Does the filmmaker give you the creative side?

Yes, in preparing the PPM the client supplies a synopsis of the story, a budget summary, and bios of the people involved. We take care of all of the legal disclosures, and all of the descriptions of how the movie business works, all the risk factors, and all the required legal notices.

What about ancillary rights of books or music? Does this go into the original package?

If you are making a feature, then ancillary rights and other sources of revenue can include home video, TV, book novelizations, soundtrack albums, merchandising, etc. The filmmaker can include these sources of revenue in the film's gross receipts and share them with investors. They can also be excluded from the revenues shared with investors, but this may discourage investors from participation in the project. At any rate, revenue from ancillary sources needs to be clearly addressed when dealing with investors.

GAP FINANCING

What is gap financing? Is it still popular?

Gap financing has to do with financing based on presales. Presales are when a filmmaker or a distributor approaches a distributor for a country, before the film is produced, and persuades this distributor to sign a contract to pay a license fee for the distribution rights to the film when it is completed. If the contracts are with reputable and solvent distributors, the filmmaker can use these contracts as collateral for a production loan. The filmmaker borrows money from a bank, which may lend 80 to 90% of the licensee fees in the contracts.

The filmmaker produces the film and delivers it to the distributors who have licensed it. The distributors pay their license fee to the bank that lent the funds to the producer. The filmmaker can make additional sales and earn profits from licenses to unsold territories.

Gap financing is when the bank is lending you more money than the value of the presale contracts. Let's say you make distribution deals for Germany, Spain, and Italy. The total face value of all these distribution deals is $500,000. But you need to borrow $600,000 to produce your film. The difference between the amount covered by licensee fees in the contracts, and the amount borrowed, is the gap. Banks charge additional interest for covering this gap because they are taking greater risk. If the film is made and you don't enter into any other licensing agreements, then the bank may suffer a loss. Gap financing is therefore more expensive to the filmmaker. Gap financing has become more difficult as prices for film licenses have fallen. Many films today are financed with a combination of equity and production incentives and perhaps some pre-sales as well. But it is very difficult today to finance films entirely with pre-sales.

BENEFITS OF AN LLC

I noticed that most producers create a Limited Liability Company instead of a C or S Corporation. Why is this?

An LLC has some advantages over a corporate form of organization in that it allows the profits and losses to be passed through to the members without being taxed at the company level. This avoids the problem of double taxation that you might have with a C corporation where the income for the corporation is taxed, and then the same money is taxed again when paid out in the form of dividends to investors. This reduces the flow of money back to the investors.

Another way to avoid double taxation is to set up a partnership, which passes profits and losses through to the partners. Here there is no taxation at the company level. But the problem with partnerships is that there is no limited liability for the general partners, only for the limited partners. So the general partners may be concerned that they may lose their houses or other assets if they are sued because the company has defaulted on its contractual obligations.

By setting up an LLC you have all of the advantages of the partnership form of business without the liability exposure imposed on the general partners. In an LLC you have managing members of the LLC, who are typically the producers, and the non-managing members, who are the investors. They both receive limited liability and there's no double taxation because the LLC can elect to have the IRS treat it like a partnership for tax purposes, that is, all the profits and losses pass through to the members. That's why the LLC form of business has become so popular. But LLCs are not always appropriate. In some instances it may be wiser to set up a corporation or a partnership, or use some other business entity.

What legal advice would you give to a first-time filmmaker?

I think it really depends on the filmmaker and their level of industry expertise. Filmmakers need to spend a lot of time perfecting their craft as a filmmaker, and also gain an understanding of the business side of the industry, including what they can and cannot do legally. They need to know what sort of rights they need to secure in order to make a film, and how to protect themselves from liability. They can do this by consulting an attorney or by reading and educating themselves.

Filmmakers also need to be aware of the marketplace for films, and whether there will be a market for their film once finished. It can be educational to visit film markets like AFM to learn which types of films attract distributors around the world.

I have written a book called *Deal Making in the Film and Television Industry*, which is a primer for filmmakers to learn about many of the legal issues involved in production.

Is this available on your website at *www.marklitwak.com*?

Yes, and at Amazon.com and most bookstores. It is widely available. The publisher is Silman-James Press.

Independent Film Financing
by Mark Litwak

The following was written and edited by Mark Litwak. (*Author's note*: These materials are offered for use as a teaching tool only. They are designed to help you understand some of the legal issues you may encounter in the entertainment business and enable you to better communicate with your lawyer. They are not offered as legal advice, nor should they be construed as such. They are not a substitute for consulting with an attorney and receiving advice based on your facts and circumstances. Moreover, the cases and laws cited are subject to change and they may not apply in all jurisdictions.)

Independent films can be financed in a variety of ways. In addition to film-makers using their own funds to make a movie, the most common methods are: 1) loans; 2) investor financing; 3) borrowing against pre-sales (a loan against distribution contracts); and 4) distributor-supplied financing.

Loans

Loans can be secured or unsecured. A secured loan is supported or backed by security or collateral. When one takes out a car or home loan, the loan is secured by that property. If the person who borrows money fails to repay the loan, the creditor may take legal action to have the collateral sold and the proceeds applied to pay off the debt.

An unsecured loan has no particular property backing it. Credit card debt and loans from family or friends may be unsecured. If a debtor defaults on an unsecured loan, the creditor can sue for repayment and force the sale of the debtor's assets to repay the loan. If the debtor has many debts, however, the sale of his property may not be sufficient to satisfy all creditors. In such a case, creditors may end up receiving only a small portion of the money owed them.

A secured creditor is in a stronger position to receive repayment. In the event of a default, designated property (the secured property) will be sold and all the proceeds will be applied first to repay the secured creditor's debt. Unsecured creditors will share in whatever is left, if anything.

The advantage of a loan, from a legal point of view, is that the transaction can often be structured in a fairly simple and inexpensive manner. A short promissory note can be used and the transaction often is not subject to the complex security laws that govern many investments. Thus, there is usually no need to prepare a private placement memorandum (PPM). Keep in mind that if the agreement between the parties is labeled a "loan," but in reality it is an investment, the courts will likely view the transaction as an investment. Giving a creditor a "piece of the back-end," or otherwise giving the creditor equity in the project, makes the transaction look like an investment.

The difference between a loan and an investment has to do with risk. With a loan, the entity that borrows funds, the debtor, is obligated to repay the loan and whatever interest is charged, regardless of whether the film is a flop or a hit. The creditor earns interest but does not share in the upside potential (profits) of a hit. Since the creditor is entitled to repayment even if the film is a flop, the creditor does not share in the risk of the endeavor. Of course, there is some risk with a loan because loans are not always repaid, especially unsecured loans that don't have any collateral backing them. That risk is minimal, however, compared to the risk of an equity investment.

In a pre-sale agreement, a buyer licenses or pre-buys movie distribution rights for a territory before the film has been produced. The deal works something like this: Filmmaker Henry approaches Distributor Juan to sign a contract to buy the right to distribute Henry's next film. Henry gives Juan a copy of the script and tells him the names of the principal cast members. Juan has distributed several of Henry's films in the past. He paid $50,000 for the right to distribute Henry's last film in Spain.

The film did reasonably well and Juan feels confident, based on Henry's track record, the script, and the proposed cast, that his next film should also do well in Spain. Juan is willing to license Henry's next film sight unseen before it has been produced. By buying distribution rights to the film now, Juan is obtaining an advantage over competitors who might bid for it. Moreover, Juan may be able to negotiate a lower license fee than what he would pay if the film were sold on the open market. So Juan signs a contract agreeing to buy Spanish distribution rights to the film. Juan does not have to pay (except if a deposit is required) until completion and delivery of the film to him.

Henry now takes this contract and a dozen similar contracts with buyers to the bank. Henry asks the bank to lend him money to make the movie with the distribution contracts as collateral. Henry is "banking the paper." The bank will not lend Henry the full face value of the contracts, but instead will discount the paper and lend a smaller sum. So if the contracts provide for a cumulative total of $1 million in license fees, the bank might lend Henry $800,000. In some circumstances banks are willing to lend more than the face value of the contracts (so-called gap financing) and charge higher fees.

Henry uses this money to produce his film. When the movie is completed, he delivers it to the companies that have already licensed it. They in turn pay their license fees to Henry's bank to retire Henry's loan. The bank receives repayment of its loan plus interest. The buyers receive the right to distribute the film in their territory. Henry can now license the film in territories that remain unsold. From these revenues Henry makes his profit.

Juan's commitment to purchase the film must be unequivocal, and his company financially secure, so that a bank is willing to lend Henry money on the strength of Juan's promise and ability to pay. If the contract merely states that the buyer will review and consider purchasing the film, this commitment is not strong enough to borrow against. Banks want to be assured that the buyer will accept delivery of the film as long as it meets certain technical standards, even if artistically the film is a disappointment. The bank will also want to know that Juan's company is fiscally solid and likely to be in business when it comes time for it to pay the license fee. If Juan's company has been in business for many years, and if the company has substantial assets on its balance sheet, the bank will usually lend against the contract.

The bank often insists on a completion bond to ensure that the filmmaker has sufficient funds to finish the film. Banks are not willing to take much risk. They know that Juan's commitment to buy Henry's film is contingent on delivery of a completed film. But what if Henry goes over budget and cannot finish the film? If Henry doesn't deliver the film, Juan is not obligated to pay for it, and the bank is not repaid its loan.

To avoid this risk, the bank wants an insurance company, the completion guarantor, to agree to put up any money needed to complete the film should it go over budget. Before issuing a policy, a completion guarantor will carefully review the proposed budget and the track record of key production personnel. Unless the completion guarantor is confident that the film can be brought in on budget, no policy will issue. These policies are called completion bonds.

First-time filmmakers may find it difficult to finance their films through pre-sales. With no track record of successful films to their credit, they may not be able to persuade a distributor to pre-buy their work. How does the distributor know that the filmmaker can produce something their audiences will want to see? Of course, if the other elements are strong, the distributor may be persuaded to take that risk. For example, even though the filmmaker may be a first-timer, if the script is from an acclaimed writer, and several big-name actors will participate, the overall package may be attractive.

The terms of an agreement between the territory buyer (licensor) and the international distributor can be quite complex. Parties may disagree about the meaning of terms used in their agreements. The following terms are standard IFTA definitions, which are generally accepted in the industry. They are used to interpret whatever document they are attached to.

Equity Investments
An equity investment can be structured in a number of ways. For example, an investor could be a stockholder in a corporation, a non-managing member of a Limited Liability Company (LLC), or a limited partner in a partnership.

An investor shares in potential rewards as well as the risks of failure. If a movie is a hit, the investor is entitled to receive his investment back and share in proceeds as well. Of course, if the movie is a flop, the investor may lose his entire investment. The producer is not obligated to repay an investor his loss.

Mark also has Independent Financing for Filmmakers on *www.marklitwak.com* and a copy is on *www.fromtheheartproductions.com* under financing information.

CHAPTER 19

DISTRIBUTION —
WHAT DISTRIBUTORS WANT

An Interview with David Vasile
President of Dazzle Entertainment

Interview with David Vasile, former President of Anchor Bay Entertainment and now the owner and President of Dazzle Entertainment, which works as a sales agent, distributor and producer for features, docs, and television.

WHEN TO CONTACT A DISTRIBUTOR

David, your company, Dazzle Entertainment, distributes excellent films. Tell me when in the filmmaking process a filmmaker or their producer or sales agent should contact a distributor?

A lot of times, you can approach too late or too early in your project development lifecycle. The right answer is: whenever it is finally prepared.

An ideal time is when you have the budget, have the cash in the bank, have your production crew, and have your cast attached, because those are the things that matter to the distributor. I think what filmmakers encounter is getting the distribution prior to having the film "in the can" can be a challenge, particularly if your team isn't tenured and doesn't have a track record of producing similar types of films.

What I recommend is you go to potential distributors when you have the funding, the cast, and something to talk about. At that point, generally, there's only one reason a distributor will make a commitment before the film is in the can. That is a belief that final production quality will be superior and that if they wait it will be more expensive and more contentious to secure distribution rights down the road. An early pickup is good for producers since this can be a major concern for many filmmakers and investors. "Will I secure distribution of the film? Will I be able to re-monetize our investment?" However, when you sell early, you often sell lower. It can boil down to your own confidence in your production. If you feel your film will be strong and compelling, securing distribution once the production is completed can often yield greater interest and stronger leverage during term sheet negotiations.

So, one of the things you can do is seriously concentrate on your PR. The best part of the film industry is we love talking about ourselves and that often provides opportunities for editorial coverage and other forms of industry recognition. If you can get some stir in the marketplace, intra-trade press coverage, like *Hollywood Reporter* or *Variety*, it starts people thinking and talking about your film. Then there's really little downside to going to a distributor and starting conversations. It's a great time to get feedback before you go into production. It's a great time to see if you can drum up a commitment or at least interest. And it helps you identify which distributors may be most interested when you've finished your film.

What materials should a filmmaker take to a first meeting with a distributor?

You want to demonstrate several things. The first thing to establish is that your project is real. You need to be prepared to talk about your funding, to show it, to show the cast and crew attachments you have, *not a series of letters of interest*. Remember, everyone in the food chain is basically looking at the same thing, and that is the marketability and merchantability of the film. They want to know how consumers will respond to the completed film. That is what's very difficult early in the process: to look at the film and make such an assessment.

So, it is important to bring with you something that shows you have an idea of the target audience for this particular film, and it needs to be credible. If you sit there and say "males from 18 to 49," okay, that's great. Then it's a very broad focus. The question is, can you credibly define your target audience? The better job you do of showing a path to consumer response and financial results, the more interest you will generate and the greater leverage you will have to negotiate fees and terms and conditions for your distribution agreements. This often impacts the marketing and promotional investments that the distribution will make during the release.

One of the most valuable exercises that I do is to give the consumer names. Sometimes it's a guy driving a pickup truck in Alabama who shops at Walmart, or a soccer mom from the Midwest who drives a minivan and shops at Target. When you really know who you're targeting, you picture them sitting in the audience and look for a moment at the film through their eyes. This is what you need to do, see the film like your potential customer and make decisions accordingly.

At the end of the day, the retailer who takes the DVD for distribution looks at it this way to decide what is going on their precious shelf space. And then, finally, the consumer will look at it to make a decision whether or not to part with their money. The broadcaster must decide if they will invest their ad revenues and schedule your film. The consumer will need to look at it and decide if they will watch your film versus the plethora of other programming options they have available. There is *nothing* more important than a consumer-focused view.

ELECTRONIC FILM MARKETING

What do you think of filmmakers who use social media like Facebook and start gathering fans while they're in production?

It's very valuable. I think that it becomes particularly valuable when there are material numbers to consider. Everyone knows that certain fan pages get millions of hits, and certain YouTube videos and trailers can generate traffic and awareness for the film, and that awareness can be invaluable. In the end, it's all about the consumer. No matter what the distributor thinks, no matter what the filmmaker thinks, ultimately, it's Joe Average American making a decision online at Netflix or making a purchase at Walmart that decides how much a film is really worth.

The audience that monetizes the film is what everyone guesses about. Everyone upstream from that moment is simply using the best information they have to try to anticipate "Joe's" purchasing response. And the bottom line is if a distributor is not excited about your project it's because they're seeing a different vision of the consumer. When you have created a Facebook page or another viral vehicle with meaningful numbers, then you've demonstrated the fact that people are interested in the movie. It's a powerful and objective way to show that an audience is there for your film. However, I encounter people all the time and say, "Well, did you tell them we have 120 fans on our Facebook page?" And I think, I know fourteen-year-olds with 5,000 fans and friends on their page but it doesn't mean they're going to be cast in the next *Home Alone*. The numbers must be meaningful.

We have a film we're working on now that we're developing in conjunction with the PGA (Professional Golfers Association of America). When we're talking to distributors and investors the fact that we have a commitment to utilize their two million membership-name database and actively promote the film to that community has a great impact because the numbers are meaningful.

Putting the film into the public eye, though, can be a harsh moment for many filmmakers. It's the moment when you really get a sense of what the marketplace looks like. And that can be a double-edged sword for you. You can get massive amounts of Facebook friends and exposure using the trailer and other promotional information and that's fantastic. But once people start giving some negative comments about it or it has light traffic, you could also be showing distributors that the marketplace for the film is thin or doesn't quite fit.

Another consideration is timing. The one thing we also know about consumers is that their attention span can be very limited. Generating market buzz and building an audience for the film can work well for you as long as your film is available to those consumers within a reasonable time frame before your film is forgotten.

However, the general rule of thumb is we want consumers to get excited about your film's release, watch it on TV, rent it or buy it. Yes, do your Facebook page, your website, and release the trailers on YouTube to begin promotion.

When it comes to promoting your film virally, electronically or through more traditional mechanisms, it is always in your best interest to put forth a whole-hearted effort. Slapping up a web page that doesn't draw traffic is not effective. And that ineffectiveness can actually hurt you in distribution. So, do it right.

THE VALUE OF A TRAILER

I know a filmmaker who just spent $20,000 for their feature trailer and made it to strengthen the financing package. How valuable is a film's trailer?

A trailer can be very important. By showing them a trailer you can demonstrate the kind of production values that can be delivered on the entire project. However, final trailers are advertising. Movies are a sensory experience. And a movie trailer allows filmmakers to expose the film visually to the consumer. It's actually funny that you asked about the importance of a trailer. Two weeks ago, we sold a film into three countries purely off its trailer. The screeners were still in transit.

So yes, trailers can be very important. And let's face it; if you're the acquisitions person at a film studio, you are seeing a tremendous volume of proposals and screeners each week. If they're not familiar with your film, it's logically a strong way to get them engaged in the content and explore further.

And then, the last thing I'll say about trailers is they often have a cost benefit to the distribution. Once a distributor looks at a film and has decided it's something they're interested in, then next they begin assessing their investment, acquisition, marketing, mastering, manufacturing, and promotional costs for the film against its earning potential. To some extent, there's a fixed pool of investment money, how much they're willing to invest. And every little bit counts. A good professional trailer can cost one of the distributors $15,000 to $20,000. So, if your trailer is good and they use it for the release, it saves them the cost of creating one. This can result in more dollars available for advances and other forms of marketing.

What is the job of a sales agent versus the job of a distributor?

Well, distributors are ultimately the people that take responsibility for getting your film in front of consumers. They have the relationships with the theater chains, retailers, websites, and broadcasters. So, for example, a DVD distributor is the one that has the retail relationships with Walmart, Target, Best Buy, etc., to actually sell the DVD. They have the relationships with the rental chains to secure placements, and often have profit sharing in those environments where they put the disks in and then take portions of the revenue. If they're helping you with your distribution to television, they're providing the sales functions and helping to leverage their relationship to get the film placed on TV. And of course, if they're handling the theatrical release, then they're the ones who are securing the screens and managing the release of the film into theaters. That's what a distributor does.

The sales agent is the person in between those two parties, the producer and the distributor. They serve a few different functions. One is that they maintain relationships between the distributors and the networks both internationally and domestically. For example, Dazzle Entertainment handles worldwide rights for most of our films. Because of our years of experience in this business, we have long-standing relationships which make it easier for us to open a door. However, the value is not just in the door opening, but also in understanding each distributor's capabilities (they vary greatly), their history of paying their royalty obligations, and each one's strength in reaching different consumer demographics and psychographics.

A lot of times, people think that opening doors is all a sales agent does for a producer. And if that is all your sales agent is doing, you don't have a good one. If you have enough tenacity, you'll probably get the phone answered or get in front of somebody by intercepting them in the hallway at AFM. But the real value is their detailed understanding of each distributor's capabilities. Each distributor has their quirks and each has their strengths. A sales agent navigates you through your options to understand more than just what's on the term. They offer a wealth of knowledge about what each distributor is capable of delivering.

They handle the front line of the negotiations for you, which again — especially when you get into things like TV which is not really driven off consumer demand, but driven off of arbitrary licensing fees that are out in the marketplace. Sales agents keep their finger on the pulse of the marketplace. That knowledge is critical in determining a good deal versus a bad deal and in insuring that you receive competitive contract terms. They are very familiar with the distribution contracts and common negotiating points. Sales agents are as critical to the business terms as lawyers are to the legal terms of such contracts.

The bad news is, no two contracts ever look alike in distribution. There are certain structures and concepts that are common. They're important concepts because distribution contracts as a whole are not defined in extraordinary detail. So, many concepts within these agreements are flexible, which can make it challenging to hold your distributor accountable for doing the job they committed to doing. A sales agent can help you, working in cooperation with your attorneys, to secure the most favorable agreements possible. And then, once a deal is completed, usually the agents continue to work with the distributors on royalty reporting, expense reporting, marketing, release, etc. on behalf of the producers.

Sales agents, such as *www.DazzleEntertainment.com*, have a good understanding of the marketplace as well. We look at royalty reports, and not only do we chase the revenue, but we can help to validate the reporting and make sure that the distributor' paperwork is accurate. So sales agents are really a support tool for the producer managing the distributor relationship and acting as your consulting resource throughout the entire process.

Agents sound valuable. Is this what Dazzle Entertainment does?

Yes. We have relationships with all of the major cable networks worldwide, all the major distributors worldwide. And we go and perform the sales function.

One of the things that make us unique in the marketplace is our consulting and production experience. Through our consulting division, we provide distribution, acquisitions, and management consulting to some of the industry's largest players as well as a number of niche distributors. We maintain direct relationships with a plethora of retailers through our consulting, which gives us unparalleled understanding and access to the "last mile" where the vast majority of the money for the film is generated. It allows us to view and understand the marketplace through the eyes of the distributor and the distributor's customers.

While we do so selectively, we also produce our own projects, which keeps us sensitive to the needs of the film makers. Since we also sell our own films, Dazzle is not just a sale agent, but we are also a client of our own services.

Your company gets involved in production on a selective basis, meaning that when you find films that you like you help raise the funds?

Absolutely. A lot of sales agents will get involved and help raise capital for films because sometimes fundraising can be done through distribution and because it is often helpful in insuring a steady flow of content for us to service. I do generally recommend that you engage your sales agents early in the filmmaking process. A lot of times, filmmakers wait to bring in their agent until the production has completed or they have had initial discussions with distributors. They make their film, and at the end of the process, they turn around and they try to get the film placed by attending AFM and guerilla marketing it. And then, ultimately, they wind up coming to a sales agent at that point.

And it's okay. Sales agents are used to it. But at that point, you've already exposed the distributors to the film presumably with less than desirable results. So now, the agent is knocking on the same distributor's door. It can be a little more challenging because you're starting with, yes, we looked at this film already. It's the old adage that you can't make a second "first impression."

My biggest criticism as a distributor and as a sales agent is that a lot of producers don't think about how to monetize their film until the very end. They've gone all the way through the process *without looking at the target consumers*, and now you have problems. Now you may have elements of the film that will be a problem with distribution or ultimately can impede consumer response. Most of our filmmakers come back and use our services for a second and third film, and on those subsequent films they sit down in the beginning to define their distribution and consumer targets as part of production planning. This most frequently results in a stronger product and, ultimately, stronger financial performance.

As a filmmaker, you control the creativity. So, it's not a matter of editing the script to make sure that it's as commercially viable as possible. It's a matter of putting these considerations in front of you so that you can make intelligent decisions based on your own criteria of what you want to accomplish with your film.

Knowledge is an asset. And bringing that knowledge into the development process earlier is something that a lot of people don't do, and sales agents welcome the opportunity. It also allows the agent to become more intimate with the project and to get distributors and broadcasters excited about the film while you are in production. So when they show back up after a few months when the film is complete, communication has already been started and the distributor has been "pre-heated" about the film.

DOCUMENTARY DISTRIBUTION

How does Dazzle Entertainment decide to be the sales agent for a documentary film?

Documentaries are traditionally one of the toughest film assets to monetize. We look at a documentary film to decide if it's suitable for television, because television for a documentary is often the most material revenue stream generated. Each documentary is different, with different subject matter and different customers. Those consumers can be geographically disbursed or are made up of small, yet highly motivated, groups which don't often fit the ideal profile for the retailers that sell the DVD. Of course, online retail makes it easier to manage this dynamic; however, the vast majority of revenue today remains in physical DVD sales. So we tend to favor programming with a well-defined audience or larger target audiences.

Getting documentaries to retail can be a real challenge. Remember for the mass merchants such as Walmart, Kmart, and Target (where at least 50% of DVD sales occur), documentary films constitute between one-half and 1% of their total DVD revenues. So the genre is just not that important to them unless your film has a large or well-defined consumer base. So, TV is always very important and DVD can be a bit more challenging. Online sales and downloads have become an excellent outlet for documentaries.

The other area we look at is international. Documentaries definitely pay differently in each international market depending on the subject matter. There are many topics that don't translate well into other countries and markets.

One of the things I always say is if you do have a documentary that's well suited to television domestically and overseas — then you probably will find that your overall financial performance will be exponentially better.

It's a great thing to run around the world and collect eighty to a hundred small checks that combined have a meaningful value. Unfortunately, the DVD market doesn't necessarily translate the same around the world. The US is a DVD-centric culture and does not have quite as many issues as other countries with piracy. So, a good strong TV documentary with subject matter that's relevant across the world can generate 200%, 250% more revenue from overseas than it did domestically.

What advice could you give emerging filmmakers for features or docs? Perhaps mistakes by filmmakers that made it more difficult for sales agents or distributors to handle?

The biggest one would be production values. I don't care what the film is, if it's not shot and edited professionally, you will encounter your greatest obstacle. This can be tough especially for first-time filmmakers, because they want to fill all the roles. They're the director, writer, producer, editor. And let's face it — it's hard to be very good at any one of those things. To be good at two, three or four is even rarer. One of the greatest challenges in this situation is that you don't have someone objective in the process.

The other is a lack of a "hook" for the marketplace. Filmmakers often will say to me that "people who see the film love it." But the larger and more frequent challenge is getting a consumer to see the film in the first place. There needs to be a compelling reason for someone to watch it, buy it or rent it. This is often marquee talent since that is truly the "brands" that consumers recognize. The real key is to develop the project with a clear sense of "why consumers will want to watch it" in the first place. It doesn't matter how good the film is, if the consumer doesn't get activated, no one will ever see it. While I am at risk of being overly redundant, I think the one thing that people sometimes forget is who their target audience is. *Sometimes they're more into the story than who's going to see the story.*

Finally, make sure that your chain of title is well assembled and clear. The filmmaking process is an exciting one; however, sloppiness in assembling your underlying rights and contracts can be fatal. Remember, you only own the rights to exploit the film when you own ALL underlying rights, so this is more than paperwork, it is a necessity.

Karen McCann on Self Distribution
http://www.karenmccann.teamasea.com

Karen, what distribution deal did you negotiate with the local theatre chain in Little Rock, for your film, *Step Away From the Stone*?

I called the local theatres and took a copy of the DVD to them and the next day they offered me a week run with hold-over options based on the box office numbers. I offered them 50% of the box office and I would do the advertising. They displayed our poster three weeks ahead and we started to find our audience from their clientele.

Why did you decide to self-distribute?

Lots of filmmakers have gotten good distribution deals and still not made money because of the distributors' "so-called expenses." I decided to try self-distribution because my most important obligation is to get the investors' money back.

How did you fill the seats without print and advertising money?

That was not as easy as I thought it would be. I expected the local actors and extras to come and bring family, etc., and that did not happen. So I got interviews on local radio stations and promoted the film on Facebook, Twitter, via emails and everywhere. We told people they could meet the actors after the screenings, we had local papers do articles about us. All this and the trailer we made really helped fill seats.

What were some of the benefits you received from the theatrical release?

First was the knowledge that I should plan ahead. I built an audience for the next film and I have theatres that will screen my next film. We were number one for two weeks even though it was a slow time. Ticket sales for *Step Away from the Stone* outsold *The American, Eat Pray Love,* and seven other movies for two weeks. I was there for most screenings and it was an exceptional moment to see people touched when the film ended.

Will you self-distribute your next feature?

I will do it the same way in towns that have independent theatres. For larger chains they may want money up front and the split is only 40% to the filmmaker, but more people will see it. Being in theatres requires money for advertising to be as successful as the majors. I will definitely self-distribute my DVDs. I believe building a fan base from day one using social media is a key to the success of your movie. Creating a website and Facebook page that shows all aspects of the film helps to create an interest in the move. Carole, I will also say that having you as our Executive Producer was instrumental in having the movie shown in theatres. You are a great mentor and I won't make a film without you!

CHAPTER 20

THE MONEY MAZE
OF PUBLIC FUNDING

WORKING WITH ITVS AND PBS

I always feel like I'm in the middle of a Monty Python movie when I look for information on those public television websites. I can see John Cleese with that comedic expression on his face looking totally baffled by all of it.

There is money here for you but you need to know how to carefully tread the path and get out of the maze before dark!

When President Johnson signed the Public Broadcasting Act in 1967, he said the creation of public broadcasting would "give a wider... stronger voice to educational radio and television by providing new funds for broadcast facilities."

The Corporation for Public Broadcasting (CPB) is the largest source of funding for public television, providing support for content development as well as individual stations and the entire public broadcasting community. PBS (Public Broadcasting Service) is a separate entity, a network of more than 340 member stations located throughout the United States. Programs that air on PBS are produced through member stations and the independent film community.

PBS has access to the General Program Fund, which typically funds programming for major mini-series, and the PBS/CPB Challenge Fund, which is designated toward co-producing major mini-series with significant funds allocated for one-hour programming. (These projects must be approved by both PBS and CPB.)

By the mid-1980s, complaints that the CPB had failed to diversify programming and give a voice to unheard minorities were at an all-time high. In 1988 Congress passed a new federal mandate challenging the CPB to negotiate with a national coalition of independent producer groups to establish a truly independent television service, and in 1991 the Independent Television Service (ITVS) was born.

PRODUCING FOR PUBLIC BROADCASTING (PBS)

The focus at PBS is on their returning strands and their icon series, with less focus on limited series programming, and even less on single documentary programming. While PBS does schedule one-off programming, 80% of their schedule is reserved for the major multi-part series (strands), which typically run four to six episodes. The strands also command the greater part of the PBS budget.

There is an upside and a downside to working with PBS. When you bring PBS a program with a $1 million budget, it will end up coming in at $1.5 million because of all of the required ancillary elements. This includes all of the activities surrounding promotion and advertising, such as on-air promos and the development and maintenance of a website, as well as those activities that are integral to PBS's philosophy, such as educational programs, audience outreach, and closed captioning. These expenses must be covered in addition to normal production expenses, so if you're going to produce with PBS, you must raise extra funds. The good news is that PBS raises funds too.

Even projects that receive significant funding from PBS usually only end up with one-fourth to one-third of the production budget, which means producers working with PBS are usually required to seek additional funding from outside sources. The program producer is also responsible for managing all aspects of a project's development and production. PBS will consider allocating finishing funds for one-off programs, though they usually do not make that decision until a project has reached the rough-cut stage of production.

PBS children's programming has a significant infrastructure with anywhere from $10 million to $20 million raised for weekday programs. These multi-million dollar productions typically run about forty-five episodes per season, which places children's programming beyond the scope of most independent filmmakers.

PBS accepts proposals on an ongoing basis. Proposals are evaluated according to the quality of the proposal, the credentials of the production team, PBS's schedule needs, and the financial commitment required by PBS. PBS wants quality programs that are journalistically sound and will reach a broad spectrum of people. If you have a project in mind, you need to make sure that your project is in sync with PBS's goals for your particular target audience.

If your proposal meets the PBS criteria, it is forwarded to the senior director for the appropriate genre, who will present your proposal to a content team. Together they will evaluate your proposal and make specific recommendations regarding your project. Your funding plan and your list of possible donors will be forwarded to PBS's underwriting department so that each of your potential funding sources can be verified as an acceptable donor. The senior programming team then reviews recommended proposals and makes the final decision on whether or not to green light the project. This team includes PBS's president and CEO and PBS programming executives in Virginia, Florida, and California.

There are other ways of getting on PBS. Some producers distribute their films on a market-by-market situation by contacting each PBS station. PBS Plus feeds programs to local stations to be picked up and scheduled on an a la carte basis. These programs are completely underwritten so they come to PBS fully funded. Producers should also consider other funding sources available for PBS through ITVS and the CPB Minority Consortia, which covers contemporary issues that fall within the five minority consortia including: Center for Asian American Media, Latino Public Broadcasting, National Black Programming Consortium, Native American Public Telecommunications, Native Public Media, and Pacific Islanders in Communications.

If you are even thinking about producing for public television you need to visit the respective website and carefully review their guidelines. They have very strict guidelines on who can underwrite programs, and if they feel even one of your underwriters has any real or perceived influence regarding the content of your project they will not accept it.

Here are funding sources on the site.

A. Funding Sources

    1. Public Broadcasting Service (PBS) *www.pbs.org*

    2. Corporation for Public Broadcasting *www.cpb.org*

       a. Program Challenge Fund

       b. Digital Distribution Fund

       c. Mobile/Handheld Digital Television Program

       b. New Voices, New Media Fund

       c. Producers Academy Scholarship

    3. Independent Television Service *www.itvs.org*

       a. LINCS

       b. Open Call

       c. Independent Lens Series — co-created with PBS

B. PBS Series

    1. American Experience *www.pbs.org/wgbh/amex*

    2. American Masters *www.pbs.org/wnet/americanmasters*

    3. Frontline *www.pbs.org/frontline*

    4. Wide Angle *www.thirteen.org/wideangle*

    5. Independent Lens *www.pbs.org/independentlens/submissions.html*

C. Minority Consortia

    1. Latino Public Broadcasting *www.lpbp.org*

    2. Native American Public Telecommunications *www.nativetelecom.org*

    3. Center for Asian American Media *http://caamedia.org*

    4. National Black Programming Consortium *http://blackpublicmedia. org/about/*

    5. Pacific Islanders in Communications *www.piccom.org*

    6. Native Public Media *http:www.nativepublicmedia.org*

II.

    1. PBS/CPB Challenge Fund *www.pbs.org/producers/funding.html*
Full proposals and project budgets must be submitted to both PBS (see Submitting a Proposal at *www.pbs.org/producers/proposal.html*) and CPB (see Submission Instructions at *www.cpb.org/grants/challengefund*)

    2. POV *www.pbs.org/pov/utils/forproducers.html*

AMERICAN PUBLIC TELEVISION (APT)

APT is the main distributor for thousands of quality series and single programs in all genres, including children's, drama, performance, comedy, music, documentaries, news and public affairs, and how-to series. They offer a wide array of marketing and distribution services and will provide promotion and ongoing carriage reports for a fee.

APT works with all 349 public television stations to help shape content, program design and pledge formats. APT has developed some of the most successful public television fundraising programs, such as *The Moody Blues in Concert at Red Rocks* and the Dr. Andrew Weil specials.

ITVS

ITVS was designed to open the door to independent producers by acting as a bridge between producers and public television. They are interested in subject matter that may be controversial and would not have been funded without their support.

Programs that air on ITVS are utilized beyond the initial broadcast, through the public education system and various public programs designed to stimulate group discussions. They want films that will promote healthy dialogue; therefore, the ITVS judges will consider your film's potential for promoting stimulating conversation as one of the most important criteria during the evaluation process. ITVS encourages emerging producers to bring their projects. While they do not sponsor student works, they are looking for individuals who want to be professionals. ITVS will embrace filmmakers who are just on the doorstep, and will accept the responsibility of nurturing emerging filmmakers as they make their way into the industry.

ITVS will be involved throughout your entire project as your executive producer. This is a full-service organization. Services include funding, creative development, feedback during production, and a comprehensive public television launch which includes marketing, publicity, website, station relations, and outreach support. They have thirteen grassroots staff members who take new projects around the country into local communities where they work on building an audience.

They have two open calls a year. It takes judges about four months during each round to read and evaluate submitted proposals. The rounds operate in either two stages or three stages. Usually there is an internal cut followed by a second phase, then the third phase, which goes to a panel. During the re-application stage, filmmakers who are selected for the last round will have an opportunity to address certain issues brought up by the judging panel. Filmmakers submit a detailed budget during this re-application period. The panel will discuss and evaluate each proposal before deciding which ones will be considered for funding. The most crucial phase in the selection process is the orientation. During this phase, producers whose projects have been selected so far travel to San Francisco where they will undergo two and a half days of intense meetings filled with essential information about ITVS's role during production. (For more personal information on ITVS, read the chapter with Jilann Spitzmiller's interview for her experience with ITVS funding *Shakespeare Behind Bars*.)

ITVS also features LINCS (Linking Independents and Co-producing Stations), a joint proposal between producers and local public television stations that provides matching production funds. LINCS is considered a very important project because it promotes collaborative effort and allows projects to reach smaller stations that do not have a competitive edge.

ITVS has a Diversity Development Fund which seeks talented minority producers to develop projects for public television. They want "to support minority artists to tell their stories and reach audiences often overlooked by conventional programming. Projects must be in the research or development phase, and cannot have begun production."

When ITVS funds a project they require a licensing fee for U.S. broadcast. This license gives them copyright over the project during the duration of broadcasting, which usually covers six releases in four years, or four releases in three years, after which all rights revert back to the producer. The producer will control the international rights, home video rights, domestic and international rights, educational domestic rights, and the international theatrical domestic rights, while ITVS will enjoy domestic rights for television broadcast.

If ITVS is the full funder they will take 50% of the royalties of other funding, their back-end share for the funding they put in, which can be considerable compared to what is available. Some of this funding comes from the Corporation for Public Broadcasting (CPB), which is ITVS's funder. There is a back-end share of revenues earned, which is put back in the production fund for future funding of other projects. If ITVS puts in 100% of the budget, they get a 50% return; if they put in 50% of the budget, they get a 25% return. They get 50% return for whatever percentage they put into the budget.

ITVS participates in foreign co-production partnerships with ZDF Germany, ARTE France, the BBC in England, and many other international distributors. This partnership allows several organizations to share the responsibility of funding, and creates a wider distribution base for films, which encourages more production.

If ITVS offers something to PBS and they turn it down they can offer it to PBS Plus. PBS Plus does not have national carriage and you can work with the individual stations. They also work with strands (such as *Frontline*) which have time slots that can accommodate additional programs. ITVS will also take programs to presenting stations such as Nebraska Educational Telecommunications (NET) or Oregon Public Broadcasting (OPB). If these options do not work out, ITVS will send the program out via satellite and will send notification to local stations letting them know when they can download the program. These stations can then air the program according to their scheduling needs. Sometimes if you work station by station you can get as much coverage as a national broadcast.

ITVS has additional calls on a year-to-year basis that address specific topics that may emerge throughout the year. For example, they commissioned thirty producers to do a one-minute piece on the aftermath of 9/11. When digital technology exploded onto the film scene, ITVS put out a special call for programs produced on DV. ITVS wanted to explore the different ways this technology would impact the industry and they encouraged filmmakers to submit applications for their DV projects. Keep watching the ITVS website for these types of calls.

INDEPENDENT LENS

Independent Lens started out as a series of ten docs that previously aired on PBS for about three seasons. In 2003 they established a twenty-nine-week national PBS series that showcases independent documentaries, dramas, experimental films, and shorts. Independent Lens is a partnership between ITVS and PBS that is designed to give independent programs a year-round presence on PBS, and is part of the program service ITVS provides to the stations. They fully expect that a large number of programs that ITVS chooses to fund will be a part of this series, and hope to use this series to showcase work that is distinctive in content. This is good news for all documentary filmmakers.

Independent Lens wants programs that are "innovative, provocative, character driven, and well crafted." Most programs are scheduled in one-hour time slots.

WNET AND WIDE ANGLE

Thirteen WNET is New York's PBS flagship station. Each department features one or more strands that are the core of PBS programming.

The news department at WNET launched *Wide Angle*, a weekly series of one-hour international documentaries that recently filled the time slot vacated by *Frontline*. WNET rarely looks at proposals for single documentaries for *Wide Angle* unless they have a solid international or current affairs appeal. If they receive a proposal that has a good science spin, or might be good material for *Frontline*, they will send the proposal off to the respective producers of these programs.

Because WNET is based in New York City, they are the most watched station in the public broadcasting system. This puts them in a very strong position at the international markets when producers are searching for foreign distribution and foreign co-production deals. Program producers at WNET have only included six or seven single one-hour or ninety-minute docs in the last few years. They occasionally acquire individual programs for the New York City market; however, this is not a place to find significant funding, as the acquisition prices are in the low few thousands of dollars. They encourage producers to bring projects with some funding already attached.

Visit *www.thirteen.org* for additional information on submission guidelines and how to pitch to WNET program producers.

Other important links are Wide Angle: *pbs.org/wnet/wideangle* and Stage on Screen *www.pbs.org/wnet/stageonscreen*.

ARTHUR DONG

Arthur Dong is one of the most well-respected documentary filmmakers in the industry today. He is a graduate of the Film School at San Francisco State University (1982, summa cum laude) and the American Film Institute's Center for Advanced Film and Television Studies (Directing Fellow, 1984). He served on the Board of Governors of the Academy of Motion Pictures Arts and Sciences, representing the Documentary Branch, and currently represents the Academy on the National Film Preservation Board. He also served on the National Preservation Board at the Library of Congress. Arthur has won numerous film awards, including a George Foster Peabody Award, three Sundance FilmFestival awards, an Oscar nomination, and five Emmy nominations, the Berlin Film Festival's Teddy Award and Taiwan's Golden Horse award.

His documentary, *Family Fundamentals*, explores the emotional issues that envelop three conservative Christian families with gay and lesbian children. The film, which was an official selection of the 2002 Sundance Film Festival, "is a deeply personal look at the 'cultural wars' over homosexuality that are being fought in families and the social/political public spheres of our nation."

Throughout production, Arthur collaborated with a diverse panel that included both gay and lesbian advisors and conservative Christian advisors. He challenged members of the panel to engage in healthy dialogue by resisting the temptation to polarize into two opposing groups. This supported one of the major goals of participating foundations, to support projects that involve an extensive community partnership.

Arthur's film got off the ground when he won "In the Works," a grant sponsored by Kodak and POV/American Documentary, Inc. The grant, which offered $10,000 in products, services, or cash, supplied Arthur with the resources to start shooting. With this win under his belt, he forged ahead embracing a proactive strategy for funding. He completed grant applications, networked, and spent quality time taking one-on-one meetings with potential funders. His strategy worked.

In addition to subsequent finishing funds from American Documentary, Inc., primary grants came from the Guggenheim Fellowship in Filmmaking and the Theophilus Foundation, with additional support from numerous sources, including the Soros Documentary Fund (now the Sundance Documentary Fund),

Arthur's final budget for the project came in under $200,000. Funding took about two years from the onset of his original concept to its premiere at Sundance. He decided early on that the project would be formatted for an art house theatrical release alongside a campus college tour, feeling confident that even a tour's limited distribution could generate much needed revenue.

POV was instrumental in helping Arthur complete his film. They respond to Arthur because he is a filmmaker who steps out and tackles complex issues that encourage communication between diverse groups. Past Executive Director of POV American Documentary, Cara Mertes, describes Arthur as the kind of filmmaker who "takes the film out and engages people who don't have a language to talk about their very human experience and how they live that from whatever perspective they are in. We believe this is a great gift." Arthur refuses to preach to the converted.

Arthur kept *Family Fundamentals'* production cost down by shooting and editing his own footage and distributing this and his other films through his company, Deep Focus Productions, Inc. "This is a good way to build a company," Cara explained. "You are not always waiting for funds to start your project. You can be generating money and paying yourself and your crew back."

Since the initial release of Arthur's documentary *Hollywood Chinese* (2007), the film has been lauded as a landmark analysis of the Chinese in American feature films by both Chinese and non-Chinese audiences, as well as film lovers and cineastes everywhere. As with his previous films, Arthur worked with a panel of advisors that included academics in the field of Asian American history and cinema history. Major funding was provided by the Ford Foundation, the National Endowment for the Arts, the Center for Asian American Media, the California Council for Humanities and ITVS (with funds from the Corporation for Public Broadcasting.)

Hollywood Chinese had its international premiere at the prestigious Toronto Film Festival. After a year of engagements in festivals worldwide and in theatrical bookings in America, the film had its broadcast premiere on PBS's Emmy-Award winning series, *American Masters*. For more information and clips from Arthur's films, please visit his website at *www.deepfocusproductions.com*.

CHAPTER 21

MISSION, VISION, AND VALUES

A Conversation with Morrie Warshawski

On Morrie Warshawski's website, he describes himself as a consultant, facilitator and writer. He is being far too modest. Morrie is one of the best-known film fundraising gurus in the industry. His list of clients includes the Corporation for Public Broadcasting, Independent Feature Project, the John D. and Catherine T. MacArthur Foundation, the California Arts Council, the President's Committee on the Arts and the Humanities, and the New Orleans Video Access Center. He is the author of several fundraising books including *The Fundraising Houseparty: How to Party with a Purpose and Raise Money for Your Cause* (2nd edition), and *Shaking the Money Tree: The Art of Getting Grants and Donations for Film and Video Projects* (3rd edition). Morrie provides individual consultations with filmmakers, focusing either on long-range career planning or on a specific project. The advice he offers comes from years of hard-earned experience in the fundraising world. For more information on Morrie Warshawski's consulting services and his books visit his website at *www.warshawski.com*.

FIVE-YEAR PROJECTIONS

What advice do you have for filmmakers?

My major advice to every filmmaker is to step back from all of this and really try to understand why you are doing this work at all. This is why my consulting is so very different, and why when I begin a relationship with a filmmaker I make them go through something I call an initial consultation. I believe the major thrust of my work with filmmakers is to help them clarify and commit to a mission statement before they can go on with the film.

What is your mission statement as a filmmaker? Why are you making films? A corollary to this is the question of vision. What do you see yourself doing in five years? The third element I like to have clarified is, have you identified your set of core values?

Mission, vision, and values. Those three things are at the very heart of my work with everyone I work with.

I say to the beginning, the emerging, the seasoned, and the veteran filmmaker, "Have you clarified these things first? Because until you do, and unless you do, you will not be as effective at filmmaking as you could be!"

When I tell filmmakers this before we consult, they scratch their heads and wonder what I am talking about. Then I say, "Well, either we can talk about these, and you work with me, or we don't."

It's one of my few non-negotiables. This is the way I work. I guarantee if you speak to 99% of the people I consult with, they will verify how beneficial this work is.

Why do you think it is important for filmmakers to envision what they will be doing in five years?

How else can you be truly strategic and decide what you will do between now and then? How you will most effectively spend your time and money? The three rocks that are the basis of all my work — mission, vision and values — each have a different function in keeping the filmmaker or any professional productive, strategic, and forceful in their career.

You asked about vision — the importance of vision is it tells you what you need to do next because you've decided what you really want out of your future. The issue for filmmakers, especially, is that they have to put a lot of time, energy, and resources in the project they are working on right now. It is truer of a filmmaker than many other types of artists. The work they will do will take years to create and it will eat up their lives during that time. If they can't step back and have a perspective on how that one film is a piece of a larger puzzle, then they miss many opportunities for maximizing everything they do while they are making the film.

You believe that this vision will enable them to decide what films to produce?

Right, but it is actually much bigger than that. They are trying to say to themselves as they are making this film, "How can I set myself up for the next two, three or four pieces I want to make." "How can I maximize the contacts I am making now so they will help me in the future?" It also makes them step back and think whether or not they should actually be making the film that they think they should make now.

I will give you an example. Occasionally I will meet a filmmaker and we will go through the work. They have decided they want to make a documentary. When we start talking about the vision, they will say to me, "You know five years from now what I really want to do is to be making independent feature films." So the first thing I will say to a filmmaker is why are you bothering to make a documentary? Why don't you start making feature films now?

This is a real wake-up call for a filmmaker. Because for some reason they have it stuck in their mind that they have to get this documentary out. Really, lots of times they don't. They could shift it, change it, and turn it into a fiction work. See, the filmmaker thinks, "If I complete this documentary and it is successful then it will help me in my career as a feature filmmaker," and that's not necessarily true.

When this filmmaker starts looking for money for their narrative feature, the funders and investors will say, "Let me see your script." "Have you ever written a script?" "Let me see the work you have done with actors, have you worked with actors before?" The documentary filmmaker hasn't done either one of those. So they are better off making a short now and just turning the documentary into a work of fiction.

You believe knowing what is in their heart allows people to move to the future with a clear direction?

That's right. They can be much more strategic and intentional. I try to get all my clients to be strategic and intentional.

CREATING A MISSION STATEMENT

You want your filmmakers to have a mission; can you give me an example of a mission statement?

Yes, the mission has a completely different function. The function of the mission is that it's the filmmaker's raison d'être. It is why they are doing anything. It's the heart of the work. Until or unless they can identify the mission, I see my clients floundering. Getting a mission statement from filmmakers is actually the first thing I do with them. In fact, I just sat down with a filmmaker yesterday and I had to walk them through creating it.

The first thing I ask a filmmaker is, "What is your mission as a filmmaker?" It may be different than their mission in life or their mission as a husband or their mission as a daughter. I tell my clients they will be much more effective in each of their roles in life if they create a mission for it. But the only mission that I am interested in is their mission as a professional. I will give you a mission statement one of my clients wrote yesterday. She said the mission of her production company is "to promote non-violent social change through amplifying women's voices."

That's a very clear mission statement.

Yes, that's very clear and it took us an hour to find it. Some filmmakers might take six months to a year to find a statement. Her original mission statement was ten times longer than this. That's a good, clear, simple mission statement. My next question to her is, "If that is your mission" — and this is very important — "then what makes you think that filmmaking is either the only way or the best way to exemplify this mission in the world?"

This means you have to clearly define your mission and clearly forecast your future.

Yes, and this is what drives the future. With the mission and the vision you can see what you want to do in five years. The mission is what drives you towards it because you say to yourself, "Oh, this is what I am about." And you know why it is really important for non-commercial films to locate their mission is because they are going through tremendous sacrifices to create the work. There is no way around it.

You are going to have to bleed and bleed and bleed to make everything count. And if you don't have a strong reason for doing this, a mission, then it ain't gonna happen. Those are the ones who fall by the wayside, people who don't have a strong mission, a strong driving force, a reason to make the work. Every client I ever work with has to clarify their mission the first thing.

We have the mission and we have the vision. Do you ask them for a set of their values?

Yes, I do, absolutely! My task is to help them as much as I can. And what I found — and it took years to discover this — is that I couldn't really help the filmmaker in a significant, qualitative way until these things were cleared up. It seems stupid to start talking about fundraising until these things are straight. If you don't, then you are not going to get the money.

Yes, and you will be so much clearer when you write your proposal.

That's right, and the funder appreciates it because now they know they are dealing with a serious person, a person with a backbone, a person that is on a mission. They may not like the mission, but they will respect you for having one.

PROPOSAL FOR A DOCUMENTARY

What suggestions would you give to filmmakers on creating their proposal?

The most important thing is to really understand what it is you want to make and why you want to make it. Those are the two big things and everything else flows from that. It is the journey of figuring that out that begins the proposal writing process. If you can articulate those two things, you can sit down next to somebody and say it, and a good grant writer could create a good proposal for you. Of course there is a lot more that goes into it but at the very center, the very heart of the proposal is, "Why am I doing this, and what is it?" A lot of filmmakers haven't clarified these things when they start looking for money.

Right, I hear it in their pitches and I think potential donors realize they don't have a clear vision of their film.

Absolutely. Now you know of course, there are things that you can't know about the film before you make it, especially if you are a vérité filmmaker. That's okay, everybody understands this. But people have to know, what is it you are trying to accomplish with this, why are you doing it? What's it likely to look like once you have created it? Those things you really have to clarify. Then, of course, there are other things that are very important once those are done, but there are subsets. One subset is, "Who is it for?"

A subset of that, which is a crucial one, is now that you have articulated who it is for, how are you going to get to them, in other words, distribution, how will you do your distribution? It is amazing how many proposals I see that don't address this issue.

When you were teaching in L.A., you made a statement that knocked me off my seat. You said, "I can tell you within thirty seconds of listening to a pitch, which films will be funded and which won't."

Well, if you have been around the business long enough and you have met enough filmmakers, you can tell. But see, that's the role of funders, funders can tell. They get pitched all the time, they know. The beauty of getting your mission, vision, and values together is that it is so much easier and quicker for you to articulate everything you want to do. That's why that groundwork pays off in spades because then you can hone in on the thing you are trying to make. It is like the mission I gave you, when I first met this filmmaker, she couldn't articulate her mission. She had written literally paragraphs and paragraphs trying to say what she was about and that showed me there was a lot of confusion. I know that every funder that looked at her material said, "There is confusion here, what is she really about?" You have got to get down to the nub and really hone in on the thing that is driving you and this work. You have to be able to articulate this to everyone in a very succinct, quick manner, because if you can't, everybody's going to know it. That's true of the funder and the listener.

You've got twenty or thirty seconds and after that they are either with you or they are gone. That's what I find, I know within twenty seconds if I want to hear any more. Absolutely, and after that it is all commentary. I get approached by filmmakers all the time, at conferences, on the street, on the phone, and I might ask them what they are doing or they may just be telling me what they are doing. Quite often they will just go on and on and on about the work, and really they don't need to. They could give you a good twenty or thirty seconds at the most and see if I am interested. Because after that, they can keep talking, but if I have lost my interest, it is wasted time.

I tell filmmakers they have to pause after they give you a bit of information for the listener to absorb it; to remember they have been carrying the film for years and this person is just hearing it for the first time.

Yes, and they have to articulate it like they are saying it for the first time.

Yes, with the same passion and enthusiasm as they had when they first got the concept.

Now, if you sit with that for a moment and you say, "What would it take to keep me enthused and excited about this pitch?" The secret is the mission. That's one of the practical ways the mission works. You go back into your heart and it gives you the energy to get excited and you know why you are excited about the film.

Is that because you know your long-term goal?

Right, and that brings the passion out every time. You might have to give a pitch a hundred times a day and every time you have to sound enthusiastic and passionate. The little energy nugget that keeps the flame alive, that keeps the flame hot, is your mission.

TESTING YOUR FILM IDEA

When someone has an idea for a film, how do you recommend they test it to see if the film has an audience?

I recommend they test the idea by starting at square one. They need to do basic research to see if anything like the film they want to do has already been created. It is surprising how many people don't do that work. This is just as important for someone doing a fiction narrative as it is for documentaries. It is imperative because if this has already been done then no one will fund it.

Once you have this settled, the second thing is to "open it up" — a phrase I use a lot in my work. I think independents are too isolated. I say, go out and talk to these kinds of people. One is distributors, people who know the marketplace. Find a distributor who specializes in the kind of picture you are making.

Next, you want to talk to your potential audience. Ask yourself who are you making this for and then go talk to them. Tell them about the film you want to make and ask, "What do you think about this?" The whole process is just a lot healthier. Otherwise you may end up with a film that no one wants. In the past year I've actually stopped used the word "audience" and am thinking a lot more about "community" — the community of people who the filmmaker wants to get involved with the project from the very beginning of the process. This is the big change that the Internet and social networking has brought about.

GRANT PROPOSAL WRITERS

What I find is that some filmmakers are passionate about the project but are not good writers. Do you recommend filmmakers hire someone to write the proposal?

What I recommend is when they create the proposal it must be perfect. So my recommendation is do whatever it takes to make it perfect. If that means having to hire someone, then so be it. Typically filmmakers, even if they are not good at writing, can find a partner who can help them write, or they can write a rough first draft and get someone who knows about writing to create a final draft. Most of my clients have the capacity to actually create a good proposal on their own with some assistance. Sometimes it just means having someone like me look at the proposal and make suggestions for change. Occasionally if they need it, and especially if they can afford it, having a professional grant writer is fine.

Where do you find good professional grant writers?

The question is really where you find professional grant writers that know about film and video. This can be hard. There are thousands of people in the U.S. who are grant writers; take a look at the Association of Fundraising Professionals, the AFP. Everyone on this list is a professional grant writer and this is a good place to find grant writers.

The whole reason I wrote my book, *Shaking the Money Tree*, is that none of them literally know anything about film and why writing a proposal for a film grant is so different than writing any other proposal. You almost have to have been around filmmakers yourself or have done a few of them to begin to understand the process.

How you find those people is more difficult. I think the best way is to go to the media art centers around the country and see who they recommend. They are all listed at the National Alliance for Media Arts and Culture (*www.namac.org*).

You can go to the website and look by state for a media art center near you. All of the media arts centers are members of NAMAC. You can also talk to other filmmakers for names of people who are good at writing grants. Also, there are great film listserves out there now where you can post this question and get responses from other filmmakers. Doculink is one of those.

Once filmmakers have their proposal written can they submit them to you for your guidance?

Yes, I have written over five hundred grants myself. I stopped writing grants a few years ago. With my hourly rate it is too expensive to write for people, and grant writing is just not that interesting to me anymore!

An effective way to use my time is just send me the grant package. Then with my critiques almost anyone can write a second draft that will be totally effective.

DONATIONS FROM SMALL BUSINESSES

I noticed in the chapter headings of the current edition of *Shaking the Money Tree* that you have small businesses listed under funding possibilities. Can you elaborate on this?

Yes, I love small businesses because they are easy to tap for support and they are very informal. They are all around you. You are probably no more than a few blocks away from some small business that you can get support from. That is the upside.

The downside is they never give you money. They are a good source for products. For example, I worked with a filmmaker/client of mine in Chicago. She told me the story of a project she was doing with students in the neighborhood. They walked around the neighborhood with a one-page description of the project. They asked the local businesses for things they needed for the film that they normally would have had to pay for. They got free meals every day for the crew from KFC, Pizza Hut, and local restaurants.

They needed walkie-talkies and they couldn't find them and the local cell phone company let them have unlimited use of five cell phones for a week. For the script, the local Kinko's let them have free photocopies. I tell filmmakers all the time to look through their budgets and pick out things small businesses can donate to you. It is as good as money.

These small businesses are very easy to approach. You just literally walk through the door and ask for the manager and you can talk to them right there. They can make a decision very quickly. What you may give them in return is a credit on the film, or they might want an invitation to the film or a free video copy when it is released.

RAISING MONEY FROM CORPORATIONS

What about larger corporations? For example, corporations that are yielding between $12 and $20 million a year that may not have an established foundation, but are starting to get involved in the industry, perhaps advertising on PBS?

When you are dealing with a corporation and want to ask them for money, then you have to jump through a completely different set of hoops than with a small business. This is much, much harder. Most of my clients have not had much luck with corporations. I would say there are some general things to keep in mind that are true about corporations.

One thing to consider, unlike a private foundation, there is usually more than one door you can go through and it is not always clear which one you should go through. For instance, one door might be human resources, or another door that is a lot more usual is the marketing door, or the community relations door. There is another door that no one talks about and that is the CEO's door. If the CEO has a personal interest in the topic of the film, or knows someone you know, well, then that door might open to you. You need to think of all these doors before you approach the corporation.

Another thing about corporations that is difficult is that if they don't have a formal giving program or foundation it is hard to do the research. They might have given to a film before but it may not be found on the paperwork. Unlike a private foundation that has to list everything, they may have just expensed the money, as they do not have to list it separately. This makes the research difficult.

The basis of all good fundraising is savvy research. So what is a good filmmaker to do? The answer is obvious. You need a personal contact. You almost always need someone who will walk you through one of the doors if you want to get corporate money.

Let's say you decide to go for corporate money. What type of package would you need to take them?

That's the other bug-a-boo. A normal grant proposal won't work in a corporation because they never really give you the money outright. If you get a donation from a corporation it is almost always a marketing buy. Filmmakers can call it whatever they want, but as far as the corporation is concerned they are buying something. That means when you go to them you have to talk to them in a way that is very different from talking to any other donor.

With corporations you have to have a lot of demographic data and psychographic data. You need to tell them essentially who the audience is that will want to see the film. You have to show them the psychographic data. Here is the age group, here is where they live, and here is how much they spend on these kinds of products.

The corporation is thinking, "I want more good will from people who buy my products. How will your film help me impact those people I want to reach?" You have to make this connection for them.

Where do you think is the best place for filmmakers to go for funding?

Relatives — your mother, your father! You know, Carole; this is too big a question to answer generally. It depends on several factors. One factor is what type of piece are you making? Some work is more appropriate for some venues of fundraising than others. If you are making an independent narrative feature film, you probably don't want to go to private foundations. On the other hand, if you are making a social issue documentary then you absolutely do want to go to private foundations.

I am recommending that everyone go to individuals as much as they can. It is an underused resource of funding for most filmmakers. It is so proactive and there is a lot of money available, but there are some instances where individuals would be impossible, like short experimental work. Now with the Internet and social networking, this avenue has opened up more than ever before for every type of film and every type of filmmaker. There are even sites like Kickstarter and IndieGoGo (and many more coming down the pike) that make it relatively easy to use the technology to get donations from individuals.

Then you feel individuals are a good untapped resource?

Oh, yes, absolutely.

How many ways do you work with people, and how do they reach you?

The easiest way is to go to my website at *www.warshawski.com*. On my page called "Workshops" there is a detailed description of my initial consultation service. That is the fastest way to find out how I work. I am very clear and detailed about what I want from a filmmaker before we talk, and then what they will get during that initial consultation. That is how I begin every relationship with every filmmaker. After that I am very flexible. I work on a retainer by the hour or by the day if the filmmaker and I both agree we are a good match. That is one thing we discover in our initial conversation.

CHAPTER 22

BUDGETS: PRODUCTION GLUE

by Norman C. Berns

I've just read that budgeting is dead, that modern-day filmmakers only need a video camera and whatever cash happens to be in their pockets. In this newfound point-and-shoot era of "new media," the word is that film-makers can skip all that tedious budget-making...

Truth be told, I'm almost tempted. Wouldn't our jobs be so much easier if we didn't have to worry about pesky details like money and how to spend it? Alas, we do. If we hope to finish our films or have a chance of seeing profits, we do, we do, and we absolutely do.

Before we even dive into the nitty-gritty of all that, it's important to understand that owning a video camera doesn't make anyone a filmmaker. No more than owning a scalpel can magically turn you into a surgeon. Rearranging electrons on a piece of videotape or memory card is as simple as flipping a switch. But *making a movie takes serious craft and a solid understanding of the hundred-year history of filmmaking.*

That's a whole other discussion, fodder for other chapters in other books. For this chapter, I'd like to stick with the *business* end of things and leave the *show* aside for the moment.

THE PROBLEM

Making movies takes money, whether you're counting in thousands or millions. When you produce a film, you're not only in charge of the art you hope to deliver; you're responsible for the cost of getting it on screen, too. If you're the producer, it's your job to make the most of every dollar. Maybe even turn a profit. To do that, you have to know how much to spend, and, most importantly, where to spend it. You'll need a plan for the cost of things.

That operating plan for your film is the budget.

There are (at least) two universes in which money doesn't matter, in which there's no reason to bother with a budget. There's the "I'm rich and don't give a hoot" universe in which any expense can be covered. And the "I'm way too cheap to pay for anything, bring your own lunch" world in which exploitation is rampant and every expense is too much.

Neither is a very good formula for long-term survival, let alone for turning out a *viable* movie. The task isn't just to *start* your film; there's little gain in that. The plan has to be to *finish* your film. And even *sell* it and maybe turn a *profit* for all your efforts so you can afford to make another film.

To do that — to finish your film, to make a profit — you'll need to know lots of things, but the first of those is the cost of things. In our universe, in most sane universes, money actually matters quite a lot. We want to make the most of the money we have. We want to use precisely the right amount of that money, but not a cent too much, so that whatever we make can make more money. (Presumably so we can fund another film. We are, after all, totally and irrevocably addicted to this amazing business of filmmaking.)

Each budget is the blueprint for the film you're about to make. Budgets show the carefully detailed structure of your production; they explain what's important to the finished film, what's worth extra time, who has to do the work, where they'll do it, and for how long. Budgets explain how you might possibly juggle days and nights, the value you place in your crew, the worth of your cast, the importance of your story and stunts and effects.

THE CRUX OF IT ALL

The *smaller* your budget or the *tighter* your production must be or the more limited your resources, *the more important it is to get your spending right.* Big or small, high or low, no matter your budget, the odds are good that you won't have enough money to make many mistakes.

Fortunately, it won't take long for you to take command of this information, *to own it*. And put it to work for your film. That's what we're going to do here — we're going to learn how a well-made budget actually goes to work for your film, how it makes your whole production run better, smarter, faster, and smoother.

At about this point, I hear the Cry of the Documentarians: "Not *my* show — I make *documentaries.*"

While the structure is different, the process for getting it ready is about the same as any other film. You have a tale to tell, there's information to convey and a point of view you hope/want/need to share. And, if you're like most mortals, you have a very limited amount of money to meet all those objectives.

Of course, many documentary films are based on concepts instead of scripts. Most work of necessity from general (and often vague) plans instead of specific shot lists. Far too many come from a "shoot till the money runs out" attitude toward finances.

If you hope to get your film funded and shot, finished and shown, you need a better plan. Budgets provide that plan.

Not only do you have to know what you're going to do and when you're going to do it, you'll also need to understand how your film will make a profit. "Not *my* show — I don't make profits. I'm a documentarian."

Filmmakers know (or should know) that not all "profits" are counted in dollars. Instead, there can be significant (if non-monetary) returns like impact, outreach, community involvement, education, training, empowerment. They're among the myriad ways your backers might hope to extract some kind of benefit — some kind of *profit* — from your project.

If you plan to get funding — even from Federal funders like the National Endowment for the Arts or the National Science Foundation — you'll need to understand (and explain) how your film will impact society. How it will "turn a profit" as it were. If you can't share a substantial awareness of the value of your film, few investors will bother to support your work.

(Of course, if your documentary is being made *for profit*, if your investors expect a return on their investment, then all the other rules here apply.)

If your show falls under the wide umbrella of not-for-profit documentaries, you may not have a structured script. Fix that. Not only is that "script" an essential step in securing your funding, the process of creating it will help you understand the innermost corners of your film.

Because this is *your* project, you already know a great deal about your film. You probably have a solid grasp of the subject, the talent, and even most of the action. (If you're not at that stage yet, you'll need to backtrack until you're ready.) Your next task is to fill in all the blanks and connect every one of the dots from your concept, through production to the finished film.

Documentaries are often like news stories. They evolve slowly as you learn more. No one would expect a reporter to write the story before rushing out to cover the fire. But that's exactly what filmmakers are expected to do. Write the script long before the full story has been unearthed.

What can you do? You're going to invent that script. Fortunately, you won't have to build it out of whole cloth at all. You're going to gather all the things you do know. Based on your research so far, let's say you already know you'll need to film (at least) four ordinary people and (no fewer than) two experts. Let's say the odds are good that you'll have to film in three different cities and spend at least a week at each of those locations. From all that research, you have a very good idea what all these people will talk about.

Bingo!

While it may be far too early to know *who* you want on camera and you couldn't possibly predict exactly *what* might be said (or you still have no idea *where*), you know the subject of your film and you know (approximately) what people will tell you or do. That's all you need to get started.

> **We are on the main street of a small Midwestern town. Mary Jones walks past local shops.**

> **MARY JONES**
> **When I first moved to this community....**

She will continue in that vein, explaining that....

You've set the scene. The script now identifies your on-camera talent and explains how your story will develop.

Essential to your plans and costs, you've learned that you need a small town for filming. You now have to do some location scouting. You'll need local extras. Maybe you'll have to add an assistant or two for the day. Get talent releases. Make plans for extra lunches. Don't forget traffic control if you're out on the street. Better see if you'll need a film permit. Contact local police.

Of course, you might film Joe instead of Mary. The town may be even smaller. Or larger. Maybe it's in the West instead of the Midwest. But those are all small details you can fill in later.

You've uncovered a long list of facts you'll need to plan your show and make your budget. In this quick scenario, you know you are going to film some *person* in that person's *hometown.* You'll need to get to and from an airport. Make arrangements for local crews. Find a place to stay. A place to eat.

While the specifics are hugely important to your story, they won't affect your schedule or your budget. Flights to *this* town or *that* will be about the same.

As you build your "script," you'll learn more and more about the structure of your story. You'll be forced to think about transitions and the number of people you'll need each day. Even which scenes should be scheduled on consecutive days.

And you'll finally be able to make a realistic budget. Not perfect, not exact, but realistic enough to approach investors and/or funders. Not only will you know how much you have to spend to make your film, you'll have a solid, defensible plan for your production.

Because documentary "scripts" have to be created with many blanks left unresolved, they're generally much shorter than their dramatic brethren. The length depends solely on how much room you need to tell your story and explore the variables you'll face in production.

Now, script in hand, it's time to begin the budgeting process. Before we dive into the technique of budgeting (*where do all those numbers come from*), let's explore one basic example to show the value behind counting first and shooting later. Let's say our script has a scene that begins like this:

The bridge collapses.

Now that's a nicely understated bit of stage direction, isn't it?

Before you grab the camera and blow up that bridge, your first job is to figure out the value of that imploding structure. Is the bridge only background happenstance or is it central to the plotline? Is it the most important piece of your film? Or only one more little piece in the overall puzzle you're weaving?

And the scene continues.

> **A booming noise. The air is filled with choking dust.**
> **John runs into the field.**
>
> ### MARY
> John? What happened?
>
> ### JOHN
> The bridge gave way; I got across....

So does that cover it all? The bridge is gone and the only impact on production would be the sweeping up of dust and debris. Maybe a bit of concrete and a few flying beams if you want to get extra fancy about it.

Of course, the demise of that bridge could be handled in many other ways, too. For every one of those variations, you have to know if this is our only "bridge collapses" scene. You need to know if John will be crossing the bridge before it comes down. Or as it comes down. Do you need to see John climbing over rubble after the bridge is gone? Or will you be perfectly happy with John running into town covered with dust?

What if John's crossing the bridge just at the moment it gives way? What if the bridge's demise comes during morning rush hour? For those options, you'd have to add stunts and effects and a long, long day with a half-dozen cameras to cover all the action.

Your cost to film that collapsing bridge can be little more than an ordinary day with extra dust in the air. Or it could soar all the way to long-term prep, serious stunts, massive crews, and multiple cameras. Which of those you plan to use depends on the *value* of that falling bridge to your film. And, of course, the depth of your pockets. "But," you say, "There's a script. That tells me exactly what's supposed to happen."

Not even close. That's *your* job. Of course you're going to do that along with directors and cinematographers, actors and editors. While there will be many other voices, the ultimate decision about what gets shot is your job.

Even if the script says, "John makes his way across the falling bridge" it's your job to interpret that scene based on your vision of the finished film and the amount of money you can raise.

That's important enough to repeat.

YOU'RE IN CHARGE OF YOUR FILM

It's *your* film. You control the money and the vision. And, for better or worse, you're going to own the results, too.

Your job has never been to blindly follow the script, but to shape it to your needs, to look at every scene and ask, "How can this scene be filmed within my budget, from my point of view, with the talent I've assembled, in the time I have?"

Even if you wrote the script — maybe *especially* if you wrote the script — it's essential to switch jobs and view the script as *your guide* to making the film you can afford. I said *guide*, not ball and chain.

The budget, that ultimate tally of time and cost, is the framework for everything that comes after, all the way through the final mix. Film budgets explain what you can afford and what you can't. They tell you whether you need to shoot everything before week's end or you can extend your shoot for a few extra days.

Budgets separate the fantasy of film from the reality of filmmaking.

> *Production is a pitched, three-way battle between the script you own, the story you want to tell and the movie you can afford to make.*

Despite all your best intentions, not every film can be made for any budget. The pair — the script and the budget — has to be a perfect match for each other. Every project has to begin with a serious discussion between your story and your wallet. When you get good at it, you may be able to give your script a quick read and determine that vague money ballpark.

When you first read a script, when you first try to wrap your head around the problems that may lie ahead, you want to think *SPLATS*.

STARS. PROPS. LOCATIONS. ACTION. TALENT. SCHEDULES.

STARS are wonderful to have. Their names can be a great asset to any business plan, their talents can add to any film. But they come with a price tag, sometimes far exceeding their value to the show. Of course there are exceptions, but if you're booking a star for your show, be sure to add enough money to cover unscripted perks like travel, personal make-up, private attendants, over-scale per diems, even visiting family or housing for an entire entourage. Perks can add up quickly.

PROPS generally fit into your home-free calculations, easy to figure and low in cost. Unless those props need to be handmade, or if they're large or difficult to use. Unless they shoot or explode or take an entire crew to operate. The more specific or complex your props, the more they'll cost. (It's easy and cheap to find a *used car*; it's a lot harder to rent a *cherry-red '57 Chevy Bel Aire convertible with a continental kit*.) The more props you have in your show, the more crew you'll need to buy, bring, clean, prep, log, fix, store, and return them.

LOCATIONS cost time and money to get, hold, fix, clean, and use. Where there are only a few, even the lowest of low-budget films can easily stay on budget. But as you add more locations, the budget (and time) will start to soar. Every extra location means packing up, moving out, moving in, unpacking, relighting, resetting, repropping, and tweaking for sound. You might be able to make that move without adding extra crew, but you won't be able to avoid burning through a lot of time that could have been spent filming your movie.

ACTION can get out of hand quickly. Too little and your movie may stall; too much and there's little time left to shoot anything very well. When planning a day, you'll have to leave time for rehearsals and resetting as well as the actual filming. Be on the lookout for complex scenes, even when they're buried in simple script directions. "And then they fought the war," "Everyone was there" and "The mob attacked" are all quick to read, but far from simple to film. Or to reset for Take 2.

TALENT is at the heart of any film; from cast to crew, you job is to assemble the best possible talent you can afford. Until your script calls for too much *special* talent. Whatever their role in your show, it takes extra planning, time, and money to bring in specialists, whether they're mountain climbers or stunt pilots, ice skaters or weapon armorers, Steadicam shooters or crane operators. Everything outside your normal workflow means more work for you, more money to be spent, less time filming.

SCHEDULES are the structure of your filming, the big tent that holds your whole production. They tell you which day you'll be in Room A and when you'll need Actor B. The cost of things depends on how well you build your schedule. You'll face very different costs (in terms of time, money and effort) if you need someone (or thing) for five consecutive days or one day each week for the next five weeks. Careful planning can mean huge savings. And more time for filming instead of recovering.

Beyond the surface of each of these items — stars, props, locations, action, talent and schedules — it's vital to stay focused on one key concern.

Every element needs a support system.

Actors don't arrive without baggage, both literal and figurative. Props won't show up because you want them on set. Locations can be hard to find and harder to clean on the way out. Action has to be planned and rehearsed before it's filmed, then started all over again. Special talents need extra time (and often helpers) to work their magic. Schedules keep productions running if they're right or grind them to a halt when wrong.

The crux of all that is *time*. And lost time, especially on a movie set, is money that can never show up on screen. The hardest job in making your movie is apportioning your time.

> *You have to be sure that you waste as little time as possible. You want most of your time, money and effort to show up on screen, effortlessly, not in travel vouchers or location fees.*
>
> *No matter how essential that falling bridge, if you spend more time than you can afford, other scenes will suffer. Spend too little and your whole movie may collapse.*

In a typical twelve-hour day, the first hour or two (and often more) is taken up arriving, unpacking, setting up, putting out coffee, organizing props, setting the set, unpacking wardrobe, and getting actors into (and out of) make-up and onto the set.

When talent finally arrives on set, you'll probably want to rehearse for the next hour. Actors need time for run-throughs, of course, but your DP and DIT need that time, too. Ditto your sound recordist and dolly grip, art director and set dresser. Even after you have that shot in the can, every new setup means everything on set will have to be reset, adjusted, moved, tweaked, fixed.

THE COST OF THINGS

Your last task is determining the *cost* of things.

Your safest (and sanest) starting point is using a budget template, a fill-in-the-blanks list with most of the items you'll need to include in your cost analysis. Major budgeting programs (like Gorilla, Showbiz or Movie Magic) include templates used by the various studios and major production companies. Sites like reelgrok provide sample budgets for different types of shows, from low-cost documentaries to big-budget features.

If your show is very simple you might even get by using a spreadsheet or the back of a napkin, though neither is recommended.

Neither templates nor detailed sample budgets know a thing about your film. Your film is one of a kind, unlike anything that's gone before. *There are no shortcuts to an accurate budget.*

Budgets can become excruciatingly complex. Even the most basic budget includes salaries (that's the easy part) plus markups for added fees and markdowns for state tax incentives. They can include overtime and holiday pay, housing and per diems, taxes and union fringes. They'll let you budget for twenty-five, twelve-hour days, then change that (in seconds) to twenty fifteen-hour days and automatically update overtime and turnaround. You can calculate your costs in dollars, and then pay in pesos (or the reverse). The best of them track the amounts you've spent (your "actuals") and show offsets for production incentives or added income.

BUDGETING PROGRAMS ARE FINANCIAL MANAGEMENT TOOLS

Spreadsheets have exactly that kind of functionality, too, though it would take serious programming to put it all to work. It can be done, of course, if you're determined enough. It might also be possible to climb Mt. Everest in your socks, but I wouldn't recommend that either.

Top budgeting programs cost about $400. That may be serious money, but it's only a small percentage of your total film budget. The program is a tool that you'll continue to use throughout your career. Even better, if your show gets picked up by a major, your budget will speak the same language they understand.

Let's use one category to see how your budget will be built. Let's look at the CAMERA department as an example.

	Acct#	Account Description	Page	Total
1	4702	DIRECTORY OF PHOTOGRAPHY		0
2	4703	CAMERA OPERATORS - A,B,C		0
3	4704	1ST ASS'T CAMERA - A,B,C		0
4	4705	2ND ASS'T CAMERA - A,B,C		0
5	4706	CAMERA TECHNICIAN/LOADER		0
6	4707	ADD'L CAMERA CREW		0
7	4709	STILL PHOTOGRAPHER		0
8	4712	STEADICAM OPERATOR		0
9	4713	AERIAL PHOTOGRAPHY		0
10	4714	WATER PHOTOGRAPHY		0
11	4715	VIDEO ASSISTANTS		0
12	4716	ADDITIONAL VIDEO ASSIST		0
13	4785	RENTALS		0
14	4786	BOX RENTALS/CAR RENTALS		0
15	4790	PURCHASES		0
16	4795	MATERIALS & SUPPLIES		0
17	4796	LOSS & DAMAGE		0
18	4797	OVERTIME		0
19	4799	FRINGE BENEFITS		0
20		Total		0

Along the left are numbered rows that might prove handy for reference, though they're rarely used. Next to it is the account numbers and those are used by everyone from department heads to your accountants.

Our major category here is 4700 — CAMERA. Below that are the account number, 02, 03 and so on. It's okay to slip extra numbers into the column, but existing numbers should be left intact — they'll be used by the accounting department to allocate costs to the correct account. And they're the language studios speak. (This one uses Disney's Chart of Accounts.)

For example, you might want to create Account 4708 and insert it for your DIT.

There's elegance to the numbering system and it's definitely worth keeping intact. In this template, every number ending with 85 is for Rentals, 90 covers Purchases, 95 is Materials & Supplies. No matter what category you're in — Props, Sets, and Locations — 85 is *always* rentals, 90 is *always* Purchases, and so on. While many studios use different templates with different numbers, every one of them makes use of the same, consistent numbering system.

You already know how long you want to shoot. You've consulted with department heads to determine the crew makeup and you've determined how much time you need for preproduction. Your editor has told you how long (and who) you'll need in post.

Now your task is to enter that information, including extra lines for overtime, taxes, union pension, stunt adjustments, and any other costs. Line by line, person by person.

Unless you're an old hand at ordering equipment, ask your key crew for the cost of items like "Rentals" and "Purchases." As early as you can, start a relationship with your rental house, going over options and the costs involved. They want your business, they'll be happy to take your call.

> We tend to think we're intruding on rental houses and post facilities when we ask them to review costs. In reality, they're working to get our business and are generally more than pleased to help. Of course, you'll need to be as organized and professional as possible so you can be gentle with their time.

Odds are very good that your first pass at the budget will be obscenely over budget. Happens to the best of us and it's exactly what you want.

With your newfound perspective, you can start trimming. That sometimes means cutting extra people in the cast or crew, but more often takes the careful paring of unessential scenes and locations, extras and effects. When even your most egregious cuts aren't quite enough to bring your budget back to reality, you'll have to trim the number (and length) of your shooting and prep days.

If you do all this work upfront — long before the cast and crew join you — you'll have a markedly better chance of extracting your movie from the script and getting it safely (and sanely) to the screen. Of course there are a world of compromises ahead of you, but you can't know what to give up until you know what you can afford to keep.

Now you know. Your most important job will continue to be aligning your script and your budget with the reality of your show. There would be no point in scheduling more than you can shoot. Or budgeting more than you can afford.

There are two other steps you'll need to make before you're done with your budget and ready to raise funds for your film.

1. Every budget needs a contingency and 10% is the industry standard. Add it. Running a film set is filled with an endless array of variables, everything from clouds intruding on a sunny exterior to a road crew making emergency repairs outside your window. You can't anticipate everything that might happen, but you can be prepared for them.

2. When looking for funding, the amount you need to make your movie is an exact number. Your budget can never be between *this* and *that*. There is no surer way to lose a backer than losing control of your costs. Find the number you need to raise and stick to it. ONE number, never a range.

This entire process — from breakdown to budget — may seem daunting, especially when you're still new to it. It's difficult even for seasoned pros, but obviously far from impossible. Even if you're not the person making the final schedule and budget — those tasks normally fall to your Production Manager (budget) and the First Assistant Director (schedule) — every new producer should go through these steps to better understand all the production requirements. And know why it seems so expensive for such a simple job.

Aside from the details here, there are a few takeaways.

- **You're in charge.** While your total dollars may be finite, there's no end to the ways you can spend them. If you really, really, really must see that bridge blow up, start by incorporating the knowhow of the experts around you. Somehow, you'll have to pay for that explosion — it might be with dollars or by cutting other scenes or — I don't know, it's your show, you tell me.

- **The script and budget have to match.** There isn't much worse than running out of money during production. Or shooting so fast that you can't get the quality or the coverage you need. This is the time to align your vision with reality. Don't be such a slave to the script that you don't leave enough time to shoot the best possible movie.

- **Film is a collaborative art.** Start early to build your entire production team. And learn to listen to them. Making a movie takes a roomful of smart, talented people who have agreed to work together, to respect each other's talents. If it turns out that you're the smartest person in the room, bring in better people or find a better room.

Now that you've gone through all these steps, detail by excruciating detail, you know more about your show than any other person around you. Congratulations. That's the first, essential step toward being a real producer.

Much of the budgeting and scheduling software is available at deep discount on the "reelgrok" film website under "GrokShop."

Software can also be bought directly from the companies:
Movie Magic — *http://entertainmentpartners.com*
Showbiz — *http://media-services.com*
Scenechronize — *https://scenechronize.com/details.php*
ShowStarter -- *http://showstarter.com*

Files and forms, how-to discussions and sample budgets are also on reel-grok, under "Documents."

Norman C. Berns is a producer, director, teacher and facilitator. He's the go-to guy for films that need the wherewithal and the knowhow to get going, to get better or to get back on track.

CHAPTER 23

LEGAL CONSIDERATIONS

Film Financing by Hal "Corky" Kessler

Corky Kessler is a donor to the Roy Dean film grants and an attorney to many film-makers. Here are some financing tips from one of his brilliant seminars. Corky can be reached at Kessler@dlec.com or at www.dlec.com.

The first thing to finance a feature film is to make sure you have professionally compiled legal documents for investors. They should be completed by an entertainment lawyer, not a real estate lawyer or a divorce lawyer, only a professional entertainment lawyer. Typically what you need are a limited liability company set of documents, which is the LLC filing, the operating agreement, the subscription agreement, the investor questionnaire, and the manager questionnaire.

Second, investors want to know that you have a very good story. Screenplays are a dime a dozen, and it's the story that stands out. It's a story-driven business. Many times screenplays just don't have a story that is good enough to merit the investment.

The third thing that you need is to make sure that as a filmmaker, you have surrounded yourself with the proper team to move the project forward. You need credibility in the team, whether it's the line producer, the producer, the attorney or the accountant. It's building a team that has credibility. Investors want to see a successful list of team members.

The fourth thing is the business plan. Sometimes the filmmaker says, "I have a business plan and I want you to do the legal documents." I immediately want to know who drafted the business plan. Often they say, "I did it." Once I review it I usually tell them two things — first of all, it's not a business plan because it doesn't meet the qualifications that a sophisticated investor thinks is a business plan. So, I would like you to call it a business overview as opposed to a plan — change plan to overview, and they do, because I don't think that I've read a single business plan by a filmmaker that merited a business plan name.

Next, I tell them there are experts like Louise Levison (*www.moviemoney. com*) who write business plans for films. Once she does your business plan you have a third-party, independent plan that helps get money because it is credible. In that business plan, there are comparables, there are similarities, there's an analysis of the film, and there are five years of financial projections. All of which give credibility to your package when you talk to investors.

CONDITIONAL PAY OR PLAY

When you have these things in place, sometimes you're able to get talent to attach to your film. And I'm not talking about letters of intent, which is not an attachment, but to attach to your film by what I call a conditional pay or play deal where the talent agrees on a salary and other necessary terms and you're given two to three months to raise money. This way they know that you're not just shopping them. And typically, many of them will agree to sign and this can help raise financing.

It's called a conditional pay or play. It doesn't obligate you unless you get the money. And it doesn't obligate the talent because it is not exclusive. The talent, by the time you get the money, may have something else that conflicts with your time schedule. So, it's a way to claim that you have an attachment without a legal obligation.

FUNDING SOURCES

We're in a climate now where you can get very credible talent on projects that have $2 to $5 million budgets. People should not be afraid to have one of their team members secure talent this way.

There are funding sources all around today that will give from 75% of the budget to your 25% or give 50% of your budget to your 50%. There's a billion and a half dollars that China has and they want to bring to the United States for co-productions. So it's a very, very good time for people to get projects done. The Chinese do not necessarily care what the budgets are. They care more about the people that are involved. They're very people oriented. Trust is a major factor. I just came back from Beijing. I was the only U.S. lawyer that China invited to be a speaker at the Beijing International Film Festival and I established some very good friendships.

To approach the Chinese you need to have someone on your team that knows these people, someone who has established a relationship. It's hard to establish a relationship without getting to know them and spending time with them. You want to find someone that over time has known them and has established trust. At this point there are very few of us who have their trust.

CHAIN OF TITLE

There is one more thing I want to mention, when I do my panels at Sundance, the moderator of our panel asks everyone, "What do you think is the one thing that independent filmmakers don't pay enough attention to?" For me, it's chain of title and chain of document issues.

Many filmmakers do not know how to preserve the chain of title; they don't know what to do. Any break in the chain will cause them the inability to get errors and omission insurance. It will give them the inability to get a distribution deal, and similarly, the chain of documents — if they don't have the right documents drafted by an entertainment lawyer they won't get errors and omission, and they won't get a distribution deal.

I had a client who called me up and said he couldn't get errors and omission insurance from his insurance broker, and I asked him why. He said, "Well, we already made our movie." I said, 'So that shouldn't stop errors and omission.' And what he told me was that he did not have one single agreement. He had no literary purchase agreement. He had no actor agreement. He had no production agreement. He had no director agreement. He had no editor agreement. He had nothing. So, nobody was going to give him insurance.

I said to him, "How could you make an entire movie and not have a single contract?" He explained he made the film with his cousin, aunts, sisters, etc. and other family members so he didn't get any contracts. I said, "Now you know why you can't get any errors and omission insurance and now you know why the distributor said they won't distribute your movie." I think it's either the naiveté of the filmmaker or the stupidity. I can tell you, the subtitle to my Film Funding seminar is "Let me empower you" to know things that your lawyer doesn't want you to know or doesn't care for you to know.

One more thing that can ruin a production is if anyone on your team has a separate agenda, it can be a cancer that grows. You have to eliminate that person as soon as possible.

Another seminar tip that I give in detail is filmmakers have to know there's money out there. But, I tell them to get out of L.A. Every city in every state has rich people and rich companies. They want to see you, they want to help you, and they want you to bring your film and your money to their community.

Hal (Corky) Kessler of Deutsch, Levy & Engel, Chartered Accountants, Chicago, IL (312) 346-1460. Corky joined DLE in 2010. He has extensive entertainment law, corporate and worldwide entertainment industry experience. Corky regularly speaks on the business and legal aspects of feature film development and tax incentives in connection with the entertainment industry and has participated in seminars and conducted speaking engagements all over the world.

LEGAL BASICS OF FILMMAKING
BY PAIGE GOLD

I often receive calls from emerging filmmakers, some recent film-school graduates, others with substantial professional experience who are embarking on their own first projects. Most of them know the technical aspects of filmmaking, but haven't given much thought to the business and legal aspects of producing.

Here are a few general pointers that I give them:

BUSINESS ENTITY FORMATION

Once the project is about to be up and running, you'll need to form a business entity (LLCs are the most common these days) for a number of reasons. You'll need one when you go to get a distributor, and to protect yourself from liability in the event that a lawsuit arises. Even if you have no assets to go after, a lawsuit can hurt the project's future prospects.

Don't bother trying to save money by forming a Nevada or Connecticut corporation if you aren't based in one of those states. If your primary base of operation is somewhere other than a "no-tax" state, you are still legally required to file paperwork with the Secretary of State (or comparable state governmental department), and pay taxes for any profits you make. Registration may cost several hundred dollars, plus you'll have to file annual tax forms, regardless of whether your business entity makes a profit.

This brings me to something I find myself telling budding filmmakers all the time: Making a movie, no matter how small the scale, is a business and it must be operated like one. If you know you don't have a handle on business matters, then pull in a friend, acquaintance or relative who does. As the old saying goes, ignorance of the law will not protect you from the consequences of your failing to obey it.

INSURANCE

Your entity will need to find production insurance, in case something like an accident or mishap occurs that leads to a lawsuit. Production insurance is completely different from errors and omissions insurance, which has to do with liability that might arise from what's onscreen.

CONTRACT BASICS

Even projects produced by a group of friends should have written agreements as to what is expected from each participant. These need to be hashed out and signed before you start shooting.

You'd be amazed at how many productions start shooting without signatures on the contracts. This can lead to painful complications later, including disputes that may prevent the picture from being sold or distributed.

Before you go to download some boilerplate contract off the Internet, keep in mind that to be valid and enforceable, a contract doesn't require more than 1) the specifics of what each party plans to contribute to the project; 2) what they expect to get back; 3) the parties' signatures; and 4) the date on which it was signed. Anyone who signs the contract should get a copy of it.

While I'm on the subject of Internet research on legal matters: There is a lot of misinformation circulated online by people who don't fully understand the legal issues involved. The information may even come from someone you know, if only through a listserve. If that person does not actually practice law in the particular area with which the contract deals, be forewarned that they are most likely speaking only from personal experience, so the validity of the information they provide may be limited to their specific situation.

OPTIONING LIFE RIGHTS

Documentary makers who are profiling individuals often ask whether it is necessary to obtain a signed contract from the person, to prevent them from working with other filmmakers. As a practical matter, once the filmmaker has developed a close relationship with the person (which often happens naturally in the course of working out the proposed documentary project), this may not be necessary, and if your subject is showing any initial reluctance to be the subject of the project, requesting a signed contract may shut the door on their cooperation.

Moreover, a signed contract with the individual cannot legally prevent anyone else from making a film on the same subject using publicly available materials (such as photos that can be licensed), or information that is in the public domain (such as facts from news stories).

However, a distributor or investor may at some point request a signed contract, at which time you can explain to the subject that in order for the project to have any chance of getting a broad audience, they will have to sign some sort of agreement.

CO-PRODUCTION DEALS

Most of the small business litigation I have handled has sprung out of oral agreements between two people who decided to work together without a written contract. Things somehow went wrong; somebody lost money, and now one of them wants to sue the other for breaching the agreement. While oral contracts are just as enforceable as written contracts, they are harder to prove. In the aftermath of a partnership breakdown, people tend to remember facts differently, and often the physical evidence of the working relationship (production paperwork, receipts, film/video footage) is the only reliable evidence of what was intended.

Because of this, when people tell me they're considering a co-production, I tell them to first sit down and make a list of what they want out of the other party. On independent films, there is no such thing as a one-size-fits-all contract. A casual deal memo that includes the previously mentioned four elements (what each party will contribute and get back, their signature and a date) is just as enforceable and can be just as effective as a twenty-page agreement drawn up by a high-paid lawyer.

If the other side sends you a contract they've drafted, are the terms negotiable?

Keep in mind that some contracts are more flexible than others. For example, production insurance terms are not going to be negotiable, because the insurer knows that you need insurance to move ahead. However, in many other aspects of production you have some leverage to negotiate favorable terms for yourself, so keep this in mind when reading the contract.

What should filmmakers look for in contracts?

When you are sent a contract, *read it* before you sign it — even if it's long and parts are seemingly incomprehensible. Don't be afraid to ask the meaning of terms you don't understand. If the person with whom you're dealing tells you they don't understand, ask them to find out. And never settle for, "That part is not important, you can ignore it." If it's not important, why is it in the contract?

But don't just rely on the other party, who has a vested interest in your signing, to find out what the contract means. You should also find your own source; a third party that isn't connected with the contract but understands contracts of this sort, to help you discern the meaning. If the other party later comes back with an explanation that has no bearing on what your own source told you, that's a yellow flag that you should not ignore.

Look for specificity of terms in a contract. Any time a contract includes a term that is vague or capable of being construed more than one way, you risk confusion, because it's likely that both parties have different concepts of what is intended (or may later claim they do, after the deal goes sour). In a worst-case scenario, if the parties end up in court, a judge would likely say, "You don't have a contract here because there was never any meeting of the minds."

NEGOTIATING A GOOD CONTRACT

The amount of leverage you have in negotiating any production-related contract will directly correlate to your experience and what your ultimate aims are. When negotiating with parties who have more power than you (e.g., distributors) concerning your first or second project, you're going to have to be willing to accept terms that are less than ideal. You should never feel compelled to sign a contract you feel is exploitative, but at the same time, if you want your first project to get made and distributed, you have to keep in mind that a certain amount of dues-paying is necessary. You may be an excellent, highly respected DP, but if this is your first time producing a project, you may need to swallow your pride and accept terms that are less favorable than you'd prefer. I often find myself telling new filmmakers, "You don't want to cut off your nose to spite your face." Once this project is out in the world, you'll have a stronger basis for demanding better terms in future contracts.

MISCELLANEOUS ADVICE

When negotiating a contract with a stranger who may try and take advantage of you, never talk as though you know more than you do, but be discreet about areas you're not experienced in.

Don't start production without signed crew contracts. When you put together the crew contracts, be sure they include the all-important language that makes their employment a work for hire and states that all copyright ownership and distribution rights rest with the filmmaker.

With small films especially, filmmakers sometimes make the movie first and then try to do the contracts. This is a sure-fire recipe for a production that will never be distributed, because a minor participant can tie up the works indefinitely with the threat of an injunction, since the absence of signed contracts leaves it unclear as to who owns the copyright to the finished product.

When you're first starting out to develop your project, look around for people you've met or worked with — even if only tangentially — who have more experience than you. You want to talk to lots of other people who are a few steps ahead of you in the same type of filmmaking. But when listening to their advice, remember that there are different ways in which deals are put together on every type of project.

Paige Gold practices entertainment and media law in Los Angeles and Washington, D.C. — (213) 507-6456. Paige is well known in the filmmaking community. She is smart, creative and very concerned with protecting filmmakers and their rights. She was kind enough to share her wisdom with us.

CHAPTER 24

STRETCHING PRODUCTION DOLLARS THROUGH FAIR USE

by Michael C. Donaldson

*Michael Donaldson (*http://www.donaldsoncallif.com*) has been fighting for independent filmmakers for more than 30 years. His book,* Clearance & Copyright, *is considered the bible for any questions on clearance issues. He helped draft the Statement of Best Practices for Fair Use for Documentary Filmmakers. In fact, his work in defining, writing, lecturing, and advancing the acceptability of fair use in the film business is so extensive that he has been called the father of fair use, although he consistently gives credit to the academics who led the charge all during the last decade. That is why I asked him to write this chapter on fair use for the second edition of* The Art of Film Funding. *It is an abbreviated version of the fair use chapter from his book* Clearance & Copyright *which is used in fifty film schools across the country.*

On average, our office writes opinion letters on about 200 items a week that are being used pursuant to the doctrine of fair use. When material is used in a film pursuant to fair use, you do not have to ask permission from or pay a fee to the copyright owner. Most of the filmmakers come to us in order to tell their story their way without restrictions imposed by cautious owners of copyrighted material. Others come to us purely to save money.

FAIR USE CAN SAVE PRODUCTION DOLLARS

The number of filmmakers who just wanted to save money increased in 2006 after the *New York Times* ran a large article with pictures detailing just how much money one of our clients, Alicia Sams, saved by utilizing her rights under fair use. She produced *Wanderlust*, a clip-intensive documentary about American road movies. Clip licenses had become hugely expensive. Initial quotations for the necessary sequences came to more than $450,000. Even after the prices were cut, the film was $150,000 in the hole. We began contacting the studios offering $1,000 a title or the filmmakers would move ahead anyway. Thirteen of the eighteen copyright holders accepted the offer, including Sony Pictures Entertainment, MGM, Universal Studios, Miramax Films, and Warner Brothers Entertainment. In the end, the total clip cost was less than $50,000.

Contrast the motivation that brought *Wanderlust* into the office with the motivation that triggered Kirby Dick coming into our office with his film, *This Film is Not Yet Rated*, a ninety-minute feature documentary detailing the unfairness of the MPAA rating system towards independent filmmakers. Kirby used clips from 135 feature films to illustrate his points. You can forget about the cost ($5,000 or more per clip). Fair use was the only option because of the critical nature of the film. Studio licensing agreements prohibit negative portrayals of copyright holders, their films, or the industry.

Whether the chief motivation is money or necessity in telling a story, the truth is that wisely invoking fair use can stretch those production dollars, especially for documentary filmmakers, although fictional filmmakers are using the doctrine more and more. Also, the fair use doctrine is a lot easier to figure out and apply to documentary films than it is to fictional films. Fair use is simply an exception to the rights that the law grants the owner of a copyright. Fair use allows you to create something new and different using someone else's creation as an ingredient, a single element in a new mix. This is the most important exception to the rights of copyright owners. Fair use is the lubricant between copyright law and your First Amendment right to express yourself on any subject you like.

FAIR USE DOCTRINE IN THE U.S. COPYRIGHT ACT

The fair use doctrine is set out in the U.S. Copyright Act. But Congress still left it up to the courts to decide fair use on a case-by-case basis and to make their decisions considering *all of the facts*, not just the answers to the four questions that are set out in the statute. The language of Section 107 of the U.S. Copyright Act seems simple enough:

"The fair use of a copyrighted work... for purposes such as criticism, comment, news reporting, teaching (including multiple copies for classroom use), scholarship, or research, is not an infringement of copyright. In determining whether the use made of a work in any particular case is a fair use, the factors to be considered shall include:

1. The purpose and character of the use, including whether such use is of a commercial nature or is for nonprofit educational purposes;

2. The nature of the copyrighted work;

3. The amount and substantiality of the portion used in relation to the copyrighted work as a whole; and

4. The effect of the use upon the potential market for, or value of, the copyrighted work."

You can see from the language of the statute that there is no list of uses that are always and under all circumstances permitted under the doctrine of fair use. The language does not give definitive guidance even to the courts, let alone the lay person. Congress merely listed some of the areas in which fair use is possible and some of the questions the courts must ask. However, the judge is directed — by statute — to consider all the facts. Fortunately, there are some more helpful ways of looking at the issue, but first let's look at a couple of cases in order for you to see how the fair use claim has played out in real life with films that were caught up in litigation.

ONE PLAINTIFF, THREE CASES, SAME RESULT—THE AIP CASES

Two of the great horror masters of all time were Sam Arkoff and James Nicholson, who had a company called American International Pictures (AIP) that literally churned these pictures out during the 1960s. Nicholson retained ownership of the copyright for many of the films he made. On his death, the ownership of those copyrights passed to his widow, Susan Nicholson Hofheinz. She administered the distribution rights and the occasional licensing of clips for a hefty slate of horror films.

So it was that she licensed a number of clips to AMC for use on the American Movie Classics channel for a documentary called *It Conquered Hollywood! The Story of American International Pictures*. During postproduction, the producers decided they needed one more clip to round out their narrative. They obtained the clip and sent over a clip license agreement containing the same basic terms on which they obtained all the other clips from Ms. Hofheinz. She prepared an amendment to the previous agreement, which AMC signed and returned. Nobody was in a rush for the paperwork. They had a good working relationship, and everybody knew exactly what was going on.

Oops! After the film was locked, Hofheinz viewed the film and said, "No deal." The filmmakers cried foul and went ahead and released the film. She sued.

She lost.

The court said that one could not make a documentary about the grand masters of horror films without showing a few clips, AMC didn't take more than they needed to take in order to make their point, AMC was making a documentary, not another horror film, and they didn't adversely impact the market for the underlying film. Voilà! That sounds like fair use to me. And it sounded like fair use to the court.

Note that Hofheinz's behavior hurt her when she went to court. Fair use is an equitable relief. An equitable relief is when the court is trying to do what is fair as between the parties, often where there are no strict statutory guidelines. When a plaintiff is asking the court for equitable relief, it is important that the plaintiff has used good faith and fair dealing throughout the transaction.

So you would think that Ms. Hofheinz would have learned her lesson from the last case. She didn't. She sued A&E over a documentary called *Peter Graves: Mission Accomplished*. Early in his career, Graves appeared in several AIP films. A short clip from *It Conquered the World* was included without obtaining permission.

She lost — again. The court said that you could not make a documentary about the career of Peter Graves without showing an early clip. A&E didn't take more than they needed to take in order to make their point, they were making a documentary, not another science-fiction film, and they didn't adversely impact the market for the underlying films. Sound familiar?

As though the third time might be a charm, she came before the same court with the same kind of lawsuit against The Learning Channel, which made a documentary called *Aliens Invade Hollywood*. They used a variety of clips from various producers. They didn't seek permission from any of them, believing that if they used small snippets of various alien visitation films to demonstrate the themes and political context of the alien-visitation film genre, it would be fair use. Hofheinz was the only one who sued.

She lost — yet again. The court said that you could not make a documentary about alien-visitation films without showing a few clips featuring aliens. The Learning Channel didn't take more than they needed to take in order to make their point, they were making a documentary, not another alien film, and they didn't adversely impact the market for the underlying films. Do you think she got the message? The court is nothing if not consistent when it comes to Ms. Hofheinz's assaults on documentary filmmakers.

THE GRATEFUL DEAD CAN STILL BREAK NEW GROUND

In 2003, Dorling Kindersley published a 480-page coffee table book outlining the history and culture of the Grateful Dead. The book included stories about the band's concerts and images, such as pictures, tickets, and promotional materials that were related to each concert. Material was placed in chronological order. Some of the images were posters promoting the band's concerts, seven of which became the subject of a lawsuit. The publisher of the book had previously sought permission to use these items from Bill Graham Archives, but they couldn't agree on a price. The publisher decided to use the images anyway.

Bill Graham Archives sued. They lost.

The court sided with the publisher, holding that it used the images pursuant to fair use. The court noted that the publisher's use of the images was plainly different from the original purpose for which they were created. In other words, the publisher's use was transformative. In their original form, the images were works of artistic expression used to promote the band's upcoming concerts. In the book, the images were highly reduced and used as historical artifacts to document and represent the band's concerts and events. Even more interesting, the court said that even though in some instances the link between the image and the story was less obvious and did not enhance the reader's understanding of the text, the images still served as historical artifacts of the band's events. The court reasoned that these images were transformative in that they were significantly reduced in size and enhanced the biographical information in the book. The court also gave us a great summary of fair use: "The ultimate test of fair use, therefore, is whether the copyright law's goal of promoting the Progress of Science and useful Arts, would be better served by allowing the use than by preventing it."

Case solved. Publisher won.

Let me give you a bird's eye view of fair use that might make a little more sense out of all of this. Think of fair use as a spectrum of possibilities, rather than a bright line that provides a definitive "yes" or "no" in all cases. In fact, the courts have specifically said, in case after case, that there is no bright line, that they have to consider all relevant factors in each case. In this way, fair use is like good manners. There are situations in which a use is clearly not fair and situations in which a use is clearly fair and then there are a number of situations where reasonably well informed practitioners in the field might differ.

SAFE HARBOR

I have defined a *safe harbor* for fair use that we use with our clients. A safe harbor is a term borrowed from maritime law. If there is a storm, a boat can go into any harbor in order to safely ride out the storm and the skipper does not have to ask permission or pay a fee to the owner. It is a place you can always go and be safe from the storm. In the Federal income tax code, safe harbor is the provision that allows you to pay estimated taxes based on the previous year and be safe from penalties even if you earn a lot more money; it's a sort of penalty-free zone. The phrase fits aptly into this discussion.

Here is one situation that will provide a safe harbor. If you can honestly answer the following three questions with an objective "yes," your use will definitely, always be a fair use.

Do you need to use this item to illustrate the point being discussed at that time?

Did you only use as much as needed to illustrate the point?

Would the connection between the item you are using and the point you are making be clear to the average viewer without any further explanation?

If you answer "yes" to the above questions, you are in a safe harbor. I am using the word "need" in a strict sense, as in "necessary" as opposed to "really cool to have."

When talking to clients, I like to start with the above three questions because if the answer to each is a "yes," we don't have to go through the four-prong test set out in copyright law. And there is a lot of fair use room left over. Refer to the chart below. Note that the safe harbor is on the far right of the chart. Review the cases listed on the right-hand end and you will see exactly what we are talking about. And there are a lot of situations that are comfortably fair use between the safe harbor and the gray area.

It's always best to have more than one road to a destination, more than one way to look at things, more than one way to analyze a legal problem. Under the leadership of Professors Pat Aufderheide and Peter Jaszi of American University financed by grants from the Rockefeller and MacArthur Foundations, documentary filmmakers created a booklet entitled *Documentary Filmmakers' Statement of Best Practices in Fair Use*. I was one of the two attorneys in private practice who were invited to join the academic legal scholars on the legal advisory board to this project. This statement is organized around four classes of situations that documentary filmmakers regularly confront in making their films. These four classes reflect the most common kinds of situations that documentarians face. The document is fairly long, so I have seriously abbreviated it for your convenience.

SUMMARY OF BEST PRACTICES FOR DOCUMENTARIES

Classification	Employing copyrighted material as the object of social, political, or cultural critique	Quoting copyrighted works of popular culture to illustrate an argument or point	Capturing copyrighted media content in the process of filming something else	Using copyrighted material in a historical sequence
Description	Specific copyrighted work is held up for critical analysis in the same way that a newspaper might review a new book and quote from it by way of illustration. This activity is at the very core of the fair use doctrine as a safeguard for freedom of expression. So long as the filmmaker analyzes or comments on the work itself, the means may vary, the use may be as extensive as is necessary to make the point, permitting the viewer to fully grasp the criticism or analysis.	Here material of whatever kind is quoted not because it is, in itself, the object of critique but because it aptly illustrates some argument or point that a filmmaker is developing-as clips from fiction films might be used (for example) to demonstrate changing Americana attitudes towards race. The possibility that the quotes might entertain an audience as well as illustrate a filmmaker's argument takes The filmmaker is not presenting the quoted material for its original purpose but harnessing it for a new one	Documentarians often record copyrighted sounds and images when they are filming sequences in real-life settings. Common examples are the text of a poster on a wall, music playing on the radio, and television programming heard (perhaps seen) in the background. In a documentary, the incidentally captured material is an integral part of the ordinary reality being documented. Where a sound or image has been captured incidentally and without prevision, as part of an unstaged scene, it should be permissible to use it, to a reasonable extent, as part of the final version of the film.	In many cases the best (or even the only) effective way to tell a particular historical story or make a historical point is to make during the events in questions, music that was associated with the events, or photographs and films that were taken at the time. In many cases, such material is available, on reasonable terms, under license. On occasion, however, the licensing system breaks down.
Limitation	The use should not be so extensive or pervasive that it ceases to function as critique and become, instead, a way of satisfying the audience's taste for the thing (or the kind of thing) critiqued. In other words, the critical use should not become a market substitute for the work (or other works like it).	Documentarians should assure that the material is properly attributed, to the extent possible quotations are drawn from a range of different sources, each quotation is no longer than is necessary to achieve the intended effect, the quoted material is not employed merely in order to avoid the cost or inconvenience of shooting equivalent footage	Documentarians should take care that the particular content played or displayed in a scene being filmed was not requested or directed, incidentally captured media content included in the final version of the film is integral to the scene/action, content is properly attributed, the scene has not been included primarily to exploit the incidentally captured content in its own right, and the captured content does not constitute the scene's primary focus on interest, in the case of music, the content does not function as a substitute for a synch track (as it might, for example, if the sequence containing the captured music were cut on its beat, or if the music were used after the filmmaker has cut away to another sequence).	Documentarians show that: the film project was not designed around the material in question; the material serves a critical illustrative function, and substitute exists with the same general characteristics; the material cannot be licensed, or the material can be licensed only on excessive terms that relative to the reasonable budget for the film; the use is no more extensive than is necessary to make the point in question; the film does not rely predominantly or disproportionately on any single source for illustrative clips; the copyright owner of the material used is properly identified.

Fair Use in other situations		Some common misunderstandings about Fair Use
The four principles just stated do not exhaust the scope of fair use for documentary filmmakers. Inevitably, actual filmmaking practice will give rise to situations that are hybrids of those described above or that simply have not been anticipated. In considering such situations, however, filmmakers should be guided by the same basic values of fairness, proportionality, and reasonableness that inform this statement. Where they are confident that a contemplated quotation of copyrighted material falls within fair use, they should claim fair use.		Fair use need not be exclusively high minded or "education" in nature. A new work can be "commercial" – even highly commercial – in intent and effect and still invoke fair use. Most of the cases in which courts have found unlicensed uses of copyrighted works to be fair have involved projects designed to make money. Fair use doesn't have to be boring. If a use otherwise satisfied the principles and limitations described in the Statement of Best Practices in Fair Use, the fact that it is entertaining is irrelevant. A documentarian's failed effort to license rights doesn't hurt a claim for fair use. Often, there will be good reasons to seek permissions in situations where they may not be required. It never hurts to try, and it actually can help demonstrate the filmmaker's good faith. And sometimes (as in connection with Principle Four) it can be critically important.

INSURANCE TO THE RESCUE

Until February of 2007, the standard insurance policy covering the content of a film specifically excluded anything for which you did not have a written release. Fair use was not considered and was not covered unless you happened to have stumbled over an entertainment attorney who had the reputation and the moxie to negotiate with the insurance company. All that changed when a leading insurance company announced a fair use rider that would be sold as part of the errors and omissions insurance policy for filmmakers.

All you need is a letter from a recognized law firm that the unlicensed material used in your film falls within the purview of the fair use doctrine of U.S. copyright law. Our law firm is proud of the fact that we are the only law firm to appear on all of the published lists that have been put out by the various insurance companies that issue this type of coverage. Insurance won't keep you from receiving a claim, but it is very persuasive with folks making claims and it is most comforting if your lawyer is unable to persuade the claimant that you are right.

Today, there still is a real dearth of cases involving music, but with the Statement of Best Practices and more fair use cases in related areas, it is easier than ever before to qualify music as fair use under certain circumstances. I will list four situations in which I have been successful in obtaining E&O insurance coverage, even though a specific case covering this exact situation did not exist. Note that each of these examples is for a documentary film.

1. Music is playing in the background. You did not arrange it and have minimized the sound to the extent possible. You did not cut to the music and did not use the music outside of the scene in which it existed naturally. This is the third example set out above in the Best Practices chart and there actually is one case on this point.

2. A portion of the soundtrack of a film that is part of a clip that was used pursuant to fair use. This doesn't include third-party music that is on a clip used pursuant to fair use.

3. A short portion of a piece of music in a biographical documentary in order to illustrate that the performer of the music played or sang the music at a certain time and place.

4. A short portion of a piece of music that is discussed in the film and played to illustrate the point that is being made about the music can be used very conservatively.

The last example was confirmed by the New York federal court when it found the use of fifteen seconds of a master recording of John Lennon's song "Imagine" to be a fair use. The film was called *Expelled*. It dealt primarily with the harsh treatment of anyone in the academic community who wanted to promote the concept of intelligent design as it applies to the creation of earth and man. The film also explored the position of some scientists who think that the role of religion should be reduced or eliminated. Ben Stein (the narrator of the documentary) commented that the thought is nothing new and in fact "takes a page from John Lennon's playbook." Immediately after those words, the fifteen seconds from "Imagine" plays with the lyric printed out on the screen over four stock shots: "Nothing to live or die for and no religion, too".

Our office issued the opinion that this use of a master recording was a fair use. Not only did we think it was a fair use, we thought it fit into the safe harbor that is discussed in *Clearance & Copyright*. The particular clip of music is the best proof of the point that Ben Stein was making, so the filmmakers needed it to make the point. They only used as much as necessary to make the point. And the point they were making would be clear to anyone viewing the film without any further outside explanation. The film was released on a thousand screens. Immediately, a storm of discussion raced across the Internet, most of it by people who did not understand fair use.

Yoko Ono sued.

Yoko lost. In the thoughtful chambers of a federal court in New York, the judge's careful analysis resulted in a finding that we were right in our fair use assessment.

CHAPTER 25

MOTION PICTURE INSURANCE

—— ❦ ——

by Kent Hamilton

Kent Hamilton, Executive Vice President and Production Insurance Broker at Truman Van Dyke Company (Kent@tvdco.com) discusses and outlines the most used production insurance products.

Insurance is a key element for all productions large and small. It is very important to get an experienced and trustworthy professional entertainment insurance broker involved with the production as soon as possible. The insurance broker works for you, not the insurance companies. It is the insurance broker's job to find you the least expensive and best coverage for your specific project. Make sure the broker truly understands the budget, story, locations and any complexities like artist problems, stunts, pyros or the use of boats or aircraft. In most instances the broker should be able to supply you with several quotes for the production so you can pick the best. Generally one broker is all you need, as only one broker can go to the different insurance markets at a time.

Note that a production company can't legally sell you production insurance; only a licensed insurance broker can sell insurance. Below is the basic information that would be needed by a broker to begin to decide how to best insure your project:

- Name of production company
- Address of production company
- Name of owners
- Name of production

- FEIN
- Gross production cost (forward budget if available)
- Amount of rented equipment needed
- Brief summary of what your filming (synopsis/treatment)
- Shoot dates
- Where you will be filming
- Will you be using a payroll services for workers' compensation? If not, please advise the anticipated payroll and number of employees (include non-paid/volunteers in employee count)
- any stunts, pyros, animals or boat use

OVERVIEW

Insuring a feature film, television production, documentary, commercial, music video, industrial or webisode may require one or more of the following insurance policies:

- General Liability/Non-Owned and Hired Auto Liability (needed to get on a location and to shoot in most cities)
- Equipment Coverage (often a part of the production package but can be obtained separately)
- Production Package/Portfolio (a group of coverages specially designed for a filmmaker)
- Workers' Compensation (the only coverage required by law)
- Errors and Omissions

GENERAL LIABILITY

Protects the production company against claims of bodily injury or property damage arising out of filming activity. This coverage is generally required prior to filming on any city property and by most locations and vendors. The cost of commercial general liability for productions is based on the budget of the insured production. The standard cover in the industry is $1 million single limit and $2 million in the aggregate ($1 million/$2 million).

Non-Owned/Hired Auto Liability
Hired Auto Liability replaces or augments the liability coverage offered by the company that rents you the vehicles used in your production. It covers

bodily injury and property damage caused by a vehicle rented by the production company and being used on an insured production.

Non-Owned Auto coverage protects you against bodily injury or property damage caused by someone's personal car if it's being used while that person is working on an insured production.

Umbrella Liability is additional liability insurance that sits on top of the basic liability cover in order to better protect the company. This is purchased in $1 million increments.

WORKERS' COMPENSATION

If someone is injured, killed or becomes sick as a result of working on an insured production, this coverage will pay for medical or funeral expenses incurred within one year of the accident date.

Workers' compensation coverage is required by state law and applies to all temporary or permanent cast or production crew members including 1099 who do not have proof of their own coverage. Coverage provides medical, disability or death benefits to any cast or crew member who becomes injured in the course of their employment. Coverage usually applies on a 24-hour per day basis whenever the employees are on location away from their homes. Even though a production company may be using a payroll service company, which usually provides workers' compensation insurance to all payroll employees, the production company should always consider carrying a backup policy of their own. This will protect the production company for any unpaid interns or others who might not be on payroll.

The only people who can choose not to be covered by workers' compensation are the owners and officers of a company. Everyone else has to be covered.

ERRORS AND OMISSIONS

An Errors and Omissions policy covers legal liability and defense costs for the production company against lawsuits alleging unauthorized use of title, format, ideas, characters or plots, plagiarism, unfair competition or piracy. Errors and Omissions also protects for alleged libel, slander, defamation of character, or invasion of privacy.

Once a film, television pilot, series of television shows, or documentary is finished, the next step is normally distribution. Most distributors will require the production company obtain an Errors and Omissions policy on the production. If you are a distributor, you should always carry your own E&O policy, in addition to requiring each of the productions you distribute to be covered.

PRODUCTION PACKAGE

The production package policy protects you against loss incurred during the production of a feature film, television series or television pilot. A production package policy has much coverage and generally comes in a package with or without cast insurance. The amount of coverage is directly related to the production cost of the film.

Cast Coverage

- Usually provided for motion pictures or television productions. However, sometimes they are also needed for webisodes, commercials, and music videos. The coverage reimburses the production company for any extra expense necessary to complete principal photography of an insured production due to the death, injury or sickness of any insured performer or director.
- Insured performer or director must take a physical examination prior to being covered by this insurance.
- Physical examination cost to be paid by the production company.
- Coverage usually begins two to four weeks prior to the beginning of principal photography.
- It is the production company's responsibility to inform the insurance broker as individuals are cast.
- If a cast member is declared, but the insurance broker has not received a medical examination declaration for a declared cast member, that cast member is covered for accident only.
- Medical coverage does not apply until a cast member's medical examination is submitted and approved.

Faulty Stock & Camera

(Note: this is an old term and includes digital activity and animation)

Covers loss, damage or destruction of:
- Raw film stock or video tape or digital or animated information
- Exposed film (developed or undeveloped)
- Recorded videotapes
- Sound tracks and tapes caused by or resulting from fogging or the use of faulty materials (including cameras and videotape recorders and digital cameras); faulty sound equipment; faulty developing; faulty editing or faulty processing; and accidental erasure of videotape recordings.

Coverage does *not* include loss caused by errors of judgment in exposure, lighting or sound recording, from use of incorrect raw stock, or faulty manipulation by the cameraman.

This coverage can only be purchased with Negative Film and Video Tape coverage.

Negative Film & Video Tape
(Note: this is an old term that includes digital and animation activity)
Covers against risks of direct physical loss, damage or destruction of:
- Raw film or tape stock or digitized information
- Exposed film (developed or undeveloped)
- Videotape
- Software and related materials used to generate computer images
- Sound tracks and tapes used in connection with a production, up to the amount of the insured production cost.

Coverage does *not* include loss caused by fogging, faulty camera or sound equipment, faulty developing, editing, processing or manipulation by the cameraman; exposure to light, dampness or temperature changes; or errors in judgment in exposure, lighting or sound recording, or from the use of incorrect type of raw stock or tape.

Props, Sets and Wardrobe
Provides coverage on props, sets, scenery, costumes, wardrobe and similar theatrical property against risks of direct physical loss, damage or destruction occurring during the production.

Third-Party Property Damage

Pays for damage or destruction of property of others (including loss of use of the property) while the property is in the care, custody or control of the production company and is used or to be used in an insured production.

Coverage does *not* apply to destruction of property caused by operation of any motor vehicle, aircraft or watercraft, including damage to the fore-going; liability for damage to any property rented or leased that may be covered under Props, Sets and Wardrobe, or Miscellaneous Equipment coverage.

This coverage is *not* provided by a General Liability Policy. Property damage coverage written as part of a Commercial General Liability Policy excludes damage to any property in the production company's care, custody or control.

Miscellaneous Equipment

Provides coverage on rented or owned camera, camera equipment, sound and lighting equipment, postproduction and editing equipment, portable electric equipment and generators, mechanical effects equipment, grip equipment, mobile dressing rooms and honey wagon trailer units, and similar miscellaneous equipment against all risk of direct physical loss, damage or destruction occurring during a covered production, including loss of use to a rental company.

Extra Expense

Provides reimbursement to the production company for any extra expense incurred to complete principal photography of a covered production due to loss of, damage to, or destruction of property or facilities contracted by the production company for use in a covered production.

Non-Owned & Hired Automobile Physical Damage

This coverage can be added to the Production Package Policy or sold in conjunction with the liability policy. It covers physical damage to your rented vehicles, film trucks, mobile studio units, dressing rooms and other trailers, grip trucks, and other autos rented and used in connection with your production.

Animal Mortality

Provides reimbursement to the production company for the declared value of the insured animal due to death and illness or disease resulting in the death of the animal.

Office Contents

Provides coverage for the production company's office, its furniture, fixtures, equipment and supplies against all risk of direct physical loss, damage or destruction while property is on the scheduled premises or at other locations used during the production and while in transit between the two. Office contents coverage is usually needed to cover the temporary production offices set up for feature films.

Third Party Property Damage

A common problem encountered during a production of a film or television is damage caused to locations used. The property damage coverage will compensate the property's owner in the event that you damage their property during the filming of an insured production. The compensation includes:

- Physical damage to the property
- Loss of use of the property

More information on insurance available for films is on *http://www.fromthe-heartproductions.com/interviews.shtml.*

See: Important insurance information by Truman Van Dyke Insurance Co. or call Truman Van Dyke Insurance Brokers at (323) 883-0012 / Fax (323) 883-0024.

CHAPTER 26

LIGHTS, CAMERA, ACTION!

Studio & Lighting:
An Interview with Britt Penrod,
Vice President of Business Development
Raleigh Film and Television Studios
(www.RaleighStudios.com)

Raleigh Studio has been a donor to From the Heart Productions and to our film grants for over ten years. They are very concerned with independent and documentary filmmakers and give wonderful prices and great service. Many times Raleigh has given From the Heart free screening rooms for documentary nights where we see filmmakers' work on the big screen and learn trailer editing with Bill Woolery. For features or documentaries, production or screening, this studio takes good care of filmmakers.

Britt, please give us some advice on how to create the best relationship with a studio.

Building some form of positive relationship with vendors and service providers is beneficial in the short and long term of a production career. While it is true that effective Line Producers will do whatever they can to keep a production within its budget, encouraging participation from the hosting studio facility will forge a partnership that can incur financial benefits for many years and many productions to follow. That is not to say a production should pay more for services within the studio in order to secure a long-term accomplice. It is to say that requesting bids for additional services within the studio's structure and accepting competitive bids for those services will win friends and favor in the process of production and those productions yet to come.

What's new in studio services?

What has evolved in recent years are geographic options now available to producers. Canada's initial incentive program in 1997, later spurring the "Runaway Production" phrase, is now a commonly legislated endeavor to secure jobs and revenues associated with production within a specified region. The subsequent documentation used to qualify production expenditures within a region are now extensively researched, published, and in the most favorable locations reveal measurable economic impacts (Profile 2010: An Economic Report on the Screen Based Production Industry in Canada). Also well documented are the production jobs created in the process of securing consistent production revenues within the region. As a result, almost every state in the U.S. has legislated some form of production incentive in an attempt to realize financial impacts in their respective boarders.

New Mexico implemented a film incentive program in the late 1990s and Louisiana commenced a sizeable program in 2002. Since then, both states have steadily increased production activity, talent pool, studio facilities, service providers and production spend (Fiscal & Economic Impact Analysis of Louisiana's Entertainment Incentives: 2010). A major studio production with a budget exceeding $100 million is no longer uncommon in those areas and increasingly common in numerous states, and now, numerous countries.

ECONOMIC INCENTIVES FOR PRODUCTION

Where can you find economic incentives for production and talented crews?

Canada, the U.K., Hungary, France, Germany, Puerto Rico, Singapore, Australia, and on and on, have been or are now laying the foundations of a local production infrastructure with economic incentives that will lure production to their countries. Production is indeed lured across the globe as each location builds a formidable reputation with all the right reasons to consider: talent, infrastructure, cost effective, and livable.

For the independent filmmaker, options have vastly increased. There is every reason to believe that a production can be successfully undertaken in various parts of the world and at a *competitive price point*, even when accommodating keys from the U.S. It would seem inevitable: "All the world's a stage" for production.

As studio operators and service providers, Raleigh Entertainment has made the decision and tremendous efforts to place ourselves where productions frequent and has now expanded into various parts of the incentivized world. Although the presence of a Raleigh studio doesn't necessarily equate to increased activity within any specific zone, it does have a distinct advantage by capitalizing on its service-oriented reputation and Hollywood practices in defined regions outside Los Angeles. Much like production, this broadened scope of business is born of demand, fueled by competing incentives.

I understand that Line Producing services are now offered through Raleigh Film and its renowned production heads in order to maintain connections to Hollywood when filming abroad.

Yes and likewise, several service companies have partnered with Raleigh to branch out in active areas rather than idly ignore the creation of competing entities further removing production dollars from their base of operations. Aside from Hollywood Rentals, a Raleigh-owned and substantial lighting and production service company, heavy equipment companies, transportation, trussing, backings, prop companies are all coming to grips with the fact that production is mobile and increasingly comfortable lensing in remote locations. As such, those companies are traveling with production to various locations and establishing satellite facilities to accommodate the activity. The mobility of experienced, respected service providers does provide additional comfort to productions filming outside Hollywood. Beyond mere comfort is the need to get the film/television program shot with quality and efficiency, which is how each of these companies has built their reputations.

What all this means to anyone preparing a production is that the geographic location where getting all the shots necessary and within a specific budget range can now be explored on a global basis and oftentimes with the support of experienced Hollywood professionals already on site.

NEGOTIATING WITH A STUDIO FOR STAGE AND LIGHTS

We want to know how to approach a studio for the best price for stage and light rental.

An individual is more likely to be the recipient of generosity than a good story. Like all people, studio employees like helping people make their projects more than supporting the theme of the project.

You should be prepared to get down to brass tacks quickly. It starts with a phone call to a facility to check on rates and availability. Calls are better than email because you have an opportunity to form some kind of memorable bond with someone in studio operations that helps filmmakers for a living, by proxy alone. Emails don't give you that human connection and that connection is the beginning of a positive relationship.

Those whose job is to fill sound stages and provide as much of the necessary services to production as we can are under pressure to accomplish that goal while attempting to handle a multitude of studio projects that always happen simultaneously. The last thing anyone wants to hear in the midst of phone calls, emails, and deadlines is a synopsis, followed by a log line, followed by dialogue from the script and the number of people who agreed to work for free to get it in the can. There are plenty of seasoned UPMs on well-funded projects who beg, grind, and leverage every line in the budget for whatever rate they can negotiate. (Many do so with great joy in the negotiating process.) The "story" is less motivating than the individuals who are making the film, and the intent to build lasting relationships with repeat customers is inherent in the business. Get to know service providers as individuals. The results of the project will speak for itself later.

One of the greatest things we can say, and always do say, is "What can we do for you?" You should be prepared to answer that question. When you think about it, how many people would ask that question and then listen to see if they can do something to help get the project done?

You should have an idea of everything you're going to need, would like to have, and at least some funds allocated to that portion of the project. Do you need a sound stage? When, and for how long? Do you need production office space? When, and for how long? What is your budget?

Do you have your preproduction, materials, postproduction, equipment and services secured?

At Raleigh Studios, one of the responsibilities is to supply bids for goods and services other than stage and offices. If a filmmaker is able to utilize the studio for several production needs, the better deal they're able to negotiate for each individual expense, including stages and offices. Once you know what you need, check with the studio for everything you need to spend money on. It will give you bargaining power. Obviously, if you've gotten a free editing system that came with your editor, you're going to take it. However, if there's any item, whether it's digital storage or tape decks, that is ancillary to that part of the project, let the studio know you are interested in getting a quote for those items.

It lets them know you're trying to keep your project within their family of businesses. You have to do what's in the best interest of your project, but don't count out the studio. When the studio is able to save a filmmaker some money, it can be a lot of money.

We've had people call and say they only have $250 and they need an exterior shot inside the studio. If there is nothing going on and they can do it on a Sunday at four o'clock in the afternoon when no one is around, we might be able to make that happen.

Everyone's story is worth telling — okay, that might be a stretch, but hopefully you've convinced your investors that you're the only one ready, willing, and able to tell it. Keep reading Carole's book on funding (I've read it a few times) for a little insight on how to make that happen. Once you have some kind of budget, please give us a call.

What facilities does Raleigh have?

Raleigh Studios is now the largest independent studio operator and service provider in the world. Currently, Raleigh Studios consists of close to seventy sound stages in Hollywood, Manhattan Beach, Playa Vista, Baton Rouge, Atlanta, Detroit, Budapest, and development projects in Singapore and Indonesia.

Raleigh is great for many reasons, especially the mindset of a family-owned business that is extremely service oriented. The company culture of "service" permeates every level of every department. Fostering that "family" atmosphere from the studio to its regarded clients is one of the great reasons shooting on a Raleigh lot is preferred.

The last few years has seen the development of Raleigh's studio services and Raleigh Film, along with numerous production-related, reputable partner companies that provide goods and services to production. Raleigh now packages services for every aspect of production, from preproduction through postproduction. Raleigh has a vested interest in the success of these companies and is selective in what companies they want to refer to their clients. Most of these services are not mandatory when shooting at the studio. However, given the opportunity to bid on a production, we're confident the rates and service provided will beat any competing studio facility.

Raleigh's independent status also provides a more tolerant environment for union and non-union productions. I would strongly suggest a tour and brief meeting to find out just how much the studio can assist in getting a project completed. There should be no reason to go outside the studio for production-related services.

How does that differ from the major studios?

The well-known major studios vary in their requirements for in-house services, and do open their doors for independent union production, albeit at a much higher cost to production. If a budget provides for that environment you're in good hands. But you can house a union or non-union production at Raleigh, rent the same state of the art equipment and stages, utilize the same crews, and have all the services you may need provided for you, all at a much lower cost to the project.

With a base in Los Angeles and branches in Charlotte, Baton Rouge, Detroit, Orlando, and Budapest, and other locations on the horizon, we're confident in our ability to provide options in any part of the country and increasing options in Europe as well. Offering those services with known entities and proven track records separates Raleigh from most L.A.-based companies.

SAVING MONEY ON STAGE AND LIGHTING RENTALS

If I was a producer and needed a medium-size stage, I would come in and say, this is my budget and I need a stage, lights and grip equipment. Then would I rent my camera and bring it on the set?

You do have to use the studio grip and electrical equipment so no one can bring a lighting package into the studio. The way to stretch your dollar is to use any service the studio can provide and this is the pitch we use, from major TV shows to a small independent feature. If you rent the sound stage for two weeks and you also agree to rent video gear from a partner company, we are able to offer reduced rates for larger ticketed items, like sound stages — and you wouldn't be paying any more for the video gear either. On one occasion a Digital Intermediate bid for a feature was $50,000 less than any outside bid, so the money saved was substantial, and the stage rate was reduced as well. The same production received financial considerations for location fees, a swing stage, and their location grip and lighting package from Hollywood Rentals. That kind of savings wouldn't be possible at a major studio.

I really couldn't tell you how hard we try to make it work when presented with requests and at least some kind of budget.

$50,000 is an incredible savings!

Yes, and the next time that filmmaker goes to shoot their higher budget film, the production will come back to our studio — and they do. We've been hovering at close to 100% occupancy for several years in all our Los Angeles–managed facilities, at a time when multiple stages are empty at the major studios, a testament to our efforts and company culture.

My advice to beginning producers is to be sure you know what you need, how long you need it, and the money you have to spend. This saves a lot of time.

If you need people to assist in determining your needs, be it a construction coordinator, UPM, special effects supervisor, or post supervisor, we can provide some of the best in the business in several locations. Take a tour of the studio, ask for introductions, shake hands and say hello to people you would like to work with and see everything a studio has to offer.

Do you rent to short films?

Absolutely. We just accommodated a short films request for an interior shoot and all he could afford was the insurance and the studio guard. The filmmaker was polite, to the point, and professional. It's always a pleasure to help decent people out and hope they experience much success and come back often.

What if a short wanted to shoot over the weekend, came in Friday and was out by Sunday night?

As long as there is some kind of budget and the studio activity for that period is accommodating, we will do our best to work with a professional and considerate group. There is no guarantee that every weekend will be available, but the request will be taken as seriously as any large budget production.

What about documentary filmmakers who need a small set with a black screen for interviews?

That is not an uncommon request. Raleigh's screening rooms are frequently utilized for interviews for major television networks and independent documentaries alike. It's an affordable soundproof alternative. We've even arranged film shoots in adjacent properties for productions that didn't necessarily need or have the budget for a sound stage.

Even if we don't have it at Raleigh, we either make phone calls to other businesses we know or put you in contact with someone that can help find rooms available for you. We have done this numerous times when we were too full or when we knew someone else had what they needed at a very low cost. Someday when they are on a higher budget show they will come back to us because of a sincere interest in their production.

I find this industry to be full of people like you, Britt, who sincerely care about filmmakers.

That's good to hear. Although, in my experience, there are only a few people who open a door to a brighter career and you are one of them to me. I couldn't thank you enough and hope to pass it on to as many as I can.

CAMERA EQUIPMENT:

An Interview with Maia Kaufman

Maia Kaufman, Rental Agent / Marketing, AbelCine, Professional Motion Picture Equipment Rental Company (New York City and Burbank, CA), *www.abelcine.com*

Maia, AbelCine's name is often mentioned by filmmakers. You seem to have good "word of mouth" in the industry. What do you think contributes to this?

AbelCine has always strived to be a complete resource for filmmakers and producers. This is evident in the range of services we offer — not just sales and rental, but also equipment maintenance, product development, digital media services, and training. These last three are new departments we've launched in 2011.

Our expertise and gear covers a broad range of formats from film to digital cinema to 2/3" broadcast and all of the smaller cameras. This allows us to make sure we can supply every project with the technology that best fits its creative and budgetary requirements.

We also put a great deal of emphasis on customer service. Our staff has a sincere passion for technology and many people work on their own creative projects in their free time. I think this deep creative connection to the industry contributes to the level of care we put into each rental.

CAMERA TRENDS

Tell us about the benefits of the most popular cameras.

The nature of the industry has changed a lot over the last few years. New technology and camera models are being introduced more rapidly now than ever before. At the same time, cameras are becoming more technically capable at lower price points.

On the higher end of the spectrum, there has been tremendous growth in digital cinema cameras such as Phantom high-speed, ALEXA and RED replacing 35mm and 16mm film cameras. On more modest budgets, we've seen a strong trend towards small, large-sensor cameras such as the Sony F3 and Panasonic AF100, as they begin replacing Canon 5D and 7D HDSLR cameras, which have been popular with productions looking for an affordable way of achieving a Super-35 film look. We've dubbed this emerging, new sector "Compact Cine," because the cameras combine a large sensor size with a compact form factor. All cameras have their own merits and limitations, of course; it's really a question of what tool is best for each particular production.

Maia, can our readers call you for information on current camera rentals?

Carole, this is part of our service. Contact us at *rentals@ablecine.com* or (888) 223-1599 in New York and (888) 700-4416 in L.A.

ECONOMICAL CAMERAS

What are the most economical cameras to rent?

The most affordable cameras tend to be compact HD cameras that were yesterday's hot models, but have been since trumped by something new. They are still perfectly viable tools, but can be rented more affordably.

The Panasonic HVX200 was the first compact HD camera that the world saw, and it continues to be a very effective camera for a great range of applications. We have seen a huge upturn in the compact HD market in the last few years, especially with the addition of the Sony EX3, which has proved a versatile camera for filmmakers. This is a great economical option for a client who wants a very professional look without making the price leap to a full-bodied camera. The EX3 has an interchangeable lens mount, and therefore can be used with the stock lens, HD ENG and Cine Style Zoom lenses, as well as 35mm-format cine lenses.

Since the still world and film world have collided in the form of the HD-SLR market, these cameras have proved to be among the most economical route for emerging filmmakers. Often students and indie clients own their own HDSLR cameras, but come to us for outfitting them with lenses and cine-style accessories. This has given many people the opportunity to shoot high-quality HD footage, where even just a couple of years ago, they wouldn't have had nearly the amount of options at this price range.

The Panasonic AF100 and Sony F3 combine the look of digital cinema with the ease of Compact HD. They both have smaller, handheld style bodies, with large sensors. Both record to solid state cards, and have the ability to utilize the array of lens options out there. We are currently renting them both with PL mounts, so the client has their choice of our wide selection of 35mm format prime and zoom lenses. We also have plans to offer Nikon and Canon mounts in the future.

SAVING ON RENTAL COSTS

What advice can you give filmmakers that can save them money on their rental costs?

If you are able to reserve gear well in advance, we can offer better prices. The closer to a shoot you get, the less likely it is that we will have everything you need available. When jobs are last minute, extra costs tend to come up, such as shipping gear from our other locations or buying components to make a rig work.

If you don't know what you need, but you have the time to do so, we strongly recommend calling ahead to speak with one of our technicians or rental associates about what gear would work best for your project. If you can be open to working with the equipment we have available, instead of being set on one particular piece, you may find yourself saving some money. Often, there is comparable, cheaper gear, which may be less popular, but works well for your project, and can save you money in the process.

Another piece of advice is to do your checkout through an AC or DP you trust. A lot of money spent in overtime both on set and in post can be avoided by prepping the camera system properly and making sure all your gear works together as intended.

What future trends do you see from the marriage of electronics and motion pictures?

The rise in popularity of digital cinema cameras and solid state recorders is probably the most dramatic new trend that we see, and which we think will continue to transform the industry.

The use of RED One and now the ARRI ALEXA on major motion pictures is more commonplace than ever before and is proving to be a viable option at the highest level of production.

When we introduced the first Phantom high-speed camera to the market, it was used predominantly as a special effect B-camera on sets where the A cameras were film. Now we're seeing Phantoms married to digital cameras all the time. It's more the norm than the exception.

Is AbelCine noticing more production in low-budget, digital, indie films?

I wouldn't say we're seeing more indie films as opposed to commercial or studio projects, but I'll say that we're just seeing more in general. The number of rentals we have per day has increased exponentially over the last few years, and we've seen a huge upturn in production industry-wide, despite the economic downturn we just endured.

I think there are two factors in this resiliency. First, cameras are becoming easier to use and more affordable. This has allowed more projects at all budget levels to get off the ground. At the same time, the Internet has created a new outlet for self-distribution of straight-to-web entertainment content through personal websites, corporate sites, or channel sites like YouTube and Vimeo.

The entire complexion of the production industry has changed in the past decade, and the indie crowd has embraced it whole-heartedly. Many people today are successfully producing films on tiny budgets with little or no crew.

STUDENT DISCOUNTS AND TRAINING

I notice on your site, www.abelcine.com, that you sponsor many events for the film community. Is that part of AbelCine's mission, to give back to the filmmaking community?

We have always been and will continue to be a resource for all types of filmmakers. Although we cater to larger productions, we will always look to encourage emerging directors and cinematographers however we can.

We offer competitive student discounts to any student, regardless of their affiliation. We also work in tandem with institutions like Columbia University and NYU to provide New York film students with a place where they feel comfortable asking questions, testing gear and learning the ropes working in the industry.

Our technical blog (*http://blog.abelcine.com*) is another great free resource for anyone looking to stay on top of industry trends and new gear. Lastly, we continue to sponsor industry events and grants. We're always open to working with new and independent filmmakers, and we love to see the fruits of our labor (and theirs) on screen.

APPENDIX

PRODUCTION RESOURCES FOR PUBLIC TELEVISION

American Public Television Producer's Handbook
http://www.aptonline.org

Enhancing Education, a Producer's Guide
http://enhancinged.wgbh.org
If you are going to get funding for your public television program, you will need to have an educational outreach plan. This site is essentially a producer's guide on how to maximize the educational impact of their projects. The guide will give you a deeper understanding of how public broadcasting approaches educational theory. You can see what other projects have developed as educational enhancements, and how they've done it, and discover the basics of educational outreach by exploring various educational formats.

Public Broadcasting Service (PBS)
http://www.pbs.org
Tel. (703) 739-5000 Fax: (703) 739-0775

Producing for PBS
http://www.pbs.org/producers

Independent Television Service (ITVS)
http://www.itvs.org
Tel. (415) 356-8383 Fax: (415) 356-8391
Email: itvs@itvs.org

Latino Public Broadcasting (LPB)
http://www.lpbp.org
Tel. (323) 466-7110 Fax: (323) 466-7521

National Black Programming Consortium
http://nbpc.tv
Tel. (212) 828-7588 Fax: (212) 828-7930
Email: *nbpcinfo@blackstarcom.org*

Native American Public Telecommunications, Inc. (NAPT)
http://www.nativetelecom.org/
Tel. (402) 472-3522 Fax: (402) 472-8675
Email: *fblythe@unlinfo.unl.edu*

Pacific Islanders in Communications (PIC)
Tel. (808) 591-0059 Fax: (808) 591-1114
Email: *info@piccom.org*
Website: *http://www.piccom.org/*

National Science Foundation (NSF)
Email: *info@nsf.gov*
Website: *http://www.nsf.gov*
Tel. (703) 306-1234 Fax: (703) 306-0250

National Endowment for the Arts (NEA)
http://www.arts.endow.gov
Tel. (202) 682-5400

National Endowment for the Humanities (NEH)
http://www.neh.gov
Tel. (800) NEH-1121 / (202) 606-8400

U.S. Department of Education
http://www.ed.gov

The Carnegie Corp of New York
http://www.carnegie.org

The Ford Foundation
http://www.fordfound.org

MacArthur Foundation
http://www.macfound.org

The Pew Charitable Trusts
http://www.pewtrusts.com

Rockefeller Foundation
http://www.rockfound.org

WNET
http://www.thirteen.org

INTERNET SEARCH TOOLS

About.com (*http://about.com*)
Metacrawler (*http://www.metacrawler.com*)
Northern Light (*www.northernlight.com*)
Search Engine Watch (*www.searchenginewatch.com*)

DATABASES & RESOURCES

Free Databases

Action Without Borders
http://www.idealist.org
Searchable index to more than 21,500 nonprofit and community organizations in more than 150 countries, search by organization name, location, or mission keyword.

Charles Steward Mott Foundation
http://www.mott.org
Detailed fact sheets on every grant made by the foundation since 1995.

FastWeb
http://www.fastweb.com
Searchable database of more than 400,000 private sector scholarships, fellowships, grants, and loans from more than 3,000 sources for all levels of higher education.

Ford Foundation
www.fordfound.org
http://www.fordfound.org/grants_db/view_grant_by_keyword.cfm
Includes three years of grants made by the foundation, updated quarterly. Search by program or keyword. A good place to check out who got funded!

Foundation Finder (Foundation Center)
http://lnp.fdncenter.org/finder.html
Search by name for basic information about foundations, it has more than 70,000 private and community foundations in the U.S.

Foundations On-Line
http://www.foundations.org/index.html
Browse the foundation directory, pick a listed foundation, search any foundation's information page or search any foundation's home page. Foundation home pages may contain downloadable information such as grant applications, periodical and financial reports, and email capabilities.

Kellogg Foundation Online Database of Current Grants
http://www.wkkf.org
To access database select "grants" then "search database." Includes all of Kellogg's grants since 1991.

Pew Charitable Trusts Grants Database
http://www.pewtrusts.com
Includes every grant awarded since 1995.

GuideStar
http://www.guidestar.org
The GuideStar website is produced by Philanthropic Research, Inc., a 501(c)(3) public charity founded in 1994. Search grantmakers' websites by keyword. Also view tax return forms.

Fee-based Databases

Foundation Grants for Individuals on CD-ROM
Located at most major city libraries for free! Offers high-speed searching of foundations and public charities that provide support for individuals. 4,200 foundations and public charities that support education, research, arts, general welfare, and more. Search fields include: fields of interest, types of support, geographic focus, company name, school name, grantmaker name, grantmaker city, grantmaker state, and text search.

GrantSelect
http://www.grantselect.com
GrantSelect is the online version of the GRANTS Database, produced by Oryx Press, containing over 10,000 funding opportunities provided by over 3,400 sponsoring organizations.

GrantsWeb
http://www.srainternational.org/newweb/grantsweb/index.cfm

PRINT RESOURCES

The Art of Manifesting: Creating Your Future by Carole Lee Dean
www.fromtheheartproductions.com

The Directory of Corporate and Foundation Givers (Rockville, MD: Taft Group, 2004)

Directory of Grants in the Humanities (Westport, CT: Oryx Press, 2003)

Directory of International Corporate Giving in USA and Abroad (Rockville, MD: Taft Group)

Foundation Grants to Individuals by Phyllis Edelson (New York: Foundation Center)

Grant Finder: Arts & Humanities (New York: St. Martin's Press)

Guide to Private Fortunes (Rockville, MD: Taft Group)

National Directory of Corporate Giving edited by David L. Clark
(New York: Foundation Center, 2006)

Producer to Producer by Maureen Ryan
(Studio City, CA: Michael Wiese Productions, 2010)

Writing a Better ITVS Treatment
http://itvs.org/producers/treatment.html

FUNDERS

911 Media Arts Center
Website: *http://www.911media.org*
Offers access to media-making tools for artists at a low cost

A.J. Muste Institute
Phone: (212) 533-4335 Fax: (212) 228-6193
Email: *ajmusteinst@igc.org* Website: *www.ajmuste.org*
Funds for projects that promote social change.

Academy of Motion Picture Arts & Sciences
Phone: (310) 247-3059 Fax: (310) 859-9351
Richard Miller Phone: (310) 247-3000
Email: *ampas@oscars.org* Website: *http://www.oscars.org*
Send legal-size SASE after January 1 to receive entry form for $2,000, $1,500
and $1,000 awards in dramatic, experimental, documentary, animation.

Agape Foundation Fund for Nonviolent Social Change
Phone: (415) 701-8707 Fax: (415) 701-8706
Email: *info@agapefn.org* Website: *www.agapefn.org*
Western states only, funds films/videos that promote the use of nonviolence.

Alabama Humanities Foundation
Phone: (205) 558-3980 Fax: (205) 558-3981
Email: *ahf@ahf.net* Website: *http://www.ahf.net/grantsProgram.html*
Executive Director Bob Stewart rstewart@ahf.net

Alaska Humanities Forum
Laura Schue, Grants officer
Phone: (907) 272-5313 Fax: (907) 272-3979
Website: *http://www.akhf.org/grants/grants_main.html*

American Film Institute
Phone: (213) 856-7691 Fax: (213) 476-4578
Website: *http://www.afi.com*
Three-week training program for mid-career women in the media arts.

American Public Television (APT)
Phone: (617) 338-4455
Website: *http://www.aptonline.org*
Acquires finished programs and develops/produces original programming.

America at a Crossroads
Website: *http://www.cpb.org/grants/crossroads/index.html*
Email: *crossroads@cpb.org*
Promotes programs that inform and enrich dialogue on public affair issues.

Annie E. Casey Foundation Attention: Office of the President
Website: *http://www.aecf.org/about/grantguidelines.htm*
Fosters public policies, human service reforms, and community support.

Arthur Vining Davis Foundations
Phone: (904) 359-0670
Email: *office@avdf.org Website: www.avdf.org*
Provides partial support for major educational series assured of a PBS airing.

Artists' Television Access
Phone: (415) 824-3890 Fax: (415) 824-0526
Email: *ata@atasite.org Website: http://www.atasite.org*
They have equipment access available at subsidized rates.

Astraea Foundation
Phone: (212) 529-8021 Fax: (212) 982-3321
Email: *info@astraea.org Website: www.astreafoundatiion.org*
This supports issues involving lesbian, gay, bisexual, and transgender issues.

Barbara Deming Memorial Fund
Phone: (267) 350-4920
Email: *pfa@pcah.us*
Website: *http://www.artistsresourceguide.org/Barbara_deming_memorial_fund_inc*
Offers up to $1,000 per grant, open to women whose projects speak for peace and social justice.

Bay Area Video Coalition
Phone: (415) 861-4328 Fax: (415) 861-4316
Email: *awards@bavc.org Website: www.bavc.org*
San Francisco Bay Area only.

Bogliasco Foundation
Website: *http://www.bfny.org* Email: *info@bfny.org*
Phone (212) 713-7628
They grant semester-long fellowships for scholars or artists.

Cable Positive
Contact: Jesse Giuliani
Phone: (212) 459-1547
Email: *jesse@cablepositive.org* Website: *www.cablepositive.org*
Funding is for AIDS organizations with grants up to $5000.

California Arts Council
Phone: (916) 322-6555 Fax: (916) 322-6575
Email: *webmaster@cac.ca.gov* Website: *www.cac.ca.gov.index.php*
Offers grants & programs for film & media makers.

California Documentary Project
Los Angeles office: (213) 623-5993 San Francisco office: (415) 391-1474
San Diego office: (619) 232-4020
Email: *info@calhum.org* Website: *www.calhum.org*
Created to encourage documentarians to show enduring images of
contemporary California.

Carnegie Endowment for International Peace
Phone: (202) 483-7600
Email: *info@ceip.org* Website: *http://www.ceip.org*
Dedicated to advancing cooperation between nations and promoting active
international engagement by the United States.

Carole Fielding Student Production & Research Grants
Phone: (866) 647-8382 Andrea Meyer
Email: *ufvahome@aol.com* Website: *http://www.ufva.org*
Competitive annual awards. Up to $4,000 is available.

Center for Independent Documentary
(508) 528-7279
Email: *info@documentaries.org* Website: *www.documentaries.org*
Multiple Grant Programs for documentaries and may give free services.

Change, Inc.
Phone: (212) 473-3742 Fax: (212) 995-8022
Emergency grants for artists in all disciplines needing help with rent, medical
expenses, utility bills, fire damage, etc. and grants up to $1000.

Charles and Lucille King Family Foundation
Phone: 212-682-2913
Email: *KingScholarships@aol.com* Website: *http://www.kingfoundation.org*
Provides scholarships to outstanding undergraduate students in television and film production and postproduction Grants for outstanding MFA projects at the University of California, Los Angeles and the University of Southern California.

Chiapas Media Project (CMP)
Phone: (312) 504-4144
Email: *cmp@chiapasmkediaproject.org* Website: *http://www.chiapasmediaproject.org*
A bi-national partnership that provides video equipment, computers and training, enabling marginalized indigenous and campesino communities in Southern Mexico the opportunity to create their own media.

Chicago Resource Center
Phone: (312) 759-8700
Awards grants to nonprofits that serve the gay/lesbian community.

Chicago Underground Film Fund
Phone: (773) 327-FILM Fax: (773) 327-3464
Email: *info@cuff.org* Website: *http://www.cuff.org*
Promotes works that pushes the boundaries.

Chicken & Egg Pictures
New York office: 162 Fifth Ave, Suite 901 New York, NY 10010
San Francisco office: 39 Mesa Street, Suite 209 San Francisco, CA 94129
Email *info@chickeneggpics.org* Website: *http://www.chickeneggpics.org*
Email for more information and closing dates.

Cinereach Grants
Phone: (212) 727-3224
Email: *grants@cinereach.org* Website: *www.cinereach.org/grants*
Large granting program for emerging and established filmmakers. There are two letters of inquiry deadlines annually for the program, June 1 and December 1. Grants range from $5,000 - $50,000 for feature and documentary films in all stages of production.

Columbia Foundation
Phone: (415) 986-5179
Email: *carolyn@columbia.org* Website: *http://www.columbia.org/index.htm*
Priority is given to Bay Area filmmakers to further their work in human rights and sustainable communities and economies.

Compton Foundation
Phone: (415) 391-9001 Fax: (415) 391-9005
Website: *http://www.comptonfoundation.org*
There are no cut-off dates for discretionary grants, they focus most in the areas of Peace & World Order, Population, and the Environment.

Connecticut Humanities Council
Phone: (860) 685-2260 Fax: (860) 685-7597
Website: *www.CtCulture.org* Email: *info@ctculture.org*
Cultural Heritage Development Fund accepts proposals for projects $5,000 or under on the first of every month. Proposals for projects under $2,500 or less are accepted on a rolling basis.

Corporation for Public Broadcasting
Phone: (202) 879-9734 Fax: (202) 783-1019
Email: *askus@cpb.org* Website: *www.cpb.org*
Accepting proposals for the Public Television Future Fund and are open to any project that addresses large-scale opportunities to increase non-federal revenues and create new operating efficiencies.

Corporation for Public Broadcasting (CPB) Greenhouse Fund
Phone: (202) 879-9600
Email: *greenhouse@cpb.org* Website: *http://www.cpb.org/grants/greenhousefund*
It provides grants for industry training and professional development projects for public TV professionals and independent producers. Proposals may be submitted by U.S.-based film producers, production companies, training organizations, media companies or public TV professionals; must demonstrate feasibility and benefits to the public TV community.

Creative Capital
Phone: (212) 598-9900 Fax: (212) 598-4934
Email: *grants@creative-capital.org* Website: *www.creative-capital.org*
Provides grants to individual artists for specific projects, with an emphasis on experimental work. Grants up to $20,000 are given every other year.

Dance Film Association, Inc.
Phone/Fax: (212) 727-0764
Website: *http://www.dancefilmsassn.org*
Postproduction grant up to $2,000 for films about dance.

Delaware Humanities Forum
Phone: (302) 657-0650 Fax: (302) 657-0655
Email: *dhfdirector@dhf.org* Website: *http://www.dhf.org*
Supports humanities programs for the public.

Digital Media Education Center
Phone: (503) 297-2324 Website: *http://www.filmcamp.com*
For independent feature directors who are looking for a means to complete their films and offering Avid-authorized training to career editors.

Discretionary and Planning Grants
Contact: Maine Humanities Council
Phone: (207) 773-5051 Fax: (207) 773-2416
Email: *info@mainehumanities.org* Website: *www.mainehumanities.org/index.php*
Offers support for small-scale public humanities projects, such as lectures, program notes, etc., or planning, development, and research activities in preparation for larger projects.

The Durfee Foundation
Phone: (310) 899-5120 Fax: (310) 899-5121
Email: *admin@durfee.org* Website: *www.durfee.org/contact/index.html*
Provides Artists' Resource for Completion grants which provide rapid, short-term assistance to artists in Los Angeles County who wish to complete work for a specific, imminent opportunity that may significantly benefit their careers.

Empowerment Project
Phone: (919) 928-0382
Email: *media@empowermentproject.org* Website: *www.empowermentproject.org*
Provides facilities, training and consultation for independent filmmakers. Academy Award–winning director Barbara Trent is available for presentations and screenings.

Experimental Television Center
Phone (607) 687-4341 Email: *etc@experimentaltvcenter.org*
Website: *http://www.experimentaltvcenter.org/grantsIndex.html*
Finishing funds up to $1,500 awarded to individual artists.

The Fledgling Fund / Creative Media Projects
Phone: (212) 242-1680
Email: *info@thefledglingfund.org* Website: *www.thefledglingfund.org*
Supporting the creation and dissemination of innovative media projects that can play critical roles in igniting social change. Rolling deadline.

Flintridge Foundation
Phone: (626) 449-0839 Fax: (626) 585-0011
Web: *http://www.flintridgefoundation.org*
This foundation supports experimental and interdisciplinary films.

Ford Foundation
Director, Media Arts and Culture
Phone: (212) 573-5000 Website: *www.fordfound.org*
Supports public broadcasting and the independent production of film, video and radio programming.

Foundation for Middle East Peace (FMEP)
Phone: (202) 835-3650 Fax: (202) 835-3651
Email: *info@fmep.org* Website: *http://www.fmep.org*
Committed to informing Americans on the Israeli-Palestinian conflict and working toward a solution.

Frameline
Phone: (415) 703-8650 Fax: (415)-861-1404
Email: *info@frameline.org* Website: *http://www.frameline.org*
Supports lesbian, gay, bisexual, transgender, visibility through media arts.

Fund for Jewish Documentary Filmmaking
Phone: (212) 629-0500 ext. 215
Email: *Grants@JewishCulture.org*
Parent organization: National Foundation for Jewish Culture
Phone: (212) 629-0500 Fax: (212) 629-0508
Email: *nfjc@jewishculture.org*
Established by Steven Spielberg, this fund is designed to support the creation of original documentary films and videos that promote thoughtful consideration of Jewish history, culture, identity, and issues.

Glaser Foundation
Phone: (903) 583-4241
Email: *cbankston@gcsi-llc.com* Website:*http://www.gfcf.org*
Focuses on three program areas: progress definition and measurement; animal advocacy; and socially conscious media. In each of these areas, the Foundation develops and pursues its own initiatives and also provides funding support to other nonprofit organizations.

Harburg Foundation
Phone: (212) 343-9668 Fax: (212) 343-9453
Website: *http://www.choreographics.com/harburg/fdation.htm*
Advances and promotes new works of American political art.

Haymarket People's Fund
Phone: (617) 522-7676 Fax: (617) 522-9580
Email: *Jaime@haymarket.org* Website: *www.haymarket.org/index.htm*
Support for New England film/video makers for films with strong connection to community organizing work.

HBO America Undercover
Phone: (212) 512-1670 Fax: (212) 512-8051
Send proposal or tape to HBO Website: *www.HBO.com/documentaries*
Provides production funds for American indie docs; Cinemax Reel Life acquires
completed docs or offers finishing funds for partially completed projects.

Hermes Foundation
Phone: 216-751-1100
Email: *senex@msn.com* Website: *www.hermes.com*
They are especially interested in gay/lesbian issues. Grants up to $1,000.

IFP/Chicago Production Fund
Phone: (312) 435-1825 Fax: (312) 435-1828
Email: *infoifpmw@aol.com* Website: *www.ifp.org*
Win an in-kind donation of production equipment and services, valued at up
to $85,000 for your next short film. Applicants must be IFP/Chicago members,
and the film must be shot in the Midwest region.

Illinois Humanities Council Media Grants
Phone: (312) 422-5580
Email: *ihc@prairie.org* Website: *www.prairie.org*
Funding for development (up to $4,000) or production (up to $10,000). Projects
must relate to the humanities.

In the Works
Fax: (212) 989-8230
Email: *intheworks@pov.org* Website: *www.pov.org*
If you have a nonfiction project that is not yet ready for submission to the PBS
series POV, you may submit it to POV's In The Works program.

Institute of Noetic Sciences
Phone: (415) 331-5650 Fax: (415) 331-5673
Email: *ions@well.com* Website: *www.noetic.org/about/grants-and-awards*
Deadline for applications is usually March 1 and they offer an annual Hartley
Film Award of $10,000 for films that address consciousness research, mind-body
health, meditation, creative altruism, and other areas.

ITVS Research and Development Funding ITVS
Independent Television Service (ITVS)
Phone: (415) 356-8383 Ext. x258
Website: *http://itvs.org/producers/funding.html*
Accepts proposals on an ongoing basis for production funding for projects that
do not fit within the parameters of its standing initiatives (Open Call, LINCS
and DDF), including limited series. ITVS also accepts proposals on an ongoing
basis for projects in all genres in need of research and development funding.

Jane Morrison Memorial Film Fund
Phone: (207) 761-2440 Website: *http://www.mainecf.org*
Offers a fellowship and various support, including educational opportunities for filmmakers in the early stages of career development. Preference given but not restricted to those residing in Maine.

Japan Foundation
Phone: (212) 489-0299 Website: *http://www.jfny.org*
Provides film production support for production of films and TV that further understanding of Japan and Japanese culture abroad.

Jerome Foundation
Phone: (651) 224-9431 Fax: (651) 224-3439
Email: *info@jeromefdn.org* Website: *http://www.jeromefdn.org*
Grant program for supporting emerging writers living in NYC and Minnesota.

John D. and Catherine T. MacArthur Foundation
Letters of inquiry only (2-3 pages).
Requests for proposals by invitation.
Phone: (312) 726-8000 Website: *www.macfdn.org*
Partial support for selected documentary series and independent films that fall within: Human and Community Development or Global Security and Sustainability.

John Simon Guggenheim Foundation
Phone: (212) 687-4470 Fax: (212) 697-3248
Website: *http://www.gf.org*
Application deadline is October 1 for U.S. and Canadian citizens fellowship, December 1 for Latin American and Caribbean citizens fellowship. Film and video makers are eligible to apply and average grant is $28,000.

Kentucky Foundation for Women, Inc.
Phone: (502) 562-0045 Fax: (502) 561-0420
Email: *info@kfw.org* Website: *http://www.kfw.org*
Grants to Kentucky feminist film/video artists.

Latino Public Broadcasting
Phone: (323) 466-7110
Email: *info@lpbp.org* Website: *http://www.lpbp.org*
Open call for proposals for programs to air on public television. The projects should center on themes and issues that are relevant to Latinos.

LEF Foundation
Phone: (415) 499-9591 Fax: (866) 333-2953
Email: *marina@lef-foundation.org* Website: *http://www.lef-foundation.org*
Funds are given for projects that encourage "a positive interchange between the arts and the natural urban environment," and may involve visual, media, performing and literary art. Six production and three postproduction grants.

Lucius & Eva Eastman Fund
Send a letter of inquiry to : 4307 42nd Street, 5C Sunnyside, NY 11104
Website: *http://www.leefund.org*
Supports film/video on social issues with seed grants.

Lyn Blumenthal Memorial Fund for Independent Video
Website: *http://www.vdb.org/lbmf/index.html*
Awards grants for criticism and production.

Maine Humanities Council General Humanities community Outreach Grants
Phone: (207) 773-5051 Fax: (207) 773-2416
Email: *info@mainehumanities.org* Website: *www.mainehumanities.org*
Grants offer support for a wide variety of modestly sized public humanities
projects, such as exhibits, lecture and film series, reading and discussion
programs, symposia, cultural celebrations, etc. Grants are awarded in amounts
from $501-$1000. Average award: $750.

Maryland Humanities Council
Phone: (410) 771-0650 Fax: (410) 771-0655
Email: *info@mdhc.org* Website: *www.mdhc.org*
Any nonprofit organization may apply for a grant. The project must be a public
program, the disciplines of the humanities must be central to the project,
humanities scholars must be involved in the project, and funding must support
projects that would not normally occur without council support.

Massachusetts Foundation for the Humanities
Phone: (413) 584-8440 Fax: (413) 584-8454
Website: *http://www.masshumanities.org*
Media proposals are accepted only at the November and May deadlines. Makes
grants to support radio programs, films, and videos that explore humanities
themes. Media grants are available in three categories: pre-production,
production and distribution, in amounts over $5,000 and up to $15,000.

Media Rights
Phone: (646) 230-6288 Fax: (646) 230-6328
Email: *info@mediarights.org* Website: *www.mediarights.org*
A community website that helps media makers, educators, nonprofits, and
activists use documentaries to encourage action and inspire dialogue on
contemporary social issues.

Minnesota Independent Film Fund
Grants for screenwriters and filmmakers, for Minnesota residents.
Phone: (612) 338-0871 Fax: (612) 338-4747
Email: *word@ifpmsp.org* Website: *www.ifpnorth.org/services/filmmaker-services/funding*

Moving Image Fund
Phone: (617) 492-5333
Email: *kathryn@lef-foundation.org* Website: *www.lef-foundation.org*
Support for New England filmmakers.

Moving Image Fund — California Region
Website: *http://www.lef-foundation.org*
Support for individual film and video artists is a high priority of this LEF
initiative. This fund supports artists making work in all genres-animation,
experimental, narrative and documentary.

National Alliance for Media Arts and Culture (NAMAC)
Phone: (415) 431-1391 Fax: (415) 431-1392
Website: *http://www.namac.org*
Composed of diverse member organizations who are dedicated to encouraging
film, video, audio and on-line/multimedia arts, and to promote the cultural
contributions of individual media artists.

National Endowment for the Arts
Phone: (202) 682-5742
Email: *webmgr@arts.endow.gov* Website: *www.arts.gov*
NEH is an independent grant-making agency of the U.S. government,
dedicated to enriching American cultural life by promoting knowledge of
human history, thought and culture. Priorities include subjects of national
significance, projects geared to diversified audiences, collaboration with other
cultural organizations.

National Endowment for the Humanities (NEH)
Phone: 1-800-NEH-1121 Fax: (202) 606-8400 TDD: (202) 606-8282
Email: *info@neh.gov* Website: *http://www.neh.gov*
Offers grants for independent filmmakers and digital media producers whose work
address significant subjects in the humanities; reaches broad public audiences;
grows out of sound scholarship; and uses imaginative, engaging formats.

National Science Foundation
Phone: (703) 292-5090
Email: *info@nsf.gov* Website: *www.nsf.gov*
Supports media projects designed to deepen the appreciation of science and
technology and the understanding of the impact science and technology has on
today's society. Projects generally develop materials and programs that reach large
audiences and have the potential for significant regional or national impact.

Native American Public Telecommunications
Email: *native@unl.edu* Website: *http://www.nativetelecom.org*
They support program ideas that bring new perspectives on Native American
cultures to audiences, increasing the quality and quantity of Native American
television programming.

North Carolina Humanities Council
Phone: (336) 334-5325 Fax: (336) 334-5052
Email: *nchc@gborocollege.edu* Website: *http://www.nchumanities.org*
($750 or less) secures the assistance of humanities scholar/consultants to plan a
project. Allowable expenses include consultants' stipends and reimbursement for
travel, meals and lodging.

Nextpix
Phone: (212) 465-3125 Fax: (212) 658-9627
Email: *info@nextpix.com* Website: *www.nextpix.com*
Postproduction funds available.

Omni's Independent Producers Initiative
Web: *http://www.omnitv.ca/ontario/info/funds*
Omni's Independent Producers Initiative is a $32.5 million independent
production fund and seven-year funding commitment created and made
available by Rogers OMNI Television for independent producers to create
third-language ethnocultural programming.

Open Meadows Foundation
Phone: (718) 768-4015
Email: *openmeadows@igc.org* Website : *www.openmeadows.org*
Projects that have limited financial access which reflect the cultural and ethnic
diversity of our society and promote the empowerment of women and girls;
and projects for social change that have encountered obstacles in their search for
funding. Grants: up to $2,000.

Pacific Islanders in Communications
Phone (808) 591-0059 Fax: (808) 591-1114
Email: *info@piccom.org* Website: *http://www.piccom.org*
National nonprofit media organization established primarily for the purpose
of increasing national public broadcast programming by and about indigenous
Pacific Islanders. Sponsors Open Door Completion Fund and Media Fund.

Pacific Pioneer Fund
Phone: (650) 497-1133
Website: *www.pacificpioneerfund.com*
California, Washington, Oregon documentary filmmakers. Grant size: $1,000 –
$10,000.

Panavision's New Filmmaker Program
Website: *http://www.panavision.com*
Submit proposals three months before you intend to shoot. Donates 16mm and
35mm camera packages to short, nonprofit film projects, including graduate
student thesis films, of any genre.

Paul Robeson Fund for Independent Media
The Funding Exchange
Phone: (212) 529-5300 Fax: (212) 982-9272
Email: *info@fex.org* Website: *www.fex.org*
Film/video projects that will reach a broad audience and will be used for social change organizing. Grants: up to $15,000; most $3,000-$6,000.

Tribeca Film Institute
Phone: (212) 274-8080 Fax: (212) 274-8081
Email: *institute@tribecafundinstitute.org* Website: *http://www.tribecafilminstitute.org*
Youth programs, Documentary fund and TFI Slone Filmmaker fund.

Pen Writers' Emergency Fund and Fund for Writers and Editors with HIV/AIDS
Phone: (212) 334-1660
Website: *www.pen.org/writersfund*
Emergency funds in the form of grants and interest free loans of up to $1,000 are given each year to more than 100 professional literary writers, including screenwriters, facing financial crisis. Assistance is given within six weeks of application, and in urgent cases $200 can be released within 24 hours.

PEW Charitable Trusts
Phone: (215) 575-9050 Fax: (215) 575-4939
Email: *info@pewtrusts.com* Website: *http://www.pewtrusts.org*
Areas of culture, education, the environment, health and human services, public policy and religion and effecting social change.

Princess Grace Foundation
Phone: (212) 317-1470 Fax: (212) 317 1473
Email: *pgfusa@pgfusa.com* Website: *http://www.pgfusa.com*
They are dedicated to identifying and assisting young talent in theater, dance and film through grants in the form of scholarships and fellowships.

The Playboy Foundation
Phone: (312) 751-8000 Fax: (312) 751-2818
Website: *www.playboyenterprises.com*
Finishing funds for documentaries in postproduction, especially those focused on civil rights and liberties in the United States. Grants: $1,000 - $5,000.

Puffin Foundation
Phone: (201) 836-8923 Fax: (201) 836-1734
Website: *http://www.puffinfoundation.org*
Grants up to $2500 to encourage emerging artists whose works, due to their genre and/or social philosophy, might have difficulty being aired.

Resist, Inc.
Phone (617) 623-5110
Email: *resistinc@igc.apc.org* Website: *http://www.resistinc.org*
Distribution costs of film and video linked to social justice organizing.

Retirement Research Foundation
Phone: (773) 714-8080 Fax: (773) 714-8089
Email: *info@rrf.org* Website: *http://www.rrf.org*
Two award programs (ENCORE and the Congregation Connection Program) open to Chicago-area nonprofits only, and the National Media Owl Awards, a national film and video competition.

Rhode Island Council for the Humanities
Email: *bhattach@etal.uri.edu*
Website: *http://www.uri.edu/rich/grants_guides/grants.html*
For fields like media production and script development.

Robert Wood Johnson Foundation
Phone: (877) 843-7953 Ext.7953
Website: *http://www.rwjf.org/index.jsp*
RWJF's mission is to improve the health and health care of all Americans. Rarely makes grants for publications or media projects.

Roy W. Dean Grants, From The Heart Productions
Phone: (805) 984-0098
Email: *CaroleEDean@.att.net* Website: *www.fromtheheartproductions.com*
LA June 30 and LA August 30, NYC Grant deadline 4/30; Multiple grant programs for docs, shorts and low-budget indie films. We want projects that are unique and make a contribution to society.

San Francisco Film Society
Phone: (415) 516-5000
Email: *info@sffs.org* Website: *www.sffs.org*
Fiscal sponsorships and grants.

Schott Foundation
Phone: (617) 876-7700 Fax: (617) 876-7702
Website: *http://www.schottfoundation.org/drupal*
Focuses on the development of: universal and accessible high quality early care and education, excellent public schools in underserved communities, gender-healthy public schools.

Scottish Screen
Phone: (845) 300-7300
Email: *enquiries@creativescotland.com* Website: *www.creativescotland.com*

Scottish Screen develops, encourages and promotes every aspect of film, television and new media in Scotland. Our mission is to establish Scotland as a major screen production center and project our culture to the world.

Sister Fund
Phone: (212) 260-4446 Fax: (212) 260-4633
Email: *sisterfund@aol.com* Website: *http://www.sisterfund.org*
Support for programming that fosters women's and girls' economic, social, political, and spiritual lives.

Southwest Alternate Media Project (SWAMP)
Phone: (713) 522-8592 Fax: (713) 522-0953
Email: *info@swamp.org* Website: *http://www.swamp.org*
Grants and fiscal sponsorship for films.

State Humanities Councils
Website: *http://www.neh.gov/whoweare/statecouncils.html*
A total of 56 humanities councils located in U.S. states and territories support local humanities programs and events.

Sundance Documentary Fund
Beverly Hills, CA 90211
Email: *sdf@sundance.org* Website: *www.sundance.org*
Development funds up to $15,000 and production/postproduction to $50,000.

Third World Newsreel
Phone: (212) 947-9277 Fax: (212) 594-6417
Website: *http://www.twn.org*
They are committed to the creation and appreciation of independent and social issue media by and about people of color, and the peoples of developing countries.

Unitarian Universalist Funding Program/Fund for a Just Society
Phone (617) 247-6600 Fax: (617) 247-1015
Email: *uufp@aol.com* Website: *http://www.uua.org/giving/fundingprogram*
Funds film/video only if it is an integral part of a strategy of collective action for social change. Grants to $10,000; most in the $5,000 to $7,000 range.

Wallace Alexander Gerbode Foundation
Phone: (415) 391-0911
Email: *info@gerbode.org* Website: *http://foundationcenter.org/grantmaker/gerbode*
Interested in projects offering potential for significant impact. The primary focus is on the San Francisco Bay Area and Hawaii.

Women in Film and Television
Phone: (310) 657-5144 Fax: (310) 657-5154
New York Website: *http://www.nywift.org*
Offers various programs.

Women Make Movies
Phone: (212) 925-0606 Fax: (212) 925-2052
Email: *info@wmm.com* Website: *http://www.wmm.com*
Major distributor of film and videos by women, they offer fiscal sponsorship programs. They give proposal writing workshops, networking opportunities with other women media makers, and discounts at labs and equipment facilities

PRODUCTION LIST — TOP CORPORATIONS WITH A HEART

These companies donate to the Roy W. Dean film grants. Use this as your production list for quality products at excellent prices. Say you found their names in this book and were referred by Carole Dean of From the Heart Productions. Email me if you need services not on the list as we are always acquiring new donors. These corporations will service your needs and give you the best professionalservice available in the industry.

Los Angeles

Alan Audio Works Jeff Alan, film music composer
5602 Hazelbrook Ave. Lakewood, CA 90712
Phone: (310) 753-1564 Website: *http://alanaudioworks.com*

Alpha Dogs, Inc. HD mastering, motion graphics
Postproduction; surround audio mixing, color correction
Burbank, CA 91506 (818) 729-9262 x100
Website: *www.alphadogs.tv* Email: *p.cham@sbcglobal.net*

AudioKut, Affordable audio
5.1 mix/Foley/dialog edit/sound design/music prod.
Jerry Deaton, cell (818) 434-2601
Website: *www.audiokut.com*

Bill Woolery, Documentary Trailer Specialist
Studio City, CA 91607 Phone: (818) 763-1505
Website: *www.billwoolery.com* Email: *billwoolery@aol.com*

Charlie Canfield, Animator
Animation Oddment & Sundries
Website: *www.charliecanfield.com* Phone: (415) 254-0083

Copy Right Video, Duplication for all formats
Phone: (818) 786-3000
Email: *info@copyrightvideo.com* Website: *www.copyrightvideo.com*

Comtel
Digital, 16 & 35mm film & video new and recycled
Burbank, CA Phone: (818) 450-1122 Richard Kaufman
Email: *jstolo@edgewisemedia.com*

Carole Joyce Photography
Stills and head shots
Phone: (805) 984-0098 Email: *authenticvisions@yahoo.com*

Claire Papin
Voice-over talent and audio producer
Website: *www.lightedpaths.org*

David Raiklen, Film music composer
Los Angeles, CA. Phone: (310) 699-0361
Website: *www.davidraiklen.com*

Documentary Doctor
Fernanda Rossi, Story Development
Email: *info@documentarydoctor.com* Website: *www.documentarydoctor.com*

DocuMentors
Helping you make your documentary film
Website: *www.documentaryhowto.com* Email: *Jilann@documentoryhowto.com*

Edgewise Film & Video
Film, video, equipment, NYC & LA
Phone: (800) 824-3130 (Phillip Loving)
Website: *www.edgewise-media.com* Email: *jstolo@edgewisemedia.com*

Final Draft, Inc. & *Script* Magazine
USA & Canada Phone: (800) 231-4055
Fax (818) 995-4422
Email: *heather@finaldraft.com* Website: *www.finaldraft.com / www.scriptmag.com*

Filmmaking Stuff
Video On Demand distribution consulting
Website: *www.FilmmakingStuff.com* Phone: 310-746-3868
Jason P. Brubaker Email: *jason@filmmakingstuff.com*

Howard Wexler, Director of Photography
Phone: (310) 396-3416 Email: *howhowardwexler.com*
Website: *www.howardwexler.com*

Jeremy Scripter
L.A.-based documentary & feature editor
Phone: (818) 308-4648 Email: *Scripterfilm@gmail.com*

Lightning Dubbs, Hollywood, CA. 90038
Phone: (323) 957-9255
Website: *www.lightning-media.net*

Louise Levison, Film Finance Consultant
Business Plans, Business Strategies
Email: *louisel@earthlink.net* Website: *www.moviemoney.com*

Mark Litwak
Hollywood's foremost production attorney
Beverly Hills, CA 90210 Phone: (310) 859-9595
Email: *atty@marklitwak.com* Website: *www.marklitwak.com*

Marc Rosenbush, Online marketing courses
Website: *www.Internetmarketingforfilmmakers.com*
Email: *Marc@zenmovie.com*

Mason Cooper, Music Supervisor
Songrunner Entertainment, LLC
Website: *www.songrunner.com* Phone (818) 337-7435

Michael Wiese Productions
Books, consulting, seminars
Phone: (818) 379-8799 Fax: (818) 986-3408
Website: *www.mwp.com*

Morrie Warshawski
Consultant to Independent Filmmakers and Nonprofits
Phone: (707) 224-4353
Email: *morriewar@sbcglobal.net* Website: *www.warshawski.com*

Mirror Image Media Solutions, Inc
A CD & DVD replication facility
Phone: (323) 650-9195 (888) 847-8547
Email: *Loren@mirrorims.com* Website: *www.mirrorims.com*

Norman C. Berns
Producer/Director/Educator, PMD, Production Consultant
Scheduling & Budgeting
Email: *ncberns@gmail.com* Website: *http://www.reelgrok.com/normancberns*

New York Film Academy's MFA in Documentary Filmmaking
3801 Barham Boulevard, L.A., CA 90068
Phone: (818) 733-2600
Email: *studios@nyfa.edu* Website: *www.nyfa.edu*
Catalog: *http://catalog.nyfa.edu/view.html*

Otto Nemenz Corporation
Cinematographic equipment (16mm & 35mm)
Phone: (323) 469-2774 Fax: (323) 469-1217
Website: *www.otonemenz.com*

Pamela C Royal AcKean Music, publishing/promotion
Email: *pamela@ackeanmusic.net* Website: *http://www.ackeanmusic.net*

Peter Broderick helps filmmakers design and implement state-of-the-art distribution strategies
Website: *www.PeterBroderick.com* (free distribution bulletin)

Raleigh Studios
Stages, lighting & screening rooms
Phone: (323) 466-3111
Website: *www.raleighstudio.com*

Power Productions, Story Board quick program
Phone: (800) 457-0383
Website: *www.powerproduction.com*

Rapid Transcript Customized Transcription Services
Sonja Coleman
Phone (800) 200-7809
Email: *sales@rapidtranscript.com* Website: *www.rapidtranscript.com*

SJ Linking Systems
PDAs, Cells, Walkie talkies
Phone (310) 295-7728, Shasta Sowards
Website: *www.sjlinkingsystems.com*

Sam Dlugach Digital Color
Telecine and Color Correction
Email: *samdlugach@mac.com*

SkullCo Technology Solutions
Website creation
Phone: (714) 847-3470
Website: *www.SkullCo.com*

Songrunner Music Supervision
Phone: (818) 470-1018
Email: *Masoncooper@songrunner.com* Website: *www.songrunner.com*

Smart Girls Productions
Marketing services for actors and writers
Phone: (818) 907-6511
Website: *www.smartg.com*

Trac3 Productions / Yon-Ferek Harrison
Create, produce, score, mix and edit music
Phone: (323) 402-0738
Email: *yon@trac3studios.com*

Truman Van Dyke Company
Documentary & feature film insurance
Phone: (323) 883-0024
Email: *Kent@tvdco.com*

Universal Studios
Sound editing & postproduction services
Universal City, CA 91608
Phone: (818) 777-2211

Writers Boot Camp
Training aspiring and professional Film and TV writers worldwide
Phone: (800) 800-1733
Email: *info@writersbootcamp.com* Website: *www.writersbootcamp.com*

New York

AAA Communications
Motorola Two-Way Radios – Rentals and Sales
Phone: (800) 925-5437, (973) 808-8888
Email: *Lori@AAAcomm.com* Website: *www.AAAcomm.com*

AbelCine Tech, Inc.
Professional motion picture equipment rental
Phone: (212) 462-0100
Email: *info@abelcine.com* Website: *www.abelcine.com*

Analog Digital Int'l Inc.
Editing suites and videotape transfers
Phone: (212) 688-5110
Website: *www.analogdigitalinc.com*

BZ Rights & Permissions, Inc.
Clears rights for music, TV & film clips, photos, art, books
Phone: (212) 924-3000
Website: *www.bzrights.com*

East of Hollywood New York Stage Rentals
Ms. Lucille Ascanio
Phone: (718) 439-3930
Email: *info@eastofhollywoodny.com*

Entertainment Partners
Payroll, residuals & production services
Phone: (818) 955-6000
Websites: *www.productionincentives.com* / *www.entertainmentpartners.com*
Email: *taxincentives@entertainmentpartners.com*

DCTV
Cameras and classes for filmmakers
Phone: (212) 966-4510
Website: *www.dctvny.org*

DIJIFI
Photo/Video/Film digitization
Website: *www.DiJiFi.com*

Documentary Doctor
Fernanda Rossi Story Development
Email: *info@documentarydoctor.com* Website: *www.documentarydoctor.com*

Edgewise Media
All your production needs
Phone: (800) 444-9330
Website: *www.edgewise-media.com*

Hal "Corky" Kessler
Dertsch, Levy & Engel, Chartered Accountants
Chicago, Illinois 60606
Phone: (312) 346-1460
Email: *kessler@dlec.com* Website: *www.dlec.com*

Imagine Communications
Web Design, SEO and Social Media Marketing;
Specialized in websites for artists, filmmakers,
Website: *http://imagine-communications.de* (Germany)
Berlin Phone: (01149) 30-616-21468
Email: *silkem@gmail.com*

Lisa Haese Smith – Composer Film – Commercials – Commissioned Works
Email: *lisahaesesmith@gmail.com*

Metro Access, Mr. Jim Chladek
Phone: (212) 686-5386

Narativ, Storytelling techniques
Website: *http://narativ.com* Email: *Jerome@narativ.com*
Phone: (212) 971-6262 x24

Silver Sound
Phone: (212) 757-5147
Email: *cory@silversound.us* Website: *www.silversound.us*

Unilux Inc.
Strobe lighting for film & video production
Phone: (201) 712-1266

ABOUT THE AUTHOR

Forty years ago Carole Dean took a $20 bill and turned it into a $50 million-a-year business, when she reinvented the tape and short-end industry with Studio Film & Tape in Hollywood, New York City and Chicago. Carole coined the phrase "short ends" and began buying and selling film ends left from production and became the world's largest re-cycler of video tapes. She was instrumental in the birth of the Hollywood independent film community because she offered film to indies at prices they could afford, allowing many producers to go on to great success; customers like Cassavetes took chances with her raw stock and succeeded. She ran this business for thirty-three years and sold it in 2000.

As president and CEO of From the Heart Productions since 1992, Carole produced over 150 television programs, including the popular cable pro-gram, *HealthStyles*, where she interviewed some of the biggest names in the industry including Dr. Deepak Chopra, Dr. Andrew Weil and Dr. Caroline Myss, and the historical show, *Filmmakers*, now housed in the National Archives.

A sought-after international speaker, Carole is currently teaching both of her books online. *The Art of Film Funding: Alternative Financing Concepts*, and *The Art of Manifesting: Creating Your Future*, which was created as a support book for artists. In 1992 Carole created the Roy W. Dean Grant Founda-tion, which she currently manages, in honor of her late father. To date

Carole's grant and mentorship programs have provided filmmakers with millions of dollars in goods and services and have played an instrumental role in creating important films and establishing the careers of some of the industry's most talented filmmakers.

From the Heart has given over $2 million in more than forty-six grants. Carole has helped these filmmakers pursue their dreams from the original donation of raw stock, lights and camera to the current New York, LA June 30, and LA August 30 grants. From the Heart now has a partnership with IndieGoGo and works with filmmakers to create strategic alliances and develop an excellent financing campaign.

Completed films sponsored by the Roy W. Dean grants are: *All Power to the People* on Starz; *A Chance to Grow*, Discovery; *Save a Man to Fight*, History; *The Flute Player*, PBS; *Miss Navaho*, PBS, *Stolen*, Court TV; *Salvages Lives*, Discovery; *Homeland* and *Shakespeare Behind Bars*, both on ITVS; *In My Corner*, PBS; *Bam 6.6*, *Wakefield Convicted: Sentenced to Die*, BURNED. and many more. Please see the From the Heart website for current lists of donors and more information on the grants and current Information on financing your films.

SHAKING THE MONEY TREE – 3RD EDITION
THE ART OF GETTING GRANTS AND DONATIONS

MORRIE WARSHAWSKI

Shaking the Money Tree became an instant classic when its first edition appeared in 1994. Now considered the "bible" on fundraising for independent noncommercial film and video, this new expanded 3rd edition takes media makers – and anyone interested in the art of fundraising – into the 21st Century, and includes sidebars with practical advice from seasoned professionals in the field.

This new 3rd Edition contains:
· New section on career development
· Detailed advice on how to get donations from all sources – individuals and institutions
· Instructions on how to write the perfect grant proposal
· Expanded sections on the Internet and Alternative Fundraising Strategies
· New sample grant proposals with budgets
· Sidebars by 15 respected professionals in the field
· Bibliography with books and websites

"This third edition of Morrie Warshawski's classic on raising money for filmmaking, Shaking the Money Tree, *is a treasure chest of time-tested fundraising wisdom, insight, and down-to-earth guidance you can put to work today. It's chock full of examples and advice, much of it in the words of highly successful filmmakers themselves. Buy this book without delay!"*

— Mal Warwick, author of *Fundraising When Money Is Tight*

"This is the perfect fundraising book for filmmakers. Covering everything from pitching in person to fundraising on the web, this new edition is a must-own for every filmmaker – and actually for anyone raising funds, be it for a film or for their organization. While the book is geared towards filmmakers, the advice is relevant to anyone raising money in the arts. The sample grants in the appendix are worth the cost alone. This is the third time I've read this book, and I learn something new with every edition."

— Brian Newman, CEO, Tribeca Film Institute

MORRIE WARSHAWSKI is a consultant, facilitator, and writer who specializes in helping nonprofit organizations on issues of strategic planning. His work is characterized by a commitment to the core values of creativity, tolerance, thoughtfulness, and transparency.

$26.95 · 188 PAGES · ORDER NUMBER 135RLS · ISBN: 9781932907667

BANKROLL – 2ND EDITION
A NEW APPROACH TO FINANCING FEATURE FILMS

TOM MALLOY

Bankroll, 2nd Edition gives filmmakers proven methods to getting their films financed. Since the first edition was released in 2009, the financial landscape has changed so much that there are completely new approaches to funding everyone in the business must know. This book, written by a successful Hollywood producer who has raised over $20 million dollars, is for actors/producers and writer/producers to get their feature films made and includes creative approaches and guidance. This book goes into detail to explain the legal aspects and paperwork needed to create an effective pitch packet and find financing for features.

"In refreshingly frank language, Tom Malloy tells it like it is… and like it isn't. Bankroll could be the only book you'll ever need to read about independent filmmaking. Tom's energy, enthusiasm and knowledge leap off the page – if this doesn't motivate and inspire you, nothing will!"

> — Stephanie Austin, producer, *Terminator 2, True Lies, Behind Enemy Lines*

"Tom Malloy's approach is the real deal and combines pragmatism with a bit of motivational pep talk and spirituality. The book isn't written by a lawyer or ex-agent or trust-fund-gilded producer who happens to be blessed with personal wealth and endless family contacts in high places. Since Tom is a writer, actor, producer, and filmmaker, his advice comes from a unique perspective and should be mandatory reading for aspiring film producers."

> — Michael Roban, executive producer, *Secretary, Penelope, Love in the Time of Cholera*

In 1998, TOM MALLOY was one of the lead actors in the film *Gravesend*, produced by Oliver Stone. The film became an indie-cult favorite. When this film failed to make him a household name, Tom decided to learn as many facets of the movie business as he could. Over the course of eight years, he created his own method to finance films. Tom first wrote and produced *The Attic*, a thriller directed by Mary Lambert (director of *Pet Sematary* and *Pet Sematary II*), and starring John Savage, Jason Lewis, Elisabeth Moss, and Tom. Tom then wrote and produced *The Alphabet Killer*, a psychological thriller directed by Rob Schmidt (director of *Wrong Turn*). The film stars Eliza Dushku, Cary Elwes, Oscar-winner Timothy Hutton, Michael Ironside, and Tom in one of the lead roles. Tom wrote and produced *Love N' Dancing*, a dance film/romantic comedy directed by Rob Iscove (director of *She's All That*). The film stars Amy Smart and Tom, along with Billy Zane, Betty White, and Rachel Dratch. As a direct result of contacts made through the techniques of *Bankroll*, Tom recently partnered with the Han Shi group of China to produce a slate of U.S. films over the next three years.

$24.95 · 220 PAGES · ORDER NUMBER 181RLS · ISBN: 9781615930890

THE MYTH OF MWP

In a dark time, a light bringer came along, leading the curious and the frustrated to clarity and empowerment. It took the well-guarded secrets out of the hands of the few and made them available to all. It spread a spirit of openness and creative freedom, and built a storehouse of knowledge dedicated to the betterment of the arts.

The essence of the Michael Wiese Productions (MWP) is empowering people who have the burning desire to express themselves creatively. We help them realize their dreams by putting the tools in their hands. We demystify the sometimes secretive worlds of screenwriting, directing, acting, producing, film financing, and other media crafts.

By doing so, we hope to bring forth a realization of 'conscious media' which we define as being positively charged, emphasizing hope and affirming positive values like trust, cooperation, self-empowerment, freedom, and love. Grounded in the deep roots of myth, it aims to be healing both for those who make the art and those who encounter it. It hopes to be transformative for people, opening doors to new possibilities and pulling back veils to reveal hidden worlds.

MWP has built a storehouse of knowledge unequaled in the world, for no other publisher has so many titles on the media arts. Please visit www.mwp.com where you will find many free resources and a 25% discount on our books. Sign up and become part of the wider creative community!

Onward and upward,

Michael Wiese
Publisher/Filmmaker